A THEOLOGICAL INTRODUCTION TO THE NEW TESTAMENT

Eduard Schweizer

TRANSLATED BY
O. C. Dean, Jr.

ABINGDON PRESS
Nashville

A THEOLOGICAL INTRODUCTION TO THE NEW TESTAMENT

Translation from the German of Eduard Schweizer's THEOLOGISCHE EINLEITUNG IN DAS NEUE TESTAMENT, with approval of Vandenhoeck & Ruprecht, Göttingen, Germany, © 1989 Vandenhoeck & Ruprecht, Göttingen.

English translation copyright © 1991 by Abingdon Press

This book is printed on recycled, acid-free paper.

Library of Congress Cataloging-in-Publicaton Data

Schweizer, Eduard.
    [Theologische Einleitung in das Neue Testament. English]
    A theological introduction to the New Testament/Eduard Schweizer; translated by O. C. Dean, Jr. p.   cm.
    Translation of: Theologische Einleitung in das Neue Testament.
    Includes bibliographical references and indexes.
    ISBN 0-687-41469-5 (pbk.: alk. paper)
    1. Bible, N.T.—Introductions. 2. Bible. N.T.—Theology. I. Title.
BS2330.2.S37   1991
225.6'1—dc20   91-14243
                                                                        CIP

Scripture quotations in this publication are from the Revised Standard Version of the Bible, copyright © 1946, 1955, 1971by the Division of Christian Education of the National Council of the Churches of Christ in the U.S.A., and are used by permission.

MANUFACTURED IN THE UNITED STATES OF AMERICA

For the
International Baptist Theological Seminary
in Rüschlikon/Zürich
as a modest token of gratitude for the
"Scroll of Honour" bestowed on me
on 24 April 1986

FOREWORD

The older I get, the more I realize how much we do not know. Incidentally, this is also a liberating insight, and one that has arisen, and continues to arise, in many conversations with my wife. For it is at those moments of recognition that one becomes more and more thankful for those people who can do what one cannot do oneself. And thus one learns to view with serenity the limits of one's own gifts.

From that standpoint I welcomed the clearly delineated task suggested to me by G. Friedrich, the former editor of the *Grundrisse zum Neuen Testament*. Writing a "theological introduction" made good sense to me. In it one would have to take seriously the differing times and situations in which the *one* faith must be witnessed and above all lived. That is as true for the New Testament as for today's church. Immediately following my course of studies and my half year as an intern, an emergency situation in my home town of Basel required me to deputize for three pastors. My ministry was in a working class neighborhood with 13,500 church members and a hundred fifteen- and sixteen-year-old confirmation candidates, who came out of the factories and the Rhine harbor for instruction from six to seven in the evening. Since it was a time of high unemployment, many conversations with men arose during my home visits. For almost the ten following years I lived in a farming community in the St. Gallen mountains and in so doing learned—even if still insufficiently—that one must convey the same message here as there but in a very different way. That has continued to be true in my academic work. On the various continents of our earth and especially with people of all sorts of different confessions, I have had to learn ever anew to listen to very unusual testimonies and even to press forward into new territory. Included here are good experiences in the study group of the Evangelisch-Katholischer Kommentar, and also the connection with the Baptist Theological Seminary in

Rüschlikon/Zürich, from which some have come to us at the university to complete their doctoral studies. May this book's dedication be a token of appreciation for the fellowship of faith experienced there and beyond the seminary among its teachers and friends in the USA. That the seminary has chosen me as the first non-Baptist to receive its highest possible honor has moved me greatly. That we can celebrate neither baptism with the Baptists nor the Lord's Supper with the Catholics shows that we have not yet attained the unity of the church of the New Testament. That pains us. And yet in recent decades much common seeking, listening, and venturing has become apparent in all our dogmatic and ecclesiastical differences.

Thus, we want to attempt all the more earnestly to listen very intensively to the New Testament, even to what at first does not suit us at all. And because so many prejudices have left their imprint on us and our way of reading, we can only pray that God himself will free us from them more and more. Thus may my effort also be understood, and I hope that you will read it not only critically, but also with a dash of friendly humor when you discover an error. For of course you know that those who merely sit on the grass and never climb the apple tree will never run the risk of falling out of it—but they will never pick any apples either!

Eduard Schweizer

CONTENTS

CHAPTER ONE

Oral Tradition and the First Written Documents

PREFACE

Writing an introduction to the New Testament involves an a priori decision, namely, restricting oneself to the writings that have become canonical, although there are other early Christian documents that are as old or older than certain parts of the New Testament: the Gospel of Thomas, Jewish-Christian gospels, the First Letter of Clement, and so forth. Nonetheless, the New Testament texts are distinguished from these other writings by the fact that they were always read as "Scripture" and were normative for the churches[1] (cf. 32.3 [and 32.2] below).

We must not forget, however, that they were written in a quite particular time and situation. Hence, in what follows we are not going to begin with certain problems, for example, the question of what *sin* or *grace* may mean in the New Testament. We will instead proceed essentially from text to text and thus give serious consideration to the historical time and situation of each individual book. Naturally, without more extensive discussion, we can determine only very briefly what is generally accepted or contested. In the process it will become clear where the present author sees the most likely correct solution, yet without his being able to substantiate it exhaustively. For that the usual "introductions" must be consulted.[2] The real issue at stake here is what happened "theologically"—that is, what is still essential today for the faith of the church—when, for example, the oral tradition was written down for the first time; or when Matthew, in a different time and situation, wanted to replace Mark with a new Gospel; or when Paul moved from answering the strong attacks against him in Galatia to the task of preparing for his visit in Rome, where similar problems may have stood in the background but where opposition to him had at least not broken out openly; and so forth.

Thus the following treatment differs from the usual introduction in that the historical issues serve only as a foundation for perceiving as well as possible the theologically important assertions of the New Testament Scriptures. It differs from the usual theology of the New Testament in that it is not oriented toward concepts, such as sin and grace, but toward individual writings. It is thus also more definitely the presentation of a historical process and to that extent a much more modest undertaking. Here also we are not at all dealing with a single, coherent development, but rather must always point to new beginnings, alternative solutions, and corrections as well, which from the outside seem to be accidental. Nonetheless, the question of the unity of the New Testament witness—how, for example, the differing answers of, say, Paul and the Letter of James relate to each other—continues to be a live issue. Moreover, we shall also at least indicate how the present author, in a necessarily personal decision, sees the direction in which the observed tensions and antitheses in the faith and life of the church can be confronted and overcome.

1. JESUS IN THE HISTORY OF HIS TIME

1.1 Non-Christian Testimonies. There are very few extant non-Christian witnesses to Jesus. The Roman historian Tacitus[3] reports, in connection with the burning of Rome under Nero, that Christ (which he took to be a name) was executed under Pontius Pilate. Suetonius[4] (also writing around A.D. 100 or somewhat later) writes that in Rome a *Chrestos* (Greek *e* and *i* were pronounced the same then) initiated an insurrection that broke out among the Jewish population. In the writings of the Jewish historian Josephus[5] we find, shortly before 100, a longer section on Jesus, which, however, certainly could not have come from a Jew, but only from a believing Christian, perhaps one of the many Christian copyists. Yet, it is possible that a brief notice of Jesus' execution already stood in the text and became the occasion for this elaboration. At another point Josephus mentions the death of James, "the brother of Jesus, the so-called Christ." Jewish news reports[6] that are vague and hard to date speak of Jesus' "magic," of "five disciples," and of his execution on the eve of Passover (thus John 18:28; 19:14). That Jesus lived and was crucified is never doubted. The quite inconspicuous mention of Jesus' brothers in I Cor 9:5 and the difficulties—still visible in the New Testament—that the early church had in comprehending the crucifixion unquestionably show that both are historical facts. Moreover, we cannot doubt the fact that encounters of the disciples with the resurrected one—however one wants to portray them—led to a new beginning. At the burial of Jesus, which may have been the highest religious duty, only an outsider was present; and on Sunday only the women came to the grave. In all probability the disciples fled to Galilee, and thus the tradition of the first appearance of Jesus before the disciples in Galilee (Matt 28:16; Mark 16:7) is presumably historically correct. The appearance probably moved the disciples to return to Jerusalem, the center of God's history; at least they were there later, not only according to Acts, but also according to Gal 1:18-19; 2:9. That those named in I Cor 15:5-8 were convinced that they had seen the Lord (as Paul states it in I Cor 9:1) is doubtless correct, even if we can no longer establish with assurance the order of the appearances in Galilee (where presumably the first meeting with Peter also took place—I Cor 15:5; transposed to Jerusalem in Luke 24:34: cf. Mark 16:7, where Peter is named especially) and Jerusalem (thus Luke and John 20).

More cannot be said. That means, theologically speaking, that it is an act of faith when the New Testament declares that in this person, Jesus of Nazareth, who does not stand out at all in world history, God himself encountered the world and its history.

1.2 When Did Jesus Live? If Jesus was born under Herod (Matt 2:1; Luke 1:5), that had to have happened before Herod's death in the year 4 B.C. Certainly there was no governor Quirinius in Syria between 7 B.C. and A.D. 6 (Luke 2:2), but rather beginning in A.D. 6 at the time in which, according to Josephus, the first taxation was carried out in Palestine. It may be possible that Quirinius had prepared for this earlier in another capacity; yet, that cannot be demonstrated and is very unlikely because at that time the land was not yet a Roman province. Thus this statement is probably in error. The information—perhaps to be explained simply as conventional literary style—about Jesus' first appearance in Luke 3:1-2 (between A.D. 26 and 29), 3:23 (Jesus about thirty years old), and John 2:20 (forty-six years since the beginning of the building of the temple in the year 20/19 B.C.) points to the birth of Jesus in the years 7–4 B.C. Since Paul, as far as we can determine, received his calling in about A.D. 32 or at the latest 35 (see 9.1 below), one can scarcely place Jesus' death later than A.D. 30/31. According to all the Gospels he was crucified on a Friday, which was the day of Passover (Matthew, Mark, Luke) or the day before (John). Since the beginning of the month in those days was determined only after the first sighting of the new moon, it could easily have fallen one day different from the real astronomical calendar. In the year A.D. 30 the fourteenth (Passover eve) or the fifteenth (Passover) of Nisan was a Friday.[7]

This means that we can give no guaranteed correct dates—at least there is something wrong with the information on Quirinius—but it is essential to the believer that the Jesus event be datable at a certain point in our history and not simply in a foggy mythical past. Both sides of this truth are included in the statement that our system of dating is in error by at least four years, but holds fast to the theologically decisive fact that God's coming into our world is connected with a datable event.

11

1.3 Where Did Jesus Live? Jesus grew up and worked at first in Galilee, the somewhat despised part of the country that did not live strictly according to the law (Matt 4:15). What is not entirely certain is whether he went to Jerusalem only at the end of his life (Mark) or more often (John 2:13, 23; 5:1; 7:14; 11:54–12:1, 12). Sociologically speaking, Jesus and his group of disciples are clearly to be placed within the society of their time, even if not in every detail. He moved among the poorer circles but did not belong to the lowest levels of the populous. He grew up in the house of a carpenter (Matt 13:55) and was himself probably a joiner or builder (Mark 6:3). Among his disciples were fishermen, including, according to Mark 1:20, the Zebedees, who worked in a small business with employees, in which Simon (and Andrew) perhaps also took part (Luke 5:7, 10). Moreover, there was a tax collector (Mark 2:14), who presumably was a small leaseholder in Galilee[8] and thus must have had some capital at his disposal. More important, Jesus separated himself from his house and family and expected the same of the disciples accompanying him. According to Mark 2:1; 3:20; 7:17; 9:28, 33; 10:10; and Matt 4:13, a house in Capernaum (Peter's?) seems to have been available to him, and according to Luke 8:3 he was supported by women of financial means. That, however, does not change the fact that Jesus and his disciples ministered largely as a wandering group free from possessions and family ties, whereby Jesus' and his disciples' prophetic proclamation of the apocalyptically understood approach of the kingdom of God and their charismatic acts of healing are singular phenomena of their time.[9]

It was apparently important to the tradition that Jesus belonged to the lower classes, even if not to the extreme level of a slave or a prisoner of war, and that at the same time he significantly distinguished himself from this society and its visions, which also included monastic movements and prophetic figures.

2. THE ORAL TRANSMISSION OF JESUS' DEEDS AND WORDS[10]

2.1 The Tradition of Jesus' Healings. When an Israelite was healed from a lengthy illness he did not simply go happily about his work, rejoicing over his new-found health. He brought his offering of thanksgiving to God.[11] If he did not live near Jerusalem, he paid it to a priest who lived near him and who went up for Temple service twice a year. He also proclaimed the story of his healing to the congregation, perhaps immediately after his recovery or on the sabbath after the worship service, and the listeners joined in praising God. In a world that knew neither newspaper nor television, the story would make the rounds and also be retold in neighboring villages. If it was spectacular enough, merchants and traders would report the event in the more distant parts of the land or, with less striking healings, when they encountered sick people. In this way the deeds of Jesus also became known. People told how he came into a village and found a sick person (e.g., Mark 5:1-2; 6:56), how severe the illness was and how long it had already lasted (Mark 5:3-5, 25-26), what Jesus said to him and did for him (Mark 5:8-9; 8:23-25), how he became well so that all could see it (Mark 5:14-15), and then how the one healed and the bystanders in their joy praised God (Mark 7:37; Luke 7:16). That is the general schema by which the healings of Jesus are described in the New Testament.[12] Similar things were told about Hellenistic wonder workers with, of course, typical differences. At the end of these stories, there was a call to faith in the salvation-bringing god on the basis of the miraculous proof, and worship was established at the place of the miracle. Jesus' disciples, on the other hand, not only told of the often still quite tentative faith in which the sick person learned to trust Jesus (Mark 9:24; 1:24, 40; 2:3-5; 5:6, 23, 28, 34; 6:5-6, 56; 7:28; 10:47; Matt 8:8-10; Luke 17:13, 19; John 5:6-8, 13),[13] but also of the commission to proclaim (Mark 5:19-20) or of the proclamation happening even against the will of Jesus (Mark 1:28, 44-45, and elsewhere).

After Jesus' death, when for other sufferers there was no hope of direct healing by Jesus, such stories were spread in praise of the great man of God. Jesus' disciples may have repeated them in order to convince others that God was with this Jesus and therefore the listeners should join Jesus' community. Healings also took place within the community (Acts 2:43; Rom 15:18-19; I Cor 12:9, 28; James 5:15). To the extent that it was the living Lord himself who was at work in these healings (Acts 4:10-12: "in the name of Jesus Christ" equals "in him"; Rom 5:18: "Christ worked through me"), the reports of *Jesus'* deeds became indispensable. They were spread farther and farther abroad (Acts 2:22; 10:38). This is in complete contrast to the apocryphal histories of the apostles and Gnostic writings, where only the miracles occurring in the time of the apostles after Easter are important. This expresses, perhaps unconsciously, the theological perception that all of these experiences represent signs of the final, world-changing act of God in Jesus Christ and are intended to call Israel and indeed the world to repentance and faith in God's final dominion.

2.2 The Tradition of Jesus' Critique of the Law. Evidently Jesus occasionally healed on the sabbath. This is never reported of Jewish teachers, and in the post-Easter community healings on the sabbath were certainly no problem; thus the tradition goes back to Jesus. That Mark (3:1-6) and Matthew (with the addition from Q in 12:11-12; similarly Luke 14:5 on another occasion) each report this once, Luke three times, and John twice (5:9; 9:14; also taken up again in 7:23), shows how important this became to the community. When Jesus, in connection with this or a similar incident, made a statement such as Mark 2:27 ("the sabbath was made for man, not man for the sabbath") or Matt 12:11 (that one lifts a sheep out of a pit even on the sabbath), which is similar in form to the wisdom sayings that are to be found in the Old Testament and in Jewish writings, then this was handed down along with the shocking incident. The hearers probably used that at every possible opportunity as an excuse for their actions on the sabbath, or else contradicted the statement. In any case, the healing, which apparently caused a certain amount of excitement, and the saying were spread further.

Here too it was not enough just to report Jesus' saying. A story is told of how Jesus had acted thus, and it continued to be told, even when for some time it was no longer a matter of observing the sabbath, but of completely different questions. Such questions decided whether one was inside or outside the Jewish community (for example, one's position with regard to the law concerning food offerings). The theological assertion is changed simply because the same story stands in a different situation and the same statement vis-à-vis other positions. If Jesus' actions on the sabbath are seen by him symbolically in the light of the hope of an eschatological "sabbath" in God's peace and of liberation from every need,[14] then in the Hellenistic community the violation of the sabbath becomes only an ethical example for the solution of other similar problems. Nevertheless, simply by the fact that Jesus' actions are recalled, the theological perception remains implicit that such freedom was based solely in the uniqueness of the all-fulfilling act of God in Jesus. Indeed this is even made explicit when an express allusion is made to Jesus' power: "So the Son of man is lord even of the sabbath" (Mark 2:28). One can thus determine that the eschatological relevance of the sabbath healing lay for Jesus in looking forward to the now incipient, liberating act of God, and for the community in looking back to that which had already come in Jesus (see 7.5 below).

Other words of Jesus critical of the law were treated similarly, for example Luke 16:18: "Every one who divorces his wife and marries another commits adultery . . . ." This statement is also placed expressly under the unique authority of Jesus when Luke 16:16-17 speaks of the great turning point, which is marked by John the Baptist as the separation between the old and new eras, and in Matt 5:32 when the decision is introduced with "but *I* say to you . . ." The latter is presumably formed later in analogy to other statements in which Jesus himself speaks similarly: "But I say to you that every one who looks at a woman lustfully has already committed adultery with her" (Matt 5:28). However genuine such statements may be, it is certain that Jesus never introduced his sayings as the prophets did, "thus says the Lord," or as the rabbis did, "so it is written," in order then to give an interpretation. In any case, close attachment to the era-changing event of Jesus' proclamation can already be seen in that these sayings are expressly handed down as words of the earthly preacher.

2.3 The Tradition of Jesus' Parables. This conclusion is true particularly of the tradition of his parables (see 27.7 below). The kingdom of God "is like leaven which a woman took and hid in three measures of meal, till it was leavened" (Luke 13:21). That was easy to remember. It made an impression. Now, we can understand a parable only when we let ourselves be completely consumed by it and understand it from the inside.[15] The woman who heard the above parable came as close to the kingdom of God as to her regular bread baking, but at the same time it seemed to be as powerful as one hundred pounds of meal (cf. Gen 18:6), a quantity that would have sufficed for over a hundred eaters and for her would scarcely have been manageable. Had Jesus intentionally spoken so strikingly of "hiding" the leaven in the meal? Is the kingdom of God supposed to be as secret and inaccessible to human vision as the leaven in the meal? It was precisely the completely unexpected, if not impossible, traits—which include the otherwise only negatively used image of the leaven as such—that made an impression and from the beginning called attention to the fact that the topic here is far from being about something understandable and obvious to everyone, but rather is about an extraordinary, unexpected, surprising working of the kingdom of God in the words and deeds of Jesus.

This is no doubt true of all of his parables. What farmer will go on at such length about the failure of his sowing if he does not want to complain and curse (Mark 4:3-7)? What moneylender can loan out a sum that amounts to fifty million times a daily wage and simply forgive such a debt (Matt 18:24-25; cf. Luke 7:42)? What father acts like the one in Luke 15:11-32? The fact that it was precisely these striking traits that the tradition preserved, and indeed reinforced, shows how much it knew about the extraordinary nature of what took place in Jesus.

2.4 The Parables' Shift in Meaning. The message of a parable necessarily changes according to the situation in which it is told. When Jesus told of the lost sheep for whose sake the shepherd left behind the ninety-nine until he found it, it was clear that the topic was the searching love of God that was realized now in the very work of Jesus. Indeed the main point is the joy described in almost exaggerated terms (Luke 15:6-7, also vv. 9-10, 22-24, 32; Matt 18:13). When Luke introduces the parable with the reproach of the Pharisees and scribes (15:1-2), he sees in it above all the defense of Jesus' openness to all people, for example, even to the Gentiles, who are not a part of Israel. This presumably corresponds to Jesus' behavior toward those who have been pushed to the fringes of society, only that now the avoidance of false arrogance is more strongly emphasized than the invitation and joy of God. That means that at the time when it was a question of recognizing Gentiles as full members of the community, Jesus, as the living Lord, continued to speak to new issues. It was not that a prophet would simply give the answer to a question in Jesus' name, but rather he would refer back to the earthly Jesus and the Pharisees and tax collectors of his time, because the validity of the answer depended on the fact that this openness of God had become reality in him.

In this very way, however, there was also the danger that the community would complacently see itself as the herd of found sheep. The reproach against the scribes did not concern them; had they not opened the church to the former Gentiles who wanted to become Christians? Matt 18:10-14 therefore places the parable in a context that speaks of the duties of the community and makes especially clear that one must go after the erring, sinful brother or sister in order to win him or her back. In this way Jesus became an admonisher of the community living in Matthew's time, by way of reference to a parable spoken authoritatively by Jesus.

Something similar is true of Mark 4:1-20. When Jesus spoke of the sower whose sowing yielded such unheard of richness of harvest, although at first one saw only the failure, the birds of prey, the thorns, and the scorching sun, he was in fact speaking of God's activity as it was then being accomplished, surprisingly, unexpectedly, in Jesus' words and deeds. When the community retold this parable it was in imminent danger of regarding itself as the good outcome of the harvest and the outsiders as the conquered birds, thorns, and stony ground. Had not twelve hundred Christians already come from twelve disciples in their own city alone—a hundredfold yield? Were not scribes and Romans and mockers now standing there abashed? In this situation an interpretation like Mark 4:14-20 *had* to be added to let the parable again become a message that moved listeners and opened their hearts, rather than letting them become paralyzed in their self-satisfaction. It warned against birds, thorns, and stones in one's own heart.

2.5 The Christologization of Jesus' Parables. In Mark 4:10-13 explicit reference is made to the earthly Jesus. Only he can proclaim in a way that really lets God speak. Mark underlines this in verse 13, according to which even the disciples understand nothing and belong to "those outside" (see 25.5 below). Jesus speaks in parables so that all the people will really be able to understand (4:33); even here it is again Jesus himself who has to open the hearts of the disciples (4:34) and through them the hearts of all readers of Mark's Gospel.

Thus the community secured its understanding of the parable in an expressly christological manner. That is why in the language of the church the seed is equated with "the word," that is, with the proclamation of Christ (v. 14). What was implicit in Jesus' parable must become explicit after Easter: everything depends on the fact that Jesus is the speaker. His parables must, to a certain extent, be seen allegorically as the proclamation of God's action in Jesus, which in Matt 13:37, for example, becomes crystal clear: "He who sows the

16

good seed is the Son of man.''[16] For this reason the parables are heard again and again as they must be heard, namely, as the word that encounters the listeners in *their* situation and sets them in motion. This process continues in every homiletical interpretation that lets the word come alive in regard to quite particular situations, dangers, and promises. Both of these—the connection with the earthly and coming Jesus Christ *and* the ever new interpretation of what that means for the present life of the hearer—also become visible in the parables that refer to the future consummation (see 3.5-7 below; also 27.6-7; 29.5).

2.6 The Baptism of Jesus. Very early on, presumably even during Jesus' lifetime, the baptism of Jesus was offensive: It seemed to demonstrate subordination to John the Baptist. Hence we have the report of the voice of God electing Jesus (Mark 1:11). That Jesus separated himself from the Baptist and went his own way—yet without consequently rejecting John—is historical fact. We no longer know whether that was connected with a particular experience regarding his baptism, but both his baptism within the repentance movement initiated by John and the fact that God led him beyond this movement are reported again and again and have been distilled in the short report of Mark 1:9-11. The beginning with John remained significant (Acts 10:37; 13:24-25), and Jesus' passage through the baptism movement and beyond became especially important in discussions with the disciples of John (Acts 18:25; 19:3-4). Both appear in all four Gospels (also Luke 7:18-35 Q [see 7.3 below]; John 1:19-36; 3:23-30). Such reports must have been revived repeatedly, not only in actual discussions with outsiders, but also in the instruction of newly won community members and in the worship services in which the community confirmed its faith vis-à-vis other points of view.

Here, too, there is evidence of a gradually developing christological precision. In the parable of the playing children (Luke 7:31-35) John and Jesus stand side by side as envoys of wisdom; in the context of 7:22-23, 28 the unique superiority of Jesus as the "Son of man" is clear, and Matt 11:19 (cf. 11:2!) also interprets the parable in this fashion (see 26.8 below). Yet the fact that John's baptism was not simply absorbed into the Christian practice of baptism, but was remembered as such, shows the theological awareness of the beginning of a new era, which remained datable with John as boundary line and Jesus as fulfiller.

2.7 Peter's Confession of Christ. This theological awareness is decidedly present in the tradition of Peter's confession (Mark 8:27-33). Jesus' curious reticence in regard to the Christ title (v. 30) and the tradition of a much more ambiguous title in John 6:68-69 ("the Holy One of God")—as well as the sharp rebuke of Peter, which is not explainable through a later "competition mentality'' that one might be able to see behind John 21:20-22; Gal 2:11-20—are scarcely conceivable unless conditioned by some incident in Jesus' life. Then the question about the special significance of Jesus' whole existence, about the authority of his whole activity and experience, would go back to the time of his ministry and not just to the last days before his death. In any case, the fact that the episode was handed down at all shows how important this question was considered to be. At the same time, the reluctance is given up more and more. Luke 9:18-22 lacks the rebuke of Peter, and according to Matt 16:13-20 he is praised for his confession of Christ. The fact that the title *Christ* occurs over five hundred times and appears in all Gospels, but is practically never placed on the lips of Jesus, shows an astonishing faithfulness in regard to the historical facts of Jesus' life, especially since that must be seen together with the tradition of the many words and deeds of Jesus that manifest his uniqueness (see 7.5 below).

2.8 Did Jesus Found the Church? Connected with Peter's confession is the promise that Jesus will build his ''church'' (or ''community'') on the foundation of this disciple who confesses him. In all the Gospels the word for church or community appears only here and in the related passage 18:17. This promise was almost certainly projected back from the time after Easter, but it incorporates something that was already with Jesus. It is important to the whole tradition that Jesus gathered around himself both the circle of the twelve and a larger group of followers, including women (Mark 15:41; Luke 8:1-3). Since after Easter the twelve had no clear function, this group was certainly not first formed at that time. It made sense as the core of a reestablishment of the twelve tribes, which is typical certainly for Jesus, but in only a limited way or not at all for the post-Easter community (see 23.1 below). Luke 22:30 (similarly, Matt 19:28) could go back to Jesus, but in any case it shows how the later community traced its self-understanding back to the earthly Jesus and was thus still aware of its character as the Israel called back again to God. Sayings such as Mark 8:34-35 also bound Jesus to his followers. The sending out of the (twelve?) disciples; table fellowship in a broader, and on the last evening emphatically in a smaller, circle; and parables such as that of the mustard seed show how the post-Easter community in a certain (very open!) way was already present with the earthly Jesus.[17] In the talk of the ''flock'' to be reassembled (Mark 14:27-28) or of the ''brethren'' to be called together anew by Peter (Luke 22:32; cf. John 21:17), and also unmistakably in Matt 16:18 and in the further embellishment of the mustard seed parable (see 4.1 below), this community is expressly introduced as the goal defined by Jesus; and this shows—apart from the question of whether or not the words are genuine words of Jesus—how important for the tradition was the anchoring of the community in the life of the earthly Jesus.

2.9 The Lord's Prayer. Jesus taught his disciples to pray, and after Easter they followed his instruction, although not in a legalistic way: the wording of the Lord's Prayer in Luke 11:2-4 differs greatly from that of Matt 6:9-13. But the salutation of God as "Father"[18]—astonishing for a Jew in Jesus' time—is preserved in both versions. How new and unexpected this gift was is seen in the fact that the Greek-speaking community still retains the old Aramaic expression of Jesus for "Father" (*Abba*—Mark 14:36; Rom 8:15; Gal 4:6), and the whole tradition always has Jesus say either "my Father" or "your Father," but he never joins with the disciples in a common "our Father." Even Matt 6:9 means only that the *disciples* should pray, "our Father in heaven." Although Jesus stood in a unique relation to the Father, the community never forgot that he did not understand it in such a way as to raise himself above all others, but rather to express precisely in this way his subordination to God's will (Mark 13:32; Matt 11:25-27).

This indicates that the oral tradition already reflected on the special position of Jesus, which stood out above all others, and not, for example, that they saw him as the only one to instill in his disciples the courage, like him, to break enthusiastically into the cry of "Abba" and thereby transcend earthly life.

3. TRANSMISSION THROUGH PROPHETS

3.1 Radical Discipleship with Itinerant Prophets. Jesus called people to be his disciples. In sharp contrast to rabbinic tradition, where the disciple asked permission to follow the teacher in the hope that as a result of instruction in the Scriptures and the art of interpretation he himself might one day become a similarly famous or even more famous rabbi, here everything is initiated by Jesus. He also admits his disciples not into the classroom but into his fellowship with God, which is lived day by day, without offering them the prospect of any sort of higher position. In the later church, of course, there were no followers who, in the literal sense, followed the earthly Jesus. In the Old Testament there is at best a parallel in the calling of Elisha, where, however, the call occurs substantially less abruptly than with Jesus' disciples, and where it was a matter of a special case and also of the special position of a prophet for the whole of Israel after the death of Elijah (I Kings 19:19-21). For this very reason one must ask who handed down this fact. Without doubt there is in every tradition a "preventive censorship;"[19] that is, only what is meaningful and plausible to the recipient of the tradition will be passed on. This alone would seem to indicate that, at least in the beginning of the tradition, there were people who really had left home and family in order to proclaim the dawning kingdom of God. Their existence is also attested by passages such as Matt 10:41 (also 7:15, 22: when false prophets come in "sheep's clothing," there must also be genuine ones in the community); Acts 11:27; 15:32; 21:9-10 (13:1?), but above all by *Didache*

11-15 (see 9.4 below) and other witnesses into the third century (see 31.2 below). For them the rules of Mark 6:7-13 and Luke 10:3-11 (Q) with their double authority for preaching and healing or driving out demons are valid. In these groups the instructions and promises of Jesus are to be taken literally.

In this way Jesus remains the one who announces and already realizes the kingdom of God in overcoming impenitence, illness, and demonic spirits. Yet the theological significance changes. What was proclamation for Jesus is now related by the prophets to their own destiny and thus to consolation (Luke 6:22-23). Even more, it is understood in a new and different way in a time that scarcely knows such itinerant prophets anymore.[20] Everywhere, nevertheless, there is recourse to the authority conferred by Jesus, and his sayings are inserted into certain situations of his life (apothegmatization—see 7.5 below).

3.2 Prophets in the Acts of the Apostles. All the prophets named in Acts (see 31.2 below) come from Jerusalem; among those named in 13:1 is Barnabas, and Manaen is also connected with the vicinity. Paul was certainly there after his calling (Gal 1:18) and probably also earlier (Acts 7:58; 22:3). Yet Luke never speaks of the prophets in the report concerning the Jerusalem period—probably because for him they, compared to the apostles, are too unsure a foundation of the church (whereas in Eph 2:20 both apostles and prophets still form the foundation). The visions of Stephen (7:56) and Peter (10:10-16, 19-20) are also prophetic. Because Acts 1–15 is seen very much from the standpoint of later development, we know all too little about the Jerusalem church and virtually nothing about the churches in Galilee, which are mentioned only briefly in 9:31.

3.3 Enthusiastic Imminent Expectation? There is, to be sure, disagreement on the extent to which appearances of the resurrected one (see 1.1 above) gave rise to an enthusiastic expectation of an early end.[21] The early Jewish-Christian formula in Rom 1:3-4 (see 5.3 below) speaks only of the raising of Jesus to present lordship, and the Parousia (Jesus' return) appears neither in the passion and resurrection predictions of Jesus (e.g., Mark 8:31) nor in the confessional formulas and hymns (see 5.2 below). Even in Mark, according to whom Jesus will not come again until the Parousia (chap. 13), Jesus is present all the same in his "name" and "Spirit" (see 25.4 below). Besides, the delay of the Parousia is not really a problem until II Pet 3:4, although it influenced the tradition earlier, of course (see 3.5-6; 24.4 below). Nevertheless, there is much evidence that Jesus' resurrection was understood as the beginning of the end and that for that reason the disciples expected the coming of the kingdom of God in the very near future—and naturally in the holy city of God. The curious mention of the already resurrected dead who were wandering around in Jerusalem (Matt 27:52-53) still betrays something of the concept of Easter as the beginning of the end. Mark 13:30-32 and many other passages show the influence of such imminent expectation. Also, Paul's expectation that he will experience the Parousia is expressed more emphatically in I Thess 4:15 than in I Cor 15:51 and particularly more than in Phil 1:23 (alongside 3:20-21).

The twofold orientation toward the delayed coming of the Lord and toward his present activity is also seen in the cry originating in the Aramaic-speaking community, *maranatha* ("Our Lord, come!"—I Cor 16:22; *Didache* 10:6; Rev 22:20 in Greek), which was evidently so central that it was adopted by the Greek-speaking community in its original form. The adoption seems to have occurred particularly in connection with the Lord's Supper.[22] We find also the title *Lord* for Jesus in contexts where it is otherwise lacking: "Death . . . body and blood of the Lord" (I Cor 11:26-27), "Cup . . . table of the Lord" (11:23, 27; 10:21—see 5.4 below). That was, so it seems, the door through which this title entered the language of the community, where it then took on new associations from what *kyrios/lord* meant in the Hellenistic world.

3.4 Statements of Holy Law for the Present. In all three places, however, *maranatha* follows prophetic warnings: "If any one has no love for the Lord, let him be accursed"; "If any one takes away from the words of the book of this prophecy, God will take away his share in the tree of life"; "If any one is holy, let him come; if he is not, let him repent." The form of these statements is that of Old Testament words of wisdom and law ("He who digs a pit [for others] will fall into it [himself]" Prov 26:27; "Whoever sheds the blood of man, by man shall his blood be shed" Gen 9:6). These prophetic warnings are much more radical than the above statements, however, in that they pledge not earthly fortune or misfortune, but God's final judgment. To this extent one can call them "statements of holy law" (*Sätze heiligen Rechtes*)[23] in which prophets proclaim God's judgment and not, say, merely demand measures of church discipline. That means, however, that for the community the future coming of the Lord is already at work in the present. That probably goes back to such words of Jesus as, "Everyone who acknowledges me before men, the Son of man also will acknowledge before the angels of God; but he who denies me before men will be denied before the angels of God" (Luke 12:8-9—see 3.8 below). Like Paul (I Cor 3:17: "If any one destroys God's temple, God will destroy him"; cf. 11:31; 14:38), these prophets may also have re-formed such statements in worship or poured Jesus' statements into this form (e.g., Matt 5:19). In an *if* or *whoever* statement the possibility of obedience or disobedience is always named and human execution of the law is renounced, but God's judgment is expected—including the death of the sinner in extreme cases (I Cor 11:30; 5:1-5; Acts 5:5, 10). This is reflected in Rev 2–3, where the prophet, driven by the Spirit (2:7), speaks in the name of the resurrected one

(2:1) and with express reference to him, and in the process can even use the first person form: "I will come [upon you] like a thief" (3:3; cf. 16:15).

3.5 The Reshaping of Eschatological Sayings. The last example shows how Jesus' words were shaped, oriented toward new conditions and problems, "creatively re-created,"[24] but also how new instructions were given in the name of the resurrected one. If the image of the thief breaking in was first coined, perhaps by Jesus himself, as an allusion to the day of judgment (as still in I Thess 5:2, 4; II Pet 3:10)—for which it is quite appropriate with its threat—then Luke 12:39-40 shows how it was explicitly applied to the coming of the Son of man. Even if we imagine the development reversed,[25] we can see how the original image in the statement is gradually "deparabolized" and is more and more reshaped into a direct statement about Christ.[26]

The change in statements is also ascertainable with the exhortation to "watch." The image of a master who has gone to a marriage feast and will thus return home late is easy to understand. Here it makes sense for the servants to watch, so that they may receive him. That is how the little parable in Luke 12:36-38 is told. The totally unexpected thing, which appears in almost all of Jesus' parables (see 2.3 above), is here simply that the returning master himself invites his servants to sit at table and serves them. This trait, which underlines the unimaginable love and devotion of the coming Lord, is thus greatly emphasized here. In a very similar vein, Mark 13:33-37 tells of a man going on a journey, but the admonition, "Watch therefore, for you do not know when the master of the house will come, in the evening, or at midnight, or at cockcrow, or in the morning," is no longer appropriate. For this master is away on a trip, so it would be completely impossible to watch through every night until early morning. In fact, it also says that he gave each servant his work to do and only asked the doorkeeper to watch. Hence, the warning, "Watch . . . lest he come suddenly and find you asleep," is only to be understood in the figurative sense: they are to do their work dutifully in the meantime. The emphasis is thus on behavior now, in the time that everyone on earth is given, and the expectation of the master's coming only underlines the responsibility the "servants" must fulfill. Thus the community's experience of the Son of man's coming not having occurred so soon clearly colored this little parable, so that it now stresses that the work given every community member must be fulfilled on this earth. Nevertheless, the old cry "Watch!" in verses 33, 35, 37 is still raised three times. Going a step further is the much more developed parable of the ten maidens (Matt 25:1-13). Here it is clearly explained that the bridegroom is coming much later than expected; indeed, that is precisely the point without which the parable would be impossible. It no longer announces the imminent but the later coming, for which people must be prepared. So the exhortation is no longer to watch; even the wise maidens go to sleep. Although the old cry, "Watch therefore, for you know neither the day nor the hour," still closes the parable, it means something different from the original; namely, that one should acquire ahead of time so much oil that it will be sufficient even for an unexpectedly long time. Thus the community is urged to be prepared to persevere in faith and hope even over a lengthy period of time and thus be ready some day to meet their Lord.

3.6 Present Responsibility in View of the Delay of the Parousia. Still more clearly perceivable is the situation of the community in the immediately preceding parable of the master who, during the time of his absence, places one of his servants over his "fellow servants" (Matt 24:45-51). Luke 12:42-46 even calls this servant "steward," differentiating him yet more clearly from the remaining "servants." Thus the parable now describes the task of a community leader. If in this parable it is still the wicked servant who thinks it will still be a long time until the master comes (Matt 24:48; Luke 12:45), the parable of the talents, on the other hand, turns against those who expect his coming in the near future, according to Luke 19:11, and emphasizes only the importance of the service of all servants, for which they will one day be held accountable at the return of their master (Luke 19:12-27; Matt 25:14-30). His long absence is still especially emphasized in the Lukan form: he has gone into a far country, in order to receive kingly power (v. 12), just as Jesus has gone into heaven in order to return again some day as king. A historical event after the death of Herod in 4 B.C.[27] has colored the story. What happened at that time is incorporated into the parable in verse 14 and especially in verse 27, which goes beyond the context. That is, after Jesus has already interpreted the parable in first person in verse 26, in the next verse the "nobleman" of the parable suddenly speaks again and gives the order to cut down his enemies. With both verses Luke wants to stress the seriousness of the warning and the judgment that threatens those who reject the dominion of Jesus.

3.7 Shifts in Accent. Viewed theologically, in the older strata the future coming of the kingdom of the Son of man thus seems to be the actual center of the message, and surely in such a way that the coming kingdom is perceived as already working in and shaping the present. The concrete significance of this for the daily life of the hearer is secondary, however, compared to the announcement of the fact *that* it will happen. While the expectation of the fulfillment of what has already happened in Jesus remains essentially constant, the unfolding of its meaning for the present activity of the community is variable. Even at the level of oral tradition Jesus is, from the beginning, the one who announces God's final fulfillment and will play a decisive role in it (see 3.8 below); since Easter he is also the one who has set the final events in motion.

23

Yet this gradually becomes presupposed background that is taken for granted and is therefore hardly mentioned anymore in confessional formulas and hymns (see 5.2 below); instead, more and more is said about what the coming event means for the community now and for its whole way of life. Sometimes, the warning, against all too enthusiastic expectations of an early end and sometimes against a slacking of hope, moves more prominently to the center of attention.

3.8 The Son of Man as Judge. Whether Jesus saw himself as the Son of man and spoke thereof is vigorously disputed. It is probable, since the title—quite different from the *Christ* title—appears only on Jesus' lips, except for Acts 7:56 (and used merely as a comparison without the definite article in Rev 1:13; 14:14). He may have seen his future role as that of the crucial witness in the judgment, whose intercession for or accusation against a person decides the case (Luke 12:8-9). Paul also makes the same point (I Cor 4:5), without using the title *Son of man* (which would be incomprehensible to Greeks). He will disclose how things are with us, and then the "commendation" (the gracious pronouncement of judgment) will come from God. But because Jesus' standing in for us decides the case, in the same sentence Paul can designate even Jesus himself as judge (v. 4) and speak of his judgment seat (II Cor 5:10) as well as that of God (Rom 14:10). Thus whereas Jesus, according to Luke 12:8-9, spoke almost symbolically of his role in the final judgment with the puzzling phrase *Son of man,* or rather of the role that his proclamation and his behavior will play as the standard for every verdict of God, the community christologized this more and more; that is, it spoke more and more of his Parousia (his "coming," his "appearance") using a word for which the language of Jesus had no expression.

3.9 Wandering or Settled Prophets? If we look back at the entire development, then it becomes clear how from the beginning the transmission of Jesus' sayings was also "prophetically" oriented again and again toward the changing situation and statement of the problem; that is, old sayings were reformulated and new ones coined. Naturally, those in the tradition felt themselves led by the resurrected Jesus. One must be careful, however, in equating these tradition bearers with the radical wandering prophets (see 3.1 above). The only ones who are to some extent historically accessible to us are the disciples who accompanied Jesus, the twelve and perhaps a wider circle, plus the women who followed him from Galilee (Mark 15:41; Luke 8:1-3). Concerning them, however, two facts can be ascertained. First, these are the very ones who settled in Jerusalem, in distinction to those Hellenists who were forced into their wandering life-style by the persecution in Jerusalem (Acts 8:1, 4-5). This transition from the nomadic life to the settled state is also seen in a different way in the prophets of Antioch (Acts 13:1) and Caesarea (21:8-9), in contrast to Agabus (v. 10). To be sure, Agabus, Judas, and Silas also seem to live in Jerusalem and to undertake journeys from there (11:27-28; 15:32-33; 21:10). Likewise *Did.* 13:1 speaks of wandering prophets who settle down. Those named by Pseudo-Clement[28] find settled prophets who receive them into their homes, and those mentioned in the *Apocalypse of Peter* of Nag Hammadi 79:19-29 also seem to have a permanent residence. A second observation is more important: the radical understanding of the call to discipleship, according to which the called leave "everything," is not found until Luke 5:11, 28 (versus Mark 1:18, 20; 2:14; only Mark 10:28 from Peter's lips). This would indicate that at the beginning of the tradition there was no sharp separation between those who left everything, those who left their homes in order to resettle in another place, and those who only took on themselves the risk of great loss, if need be, for Jesus' sake. Perhaps the stories were told again and again, so that all the details became unimportant and—almost in wood-cut fashion—told only of his coming, his view, his call, his promise, and the obedience of the called, which seemed to be taken for granted (Mark 1:16-20; 2:14; cf., told like a short story, Luke 19:1-10).

3.10 Easter and Pentecost as a Decisive Caesura. On the other hand, the form of discipleship for those about whom we have information—the twelve, the women, and a not very clearly described wider circle—was redefined and reshaped by their encounters with the resurrected one. As far as we know, they now live with their families in Jerusalem. The prophets going out from there return again or settle somewhere else. Whether there were more radical wandering prophets in Galilee, and if so, how many, we do not know. Above all, the conviction that the risen Jesus Christ continued to speak through his prophets was very strong in the first experience after Easter; that is, it was defined by the event of the resurrection and was certainly not a more or less unbroken continuation of the Galilean activity. Of course, with the twelve in Jerusalem (Acts 2:32, etc.), as with Paul and his opponents (appearing as wandering prophets?—Rom 15:19; I Cor 12:9-10; II Cor 12:12), we see the same twofold authority to preach and to heal as in Jesus' sending-out speeches, but, completely different from the latter, that authority is attributed to the Spirit. The coming of the Spirit is linked with a post-Easter event in Jerusalem (Pentecost) and for Paul with his calling by the resurrected one. Where the work of the Spirit is explicitly mentioned in Rev 2–3 it is christologically based on the "true witness, the beginning of God's creation" (3:14), namely, the resurrected one (2:1, 8), raised as Lord and Judge (2:12, 18; 3:1, 7). In any case, Easter is understood as the inbreaking event that first makes possible the apocalyptic experience of an already dawning new world.

4. TRANSMISSION THROUGH "SCRIBES"

4.1 The Fulfillment of the Old Testament in Jesus' Parables. Early Christendom had no Bible except our Old Testament. The extent to which Jesus was already shaped by its passages and consciously referred back to them is again in dispute, but anyone in Jesus' day who knew the Bible even to a small degree found in it what Jesus was talking about and what he did and experienced. When he told of the mustard seed that became a tree (Luke 13:19 Q), those who passed on the parable were reminded of passages like Ps 104:12, which speaks of birds in the branches. By this the "tree" promised by Jesus became the fulfillment of what was already indicated in the creation, and from there the idea that Jesus' community is the fulfillment and perfection of God's creative activity lay only a step away. Perhaps Q was already influenced by the wisdom saying of the tree planted by God himself in Ezek 17:23 or by Dan 4:12, 21, which speaks of a tree and the dwelling of the birds in its branches. Then this would mean that the final perfection had now occurred. In the place of tyrants and their kingdoms, God has set Jesus and his community. The formulation in Mark 4:32 ("in its shade") comes even closer to Ezek 17:23 and 31:6. It is highly probable that in Jesus' parable Mark sees an announcement of the fulfillment of the prophetic saying that "under its shadow dwelt all great nations" (Ezek 31:6; essentially also Dan 4:21-22). Here, no doubt, we have the fruit of "scribal work," the reflection of people who can read the prophetic texts and have access to biblical scrolls, rare in those days, and time for their study (cf. 23.5 below). What was included in Jesus' authoritative telling can be shown thus: now, in Jesus and in the new people of God called forth by him, God's plans for Israel and the peoples of the world are being fulfilled. As long as Jesus himself told parables like this one, the entire emphasis was that even now God's final activity is beginning and that listeners should open themselves to it. Looking back to Jesus' work after Easter, it became important to include it explicitly in God's salvation history.

4.2 The Fulfillment of the Old Testament in the Future. Something similar can be ascertained in the community's future expectation. Jesus himself probably spoke of the coming end time only in images, above all that of the banquet (Mark 14:25; Luke 22:15-18, 24-30; 12:37; 14:15-21). This was expanded early on by the community through what they found in their Bible. Often the prophets spoke of sword, famine, and pestilence, which would come before God's final intervention (Jer 14:12; 21:7; 38:2; Ezek 5:12; cf. 14:21; I Kings 8:37). Ezek 38:19-22 also combines earthquake with sword and pestilence, and according to Amos 8:8 and Joel 2:10 the collapse of the cosmos will begin with a powerful earthquake. Times of struggle and persecution are the topic in Mic 7:6 and a Jewish writing from the second century B.C. (*Jub.*

23:19-25). That led to a whole chain of omens, as introduced in Mark 13:7-9, 24-27 (pestilence only in the parallel Luke 21:11) and quite similarly in Rev 6 (rebellion, war, earthquake, famine, pestilence, persecution, cosmic collapse). Added to this was a prediction about the fall of Jerusalem (in the heavy troubles at the end of the sixties?) and admonitions to the community, which warned against temptations (Mark 13:14-20 and vv. 5-6, 21-23) and also called for endurance in persecution (13:9-11, 13).

Whether Jesus himself was thinking of Dan 7 when he mysteriously and provocatively spoke of the "Son of man" (see 3.8 above) is uncertain. In any case, the express reference to this passage and its combination with Ps 110:1 in Mark 14:62 or with Zech 12:10-14 in Rev 1:7 are the work of community members knowledgeable of the Bible.

4.3 The Fulfillment of the Old Testament in the Passion of Jesus. A special problem is presented by the passion story. Naturally, it cannot simply be passed down to the praise of Jesus like his healings or even the parables and ethical admonitions. It became meaningful only through its interpretation. That happened very early, as demonstrated by the formulas already taken over by Paul (see 5.4-5 below). In a certain sense Jesus' passion was traumatic for the community;[29] thus it was necessary that the question of its meaning be raised. In regard to the passion story, there was never "innocent telling" (as opposed to the sinful fall of speech).[30] One wonders whether that was *fundamentally* different from the remaining stories and reports about Jesus. No one told of the healings of Jesus without at least implicitly raising the question of whether this Jesus was not the eschatological prophet or man of God or miracle worker or Messiah. Yet there it was less urgent than with the passion of Jesus to remember the Old Testament prophecies and even to refer expressly to them. Certainly the reference to them or even a gradually solidifying formula such as "in accordance with the scriptures" or "thus was fulfilled . . ." is a clear invitation to the hearer to understand the event in this way, and it no longer simply leaves open an abundance of answers. But healing stories let the question of Jesus' authority and significance emerge on their own; his passion, on the other hand, was incomprehensible without such allusions and could not be passed on without an offer such as I Cor 15:3-5 or Rom 4:25 or the very echo of Old Testament descriptions of the suffering righteous one.

The passion and death of Jesus, however, were not only attested to in such formulas; they were also recounted. This is already presupposed in I Cor 11:23. At the very least, the community knows about the night on which Jesus was betrayed and about the preceding meal with the disciples. According to verse 26 the death of Jesus is proclaimed with or in the Lord's Supper. This is scarcely conceivable without corresponding liturgical texts. It is correct that the problem of Jesus' death was not to be overcome merely "textually"—neither through narrative report nor through interpretive formula. It was repeatedly remembered in the celebration of the meal,[31] but the meal itself, at least for its part, acquired assertive power only through the text of (interpreting) words of Jesus and a short report as introduction.

4.4 Implicit and Explicit References. In Mark the passion story is still told naively to the extent that it is generally shaped by the picture of the suffering righteous one, as it would have to happen with a Jew who reports of Jesus' passion in an unreflected, matter-of-fact way. With Mark it is, as a rule, still uncertain whether or not a certain scriptural passage stands behind a report (14:18, 34, 38; 15:23/36, 29, 33). Although the words over the cup in the Last Supper point to the redemption of death "for many" announced in Isa 53:11 (Mark 14:24; also in Jesus' saying in 10:45), there is no express reference to this passage, which is also used in the pre-Pauline formula of Rom 4:25. Whether Isa 53:7, 12 stands behind 14:49, 61 and 15:27 remains uncertain. Only 14:27 (where the shepherd is struck, the sheep will scatter) refers to scripture. Clearly the aftereffect of Ps 22 is in 15:24, 34 (division of the clothes, Jesus' cry, "My God, my God . . . ") (vv. 18, 1), without the Psalm being mentioned. Only gradually do allusions to scripture become clearer (Matt 27:9-10, 34, 43; Luke 23:34-35, 46, 49) and even expressly mentioned (Luke 22:37 [Isa 53:12!]; John 13:18; 19:24, 28, 36-37). Here, as in other details, another passion tradition appears in Luke and John with certain points of contact between these two Gospels. In Matt 27:3-10; Acts 1:16-20; and Papias (frag. 3) we have three different versions of Judas's fate shaped more and more by the scripture (first Zech 11:12-13 [with Jer 18:2; 19:1; 32:7]; then Pss 69:25; 109:8; finally Pss 69:23; 109:18).[32] In view of what is already presupposed by Paul and the broad and diversified tradition, it is highly unlikely that the passion story first came into being with the written composition of the Gospel.[33]

5. TRANSMISSION IN THE LITURGY[34]

5.1 The Name of the "Lord" Who Is Resurrected from the Dead. The cry "Our *Lord,* come!" (see 3.3-4 above) is itself an expression of faith within the worshiping assembly. "Jesus is Lord" is understood as a confession of faith inspired by the Holy Spirit (I Cor 12:3). As the content of preaching II Cor 4:5 names "Jesus Christ as Lord" (cf. Acts 9:28), and in the worship service the "name of our Lord Jesus Christ" is sounded as an invocation (I Cor 1:2; cf. Joel 2:32 [3:5] in Rom 10:13 and probably also in Acts 2:21 in reference to Jesus, similarly II Tim 2:22; Acts 9:14, 21; 22:16; Jas 2:7; *Herm.* 72:4 (= *Herm. Sim.* VIII 6:4). In baptism there is an appeal to the "name of the Lord Jesus (Christ)": Acts 8:16; 19:5; I Cor 6:11; *Did.* 9:5 (versus 7:1); for "where his lordship is proclaimed, there is the Lord (*Did.* 4:1). Healings and demon expulsions were also performed "in the name of the Lord": Acts 19:13, 17 (Jas 5:14?).

The "confession of the Lord Jesus" can also be formulated as the content of "saving" faith in the form of a report: "God has raised Jesus from the dead" (Rom 10:9). God is no longer only the Supreme Being, but has now shown himself as the one who raised Jesus[35] (from the dead): I Thess 1:9-10; Rom 4:24; 8:11; Gal 1:1; II Cor 4:14; cf. I Cor 6:14. Very early on a particular person or persons are mentioned who are witnesses of this event: "The Lord has risen indeed, and has [been seen by] Simon" (Luke 24:34; cf. I Cor 15:4-5). Such confessions were presumably part of the (baptismal) worship service. In any case, God is praised in similar terms in Jewish psalms and confessions: "Bless the Lord . . . who forgives all your iniquity" (Ps 103:2-3); "I am the Lord your God, who brought you out of the land of Egypt" is even supposed to be expressed as a constant confession in the tassels of all garments (Num 15:41, cf. Exod 20:2); cf. Isa 45:6-7: "I am the Lord . . . I form light and create darkness." Independent sentences are more frequent, often introduced with *for*: "Give thanks to the Lord, for he is good" (Ps 106:1, where a long list of his deeds follows, and elsewhere); cf. Pss 111; 113 (vv. 1-2: "the name of the Lord"; v. 7: "He raises the poor from the dust"); 118; 121:2 ("My help comes from the Lord, who made heaven and earth"); 123:1 ("who art enthroned in the heavens").

5.2 Resurrection—Parousia—Judgment. In Rom 10:9 the resurrection of Jesus is seen as the beginning of his lordship. That is also true of I Cor 15:4, because the Greek form ("he has been raised") designates an event that still remains valid. In I Thess 1:10 this assertion is directly tied to his function as Savior at the last judgment. While Jesus' resurrection was understood at first, by some at least, as the beginning of the resurrection of all the dead (see 3.3 above), it soon became evident that this was not happening. The linking of the two events is hardly found outside of Paul (I Thess 4:14; I Cor 15:12-20; 6:14; Rom 8:11, 29; II Cor 4:14; pre-Pauline in Rom 1:4?—see 5.3 below) and not in the first three Gospels, presumably because the resurrection of Jesus at first meant less the overcoming of death than the beginning of his lordship and thus his exaltation (see 8.8 above). According to Paul (and also a hymn known to him?) the worldwide adoration of the exalted "Lord" will be fulfilled at Jesus' return (see 5.10 below). In the (pre-Pauline?[36]) confession of I Cor 8:6 ("one God, the Father . . . and one Lord, Jesus Christ") it is notable, vis-à-vis Jewish[37] and Stoic assertions about God, that we not only come "from" him but also exist "for" or "to" him—this with perhaps a thought toward the final consummation (versus Eph 4:6).[38] That, however, does not change the fact that although return, judgment, and consummation are, to be sure, presupposed everywhere, they are not actually found in a confession or hymn. Together with

29

faith in the one God, they belong to missionary preaching, because the sequence—monotheism, resurrection of Jesus, last judgment—appears in I Thess 1:9-10 as well as in Acts 17:22-31.

5.3 Incorporation into Israel's History and Designation as "Son of God." In Rom 1:3-4 we read: ". . . descended from David according to the flesh and [installed as] Son of God in power according to the Spirit of holiness by [the] resurrection from the dead, Jesus Christ our Lord." The rhythmical form of the parallelism, the concentration on important confessional statements, linguistic peculiarities, statements that would not be necessary from the standpoint of context, and parallels of content and language in other texts (elsewhere Paul never speaks thus of the son of David) identify the text as a quotation, perhaps expanded or slightly modified by Paul (see 23.4 below). It may come from a Jewish-Christian community, be introduced by Paul with "concerning his Son" (beginning of v. 3 in tension with what is said in the confession itself in v. 4), and be carried further with verses 5-7 (including "Jesus Christ our Lord"?). What is important is the incorporation into God's history with Israel and installation as Son of God in the resurrection. As in Ps 2:7, here *Son of God* is the title of the one called by God to lordship. It is also understood this way in Acts 13:33 (cf. 2:36). What is curious is the general reference to (literally) the "resurrection of the dead" (and not to "his resurrection from the dead"). That could go back to a time in which this was still placed entirely in the context of the resurrection of all the dead (see 3.3 above).[39] Resurrection is thus understood here in the context of sonship of David not as a cosmic event but as the beginning of the execution of his royal sovereignty over his people (not over the cosmos). Hence there is a two-step schema: the one who has already appeared as Davidic Messiah or Messiah candidate is appointed by the resurrection to full royal sovereignty, in which the additional phrase "in power" is perhaps a Pauline refinement. Thus here the assertion of the resurrection is linked, on the one hand, with the earthly activity (or only the birth?) of Jesus and his embedding in the expectation of the son of David and, on the other, with his lordship over his people, not with his final coming as in I Thess 1:10.

5.4 The Meaning of Jesus' Death. Whether there was actually a formula that spoke only of Jesus' death is uncertain. "Die for" or "for . . . sake" is pre-Pauline formulaic speech, because in Rom 5:6, 8; 14:15; I Cor 8:11 the subject is always "Christ," in I Thess 5:10 "our Lord Jesus Christ," never "Jesus" or "the Lord (Jesus)." The "death of the Lord" is proclaimed only in the Lord's Supper (I Cor 11:26) and for reasons already given (see 3.3 above). Along with this the formulation of the "delivering" of Jesus became established. In the Gospels the sentence, "Son of man will be delivered into the hands of (the sons of) men,'' is presumably the oldest (Mark 9:31) in which the use of the passive points to God's decision, which is not explained. Also Mark 8:31 (''the Son of man must suffer many things and be rejected'') does not explain the necessity of the suffering, which, as in Luke 17:25; 22:15; 24:26, 46; Acts 1:3; 3:18; 17:3; Heb 13:12; I Pet 2:21, includes dying. Rom 4:25, on the other hand, says he was ''put to death for our trespasses'' (see 5.5 and 8.7 below); similar is the Lord's Supper tradition of I Cor 11:23, where ''for you'' in verse 24 corresponds to ''for many'' in Mark 14:24. Rom 8:32 is formulated in the active voice: God ''did not spare his own Son but gave him up for us all.'' Jesus' self-giving is the message in Gal 1:4; 2:20; Eph 5:2; also Mark 10:45 (of the Son of man), and related to this is I Tim 2:6 (''as a ransom for all''). The death of Jesus was also connected with baptism: Rom 6:3; (cf. Mark 10:38; Luke 12:50). Thus, already in the pre-Pauline tradition, formulaic language in baptism and the Lord's Supper pointed to the ''death of Christ.'' Also the phrase the ''blood shed for many'' appears before Mark and (abbreviated) also before Paul in connection with the Lord's Supper; likewise, in Rom 3:25; 5:9 and often after Paul, the blood of Jesus and also the ''lamb'' are mentioned (I Cor 5:7; John 1:29; I Pet 1:19; Rev 5:6). Evidence of the Lord's Supper liturgy is provided by I Cor 11:23-26 and Mark 14:22-24; for the baptismal liturgy Rom 6:3-4 allows us to presume that one component was a corresponding formulation about Jesus' death for us.

5.5 The Double Formula of Jesus' Death and Resurrection. On a further level of development (which temporally does not absolutely have to be set later), Mark 8:31; 9:31; 10:34 expressly add being killed and the resurrection to the passion and rejection. In I Cor 15:3-5 dying for sins and being resurrected are already tied together. Those are the two salvation events, both assured through the burial on the one hand and the appearance to Cephas and the twelve on the other. Paul himself adds ''more than five hundred,'' James, all the apostles, and himself as witnesses. ''For us'' is mentioned with the dying (although the cross is not), while presumably the fulfillment of scripture, which is named in both parts, is especially emphasized with the resurrection ''on the third day'' (Hos 6:2!). Yet the Greek form shows that Christ as the resurrected one is still there for the community. Thus it is the confession of a community that thinks in terms of (salvation) history (''in accordance with the scriptures'') and for whom the decisive problem is enduring the last judgment (''for our sins''). The introduction shows that Paul ''received'' this formula in Jerusalem or Antioch and ''delivered'' it to the Corinthians. Thus the community summarized in binding fashion what the core of their faith was, and the apostle passed it on to those who wanted to join the community—presumably before baptism. That does not exclude the possibility that what is said therein must be interpreted again and again, and also that in worship new confessions can be spontaneously called out or sung, in fixed form (I Cor 12:3?) or newly formulated. Such a practice can be observed today, say, in churches in Asia and Africa, where the refrain of a song remains constant while everything else varies according to the situation and the inspiration of the singer.

Romans 4:25 also links the sacrifice of Jesus our Lord for our trespasses and his resurrection for our justification. The linking of resurrection and justification, unusual for Paul, and the sacrificial formula, which is based on Isa 53:12, point to a pre-Pauline origin. Also, in the summaries of Peter's sermons in the Acts of the Apostles, death (as crucifixion) and resurrection stand side by side, but in the configuration ''you have crucified him whom God has raised'' (or something similar): 2:23-24; 3:15; 4:10; 10:39-40 (detailed by Paul in 13:27-30). In this the exaltation to lordship and glory is tied to the resurrection (Acts 2:32-33; 5:30-31; cf. the appointment of Jesus as judge in 10:40-43; 17:31) or can replace it (2:36; 3:13). Similar to I Cor 15:5(-8), the witness of the apostles is also added in 2:32; 3:15; 5:32; 10:39; 13:31; different from that is the reference to the earthly Jesus (2:22; 10:37-38).

5.6 The Mission of the Preexistent Son. In the statement that God sent his Son so that he might save people in Gal 4:4-5; Rom 8:3-4; John 3:16-17; and I John 4:9, we have what is not a formula but a somewhat fixed form of speech that reminds us of Jewish statements about Wisdom (Wis 9:10, 17 etc.).[40] Central here is the coming of Jesus and the presupposition that he dwelt with God as Son before his birth. Admittedly that appears as unstressed background, probably because the wisdom of God, in its active involvement in creation (Prov 8:22-31; Sir 24:3-6) and in the history of Israel (Sir 24:7-12; Wis 10-12), was already regarded in contemporary Judaism as a person sent by God, similar to an angel but at the same time as the actual being of God standing over all angels. In all five passages the final clause points to Jesus' dying for humanity, yet without this being directly stated (Gal 3:13/4:5; Rom 8:3 ''as a sin offering,'' as often in Lev; John 3:14-15 par. to vv. 16-17; I John 4:10). The images of a dwelling with God before coming to earth, which were adopted from Jewish Wisdom thought, are thus not only important in themselves, but are intended to capture the idea that in Jesus' death and then also in his becoming one with human beings (Phil 2:6-8: see 5.10 below; Heb 1:3; 2:11-18: see 21.2 below) God himself really encountered the world. In Paul—with the possible exception of II Cor 8:9—a clear allusion to a preexistent Jesus is found only in set formulas (I Cor 8:6) or hymns (Phil 2:6-8; then Col 1:15-18; cf. 5.10-13 below). Thus, without express reflection on the time before Jesus' coming and the manner of his dwelling with God, Jewish wisdom language was used to express the God dimension of the Jesus event. That was important in a community for whom expectations of a Davidic king over Israel were no longer alive.

The express formula of the confession of (or faith in) Jesus (Christ) as Son of God is then found in Heb 3:1; 4:14; 10:23; I John 4:15; 5:5 (cf. 2:23); and perhaps Acts 8:37. The confession of his coming in the flesh is stressed in I John 4:2 and II John 7.

5.7 The Revelation Schema. Even the so-called revelation schema[41] is not a set formula, but the expression of a certain viewpoint with a few set motifs. It asserts that through God's decision the long hidden "mystery" (*mystērion*) has now become apparent to all people through Christian preaching. As far as we can tell it is thoroughly connected with the Gentile mission of Paul (in the later addition of Rom 16:25-27; Col 1:25-26; Eph 3:1-3, 8-11, cf. v. 6). Here the preaching of the gospel is itself understood as a salvation event, and the apostle has become something like a savior figure. This is possible and meaningful in a world that feels itself abandoned by God—"secularized" or "profane" in today's language. For that world, the new coming of God in the message of Christ, without any effort on its part, is the decisive miracle. What happened to that world is the same thing that happened to the tax collector into whose life Jesus stepped (Mark 2:14; Luke 19:5-6; cf. 5.12 below).

5.8 The Hymns of Revelation. The situation is different with the hymns,[42] because the singing of a congregational song is in itself already an act of faith, and especially because here the addressee is God or the exalted Christ himself. Thus the function of the hymn is not the delineation of proper faith vis-à-vis heresy and superstition, nor is it exhortation to a life befitting the faith; rather, it is praise of God. In praise one may and must affirm that fundamentally God has already accomplished everything, even if this is still resisted by the absence or inadequacy of human faith. The singing of the community is mentioned in I Cor 14:26; Eph 5:18-20; and Col 3:16. The models are the biblical psalms and the Jewish songs of praise, for example, in Qumran. Of course, we see less asserted of the believer's experience and more of God's action than in those models. While the short baptismal song (?) of Eph 5:14 extols the waking from sleep, the (already achieved) resurrection from the dead, and enlightenment through Christ, the songs of Revelation place worship of the cosmic Lord, who created everything (4:8, 11) and has achieved his dominion (11:17-18; 15:3-4; 16:7), beside that of the sacrificed Lamb that has purchased for God a royal priesthood (5:9-10, 12). In this song, God and the Lamb together are recipients of hymns of praise (5:13; 7:10, 14-17; 11:15; 12:10-12; cf. 15:3; 19:6-8). Old Testament forms appear in the threefold "holy," in the hallelujah, in the acclamation with the dative, in the cry "worthy art thou . . .", in the summons to worship and praise and be happy, and in the reporting of God's great deeds from the creation through the present and into a future often already anticipated in worship (4:8, 11; 5:9-10; 11:15, 17-18; 12:10-11; 19:1, 5, 6-7).[43]

5.9 Temporal and Spatial Categories. Where detailed psalms appear, they describe clearly the Christ event. In all of these, Christ's being with God before his birth and his exaltation after death are asserted or at least presupposed. The theological view is thus different from that in the confessions or in the hymns of Revelation. The common source is the knowledge about Jesus as the "Lord." Even the confessions (except in Acts 2:22; 10:38, where there is hardly a fixed formula) speak not of the earthly activity of Jesus, but of the events that frame it: birth, death, and resurrection, which point to his divine (transcendent) character; but they do it in the categories of historical events. In the hymns of praise in Revelation the sacrifice of the Lamb is central (5:9-10, 12), but is expanded back to creation (4:11: God, but cf. 3:14; 15:3) and forward to the final assumption of lordship (11:15; 12:10: God and the Lamb). So, here too, the components of time and history are decisive. In the hymns to be discussed in what follows, the model of space is more strongly at work. They speak of the reopened unity of heaven and earth, of the "heavenly" dimension of the Christ event, in which God himself—heaven—dwells on earth. They always begin (except in 5:13) with ". . . who . . ."; an original beginning "we praise him who . . ." or "Hallelujah to him who . . ." has fallen away, because in the continuity of the letter Jesus is already mentioned, and to this the content of the praise is added.

5.10 Phil 2:6-11. In a first strophe of Phil 2:6-11, the incarnation of the one dwelling with God[44] is described as humbled (see 5.6 above). Death is only the last step (presumably Paul is the first to mention the cross). The second strophe speaks of exaltation to "Lord" (with perhaps Paul again adding "to the glory of God the Father"). It remains uncertain whether the adoration of the *kyrios* "in heaven and on earth and under the earth"—which is scarcely to be restricted to angels and living and dead people, but probably includes all "powers"—was originally understood as already fulfilled through the exaltation of Jesus[45] (against this see 7.8 below). It is certain that Paul did not expect this until the Parousia. Rom 14:11 contains the same quotation from Isa 45:23; this passage and I Thess 4:15-17; I Cor 15:25-28; and Phil 3:20-21 as well as the appeal to the *kyrios* ("Lord") in Matt 7:22 and 25:11 certainly refer to the Parousia and the last judgment, which naturally also shape present-day life (see 3.4 above). Here too—in remarkable agreement with Q (see 7.7-8 below), where we find an entirely different picture of Christ—cross and resurrection are not central. Death is the final consequence of service in humiliation, and the resurrection is understood as exaltation and proves itself in Jesus' position as judge of the world, as in Q. Stressed here, to be sure, is less the temporally than the spatially unrestricted lordship.

5.11 Col 1:15-20. If the confessional formulas (with few exceptions) and hymns discussed thus far originated before Paul, that is, before ca. A.D. 50, this is no longer certain when we come to Col 1:15-20 (see 17.1 below). Different from Phil 2:6-8, here, as probably already in I Cor 8:6 (see 5.2, 5.6 above), the creation is seen as the gracious and loving openness of God to the creatures (see 5.13 below). It is precisely this gracious and loving openness that is completed in Christ. Thus the community can already understand creation as the beginning of the Christ event: in him, through him, and to him everything was created. Beside this (first) creation (vv. 15-16) comes the new creation in the resurrection of Jesus (vv. 18b-20). A short connecting strophe (vv. 17-18a) states that the whole cosmos is held together in him; the reference to the church was probably added by the letter writer. It is all the more curious that verse 20 mentions the reconciliation of all things, without speaking of a separation. Yet here the writer is not thinking at all in terms of salvation history. In the hymn the community turns directly to the exalted Lord, who is Lord of both the creation and the new creation. The temporal sequence no longer plays a role. As in 5.12 (below) the dwelling with God—there before the incarnation, here at the creation—and the resurrection or exaltation are central statements of faith. The reference to the death in Col 1:20 is, in any case, a later addition, presumably added by the letter writer. Again the reconciliation of the cosmos, the binding of heaven and earth is essential.[46]

5.12 I Tim 3:16. Presumably to be placed even later (see 20.1 below) is I Tim 3:16, a short Christ hymn that is expressly designated as a generally recognized confession of faith of the church. The creation is not mentioned here. The beginning presupposes as obvious that Christ belongs to the heavenly world of God, so that even his manifestation in the flesh is a miracle. Immediately after this is his exaltation (literally, his justification—see 29.9 below), which is developed as an appearance to the angels (in his triumphant ascension as in Col 2:15?), then, as in the revelation schema (see 5.7 above), as a proclamation among the nations and recognition through the faith of the world, and is finally reported as assumption into glory. Earthly and heavenly events are always linked together, specifically in the order a-b, b-a, a-b, which is also found, for example, in Prov 10:1-5 (good-bad, bad-good, good-bad); 11:16-20, 25-28; 29:6-10. The contemporary Hellenistic world lived with the feeling of being torn apart: heaven had moved far away, earth had become heavenless and left on its own, the Deity was unreachable, and heaven was pitiless, the sky like a brazen dome repelling all prayers and cries. Into this feeling of cosmic abandonment the community sings: earth and heaven, heaven and earth, earth and heaven have come together again in him, Jesus Christ. His coming from heaven and his return to heaven, which includes the adoration of all the angels and all nations, thus become the decisive statement of faith.

5.13 John 1:1-18. In yet another form this view is taken up in a Logos hymn that is contained in John 1:1-18. Verses 6-8 interrupt the logical flow. Verse 8 explains, "He (John) was not the light . . ."; verse 9 says that he (the Logos as in v. 5) was the true light. Since 1:6-8 speak of the Baptist, one can only relate what is said in verses 9-13 to the "Word" that has already become flesh, that is, to Jesus of Nazareth. Then, however, verse 14, with its nonetheless decisive statement, "And the Word (Logos) became flesh," adds nothing new. Quite probably, then, the evangelist already had before him a Logos hymn that, without verses 6-8, spoke in the language of Old Testament wisdom of the coming of the Word of God and his rejection by Israel, in order then to sing (in vv. 14-18) of the final devotion of God in the incarnate Word, Jesus Christ. Verse 15 (and 17?) also appears as an insertion of the evangelist. As in Col 1:15-16, the writer speaks expressly of the work of Christ—here the Logos (= "Word")—in creation. The reference back to Jewish assertions of the word or wisdom of God (Prov 3:19; 8:27-31; Wis 7:21-22; 9:1, 9; Philo *Cher.* 127) is especially clear. Thus in John 1:1-5 we see at work the motif of the prehistorical reign of wisdom, but the following assertions are shaped by the other motif of the sending of wisdom, which is typical of Q (see 7.8 below) but also of Phil 2:6-8.[47] In contrast to Col 1:15-20, the incarnation as such is the high point of the hymn. If this, as self-humiliation, was the theme in Phil 2:6-8, even there the aim was nevertheless exaltation and cosmic adoration. In other hymns and confessional formulas, too, the incarnation does not appear as such, but at best, as in Phil 2:6-8, in connection with Jesus' death (see 5.6 above) or as in I Tim 3:16 as mere manifestation. Here, however, the "glory" of Jesus Christ is to be seen (1:14) precisely in the incarnation of the Word of God, which was previously apparent only to a few (1:12-13). According to verse 18, that glory consists in the fact that the only begotten (or: begotten by the only one?) God, who is in the bosom of the Father, has made God known to us—literally, has exegeted God—whom no one has ever seen. Here the category of the wisdom teacher is still operative, although the category "God" is already used of Jesus, as in verse 1 of the preexistent one.

If all the confessional formulas and hymns discussed thus far were open toward the post-Easter community's proclamation of Christ, toward the Pauline, extra-Pauline, and post-Pauline letters, then so is the prologue of John already open from the very beginning toward the collection of the sayings of the earthly Jesus and tales of his activity, that is, to the Gospels and their precursors. We will turn to this in chapter 7. Through the insertion of the hymn into the Fourth Gospel, of course, the prospect of a future exaltation is also opened. But even when this also includes resurrection and ascension, it takes place at the cross (see 29.7 below). It is probably not accidental that we find the title *Son of man* here (see 7.5, 7 below), which is typically used by Q. Even now all judgment is already turned over to him (5:22-27). Thus, the Christ image in

Q, which pictures a wisdom teacher who will one day return as judge, is combined with that of a heavenly being, as in Phil 2, who humbles himself and becomes human in order then to be exalted again as God (see 5.10 below).

6. THE PROBLEM OF A WRITTEN GOSPEL[48]

6.1 Christ Only in Oral Proclamation? According to Martin Luther the New Testament should actually be oral proclamation, and only the Old Testament should be Scripture.[49] In the former the listener also contributes; his expectations, his understanding or misunderstanding, and his reaction of laughing or becoming reflective influence the form and tone of the speech. Especially the tone in which something is said can substantially change a document's meaning and cannot be expressed in the written word.[50] In the letters of Paul the community and its members, to whom he is writing, are still clearly detectable as his partner in a dialogue, for instance in the catchwords and views that he picks up from them. Already in the oral confessional formulas and hymns the wording is more or less fixed, even when they are occasionally changed (see 5.1-9 above) or expanded with additions (see 5.10, 11, 13 above). That gradually becomes different at least in the Gospels, although even there the situation of the author and his readership has an influence. While Paul discusses pertinent issues with his churches and in so doing also reaches back repeatedly to the Jesus event and above all to the cross and resurrection, the Gospels describe the already past time of Jesus with a view, of course, to its present significance for the lives of their readers. For Paul Jesus is also the one who lives today, who shapes Paul and his churches, so that he "will not venture to speak of anything except what Christ has wrought through me" (Rom 15:18; cf. II Cor 13:3); but for the evangelists Jesus is absent between the resurrection and the Parousia[51] (yet see 6.2 below). The question is whether the exalted one remains alive only as long as he speaks in the oral prophetic proclamation that is ever anew related to the hearers, a proclamation in which we can scarcely still distinguish between sayings of the earthly Jesus and those of the Jesus speaking now or in which newly formed sayings have been placed on the lips of the earthly Jesus.

6.2 Jesus and the First Preaching of Christ as Enduring Foundation. The distinction cannot be denied. Nevertheless, the extent to which words of prophets were unreflectively understood as the continuation of Jesus' preaching remains very uncertain (see 2.4-5; 3.8-9 above). In Paul's writings, where we can be more sure of recognizing material in seeking an answer to current questions, he occasionally reaches back to the message of the earthly Jesus, but almost always to the original "gospel."[52] In this sense Jesus Christ is the only foundation, and thus is he depicted by Paul (I Cor 3:11). It is the "gospel"—already adopted by Paul from the church and passed on to the

Corinthians "as of first importance" (or "above all")—that must resolve the conflicts concerning the resurrection (I Cor 15:1-5). It is the words of Jesus on the last evening of his life, likewise adopted by Paul, with which he attacks the problems of the celebration of the Lord's Supper (I Cor 11:23-26). Wherever the now living Christ speaks, he is to be measured by what happened in Jesus' death and resurrection. No angel from heaven escapes this criterion (Gal 1:8). Even the chief apostle Peter must be asked whether through his behavior or preaching he has endangered the one decisive fact: that "Christ . . . gave himself for me" (Gal 2:20). Moreover, for Paul Christ speaks through the Spirit; conversely, for Mark the Spirit is also present with Jesus' disciples (13:11), and the driving out of demons still occurs in Jesus' name (9:38; see 25.4 below). Naturally, everything that is said about discipleship or about the new nature of the disciples is also directly addressed to the readers (cf. Mark 10:28-30; 11:22-24; 13:10-13). Therefore, the historical details are reduced to a minimum and only the decisive traits discussed (1:16-20; 2:14); consequently, the new life is expressly based on the death of Jesus "for many" (10:42-45).

It is true that in the time of Mark a danger threatened that did not exist for Paul, namely, that the rooting of the faith in what happened in a particular time and particular place would be forgotten. For Paul the crucifixion of Jesus was such a scandal, and the experience of meeting the resurrected one the absolute foundation of his preaching, that this rooting in the Christ remained the obvious presupposition of all assertions. For Mark, on the other hand, the relationship of all past events—including not only the death and resurrection but also the preaching and activity of the earthly Jesus—to the present-day life of the readers is likewise an obvious presupposition, especially if 1:1, as is likely, is meant to say that what is written in his book is only the beginning of the continuing event of the preaching of the gospel[53] (see 25.3 below).

6.3 Ongoing Interaction Between Jesus and Community. Thus, what up to this point was silently presupposed as known, what was expressed through the incorporation of authentic or newly formed sayings into the earthly life of Jesus, what was marked by the short formula of cross and/or resurrection is fixed in writing by Mark and in part already by his predecessors (see 7.1 below). That does not mean, however, that the interaction between speaking and acting, indeed the whole activity and destiny of Jesus on the one hand and the community moved by it on the other came to an end. This interaction occurs even today wherever these things are read, because what is read is in dialogue with the situation of the reader. Canonization only establishes the idea that there is a fundamental encounter between the God who acts in Jesus and human beings, from the actual eye witnesses to Paul and the evangelists. It gives the direction in which in other times and situations the Word must be heard anew, the actions and destiny of Jesus understood anew, and at the same time the standard by which the necessary new interpretation must be measured. As Jesus' words addressed the questions and needs, longings and difficulties of his listeners, so also the message of the written Word is continually changed according to the questions and needs, longings and difficulties of its readers.

Yet these could not be allowed to become stronger than the Word itself. Therefore the Word must be unambiguously tied to what happened in the uniqueness of the life, death, and resurrection of Jesus, which may not be softened to be simply the beginning of a speaking and acting that continues on and on and is of equal value with the speaking and acting of Jesus. That is already contained in Jesus' saying that in his exorcisms God's kingdom has come (Luke 11:20), or that God's time is fulfilled in his healings, and therefore one's encounter with God is decided by one's attitude toward Jesus (Luke 7:22-23). Hence, already at the oral stage, the stories of Jesus' miracles were not prescriptions for imitators but first of all testimonies to the presence of God, which became a reality in Jesus. Therefore, even after Jesus' death they told of the healing he performed, and not only of those that continued to take place in his name (see 2.1 above). That emphasis, however, is also contained already in the parables of Jesus, in which the unexpected and striking traits show that here the subject is not something that is eternally valid that can happen again anytime and anywhere, but of the unexpected and striking action of God that is happening now in Jesus. Therefore, these very traits are also strengthened even more in the tradition, and there is an actual christologization of the parables. So too Jesus' sayings are more and more firmly incorporated into the time of his unique life, by briefly indicating where and when and to whom he said them (see 2.2-5 above, 7.5 below; cf. 4.1).

7. THE BEGINNINGS OF THE GOSPELS (Q)

7.1 The Two-Source Theory. The first three Gospels often report in almost literal agreement with one another and are only somewhat shortened or expanded compared to one another. Above all, the order of the individual sections is essentially the same, with Matthew and Luke inserting more material in between. This similarity is explicable only if they knew one another or shared a common model. The simplest assumption is the two-source theory: Matthew and Luke used Mark and a source named Q, which contained the material that is in their two Gospels but does not appear in Mark, especially sayings of Jesus. If one takes into account only the three known synoptic Gospels, the priority of Luke would be out of the question, because it would be inexplicable why parables such as those of the good Samaritan (Luke 10:30-37), the prodigal son (15:11-32), the Pharisee and the tax collector (18:9-14), the Christmas story (2:1-20), the emphasized journey to Jerusalem (9:51–18:14), and the story of the Emmaus disciples (24:13-35) were taken over by no other evangelist. However, since Papias wrote around 130-40 that, "Matthew assembled the words [of Jesus] in the Hebrew language, but each one translated them as he was best able,"[54] we would most likely regard Matthew as the oldest Gospel, if we did not take Q into account. Since a parallelism between Luke and Mark also exists where a section is missing in Matthew (e.g., Mark 12:41-44), or between Matthew and Mark when it is missing in Luke (e.g., Mark 6:45–8:21), Luke in this case would have to have known both Matthew and Mark. It is highly unlikely that Mark wrote even later than Luke, for then he would have had to use both the other Gospels and at the same time omit large and central portions. If, however, Luke knew Matthew, how could he—apart from the infancy narratives missing in Mark and told completely differently in Matthew—have torn apart the closed structure of the Sermon on the Mount (Matt 5–7) and inserted the same sayings in about ten different places in his Gospel? The opposite process, that Matthew placed them together, is easily imaginable (see 26.3 below). Or how is Luke supposed to have constructed from Matt 10:5-16 two missionary speeches and placed what is in both Matthew and Mark in one and what is only in Matthew in the other? Again, it is easy to envision the opposite: that Matthew merged the version from Mark with that from Q while Luke presents the two separately (see 26.4 below).

It is also in details that Matthew demonstrates that he is later than Mark. Mark 1:34 reports that Jesus healed "many," but Matt 8:16 states that he healed "all" (also Mark 3:10/Matt 12:15). Moreover, Matthew inserts the Sermon on the Mount and the healing of the servant in Capernaum after Mark 1:22 and thus before Mark 1:29–3:19, but Luke puts it after 3:19. That is only imaginable if Mark and his outline lay before them both. Likewise, Luke orders the discipleship sayings, the woes, and praise of the "babes" in 9:57–10:22 *after* Peter's confession, Matthew *before*. If both had Mark and Q available, they were free to choose when they wanted to leave the Markan outline and insert Q material. But if Matthew's text lay before Luke, why would he reverse things? One would then have to postulate a much shorter original form of Matthew, for example, an Aramaic minigospel, which, translated into Greek, lay before all three evangelists, or a basic gospel into which everything else was gradually incorporated. Even so, one would scarcely make it work without a second sayings source, which could, of course, look different from Q. It would be much simpler then to assume that, in the event that such a prototype existed, it was used first by Mark, and then Matthew and Luke would have had both this prototype and the Gospel of Mark before them. Then, however, we would have the two-source theory again, except that now Mark's model would have already contained what we attribute to Q—above all the sayings of Jesus common to Matthew and Luke. Though this is possible, the process would then be more complicated to conceptualize, which makes it seem less likely.

7.2 The Passion Story. Since the outline of the passion story in John is essentially the same as in Mark, but John hardly knew Mark (or Matthew or Luke), we may assume that it was already assembled before Mark. At first there were perhaps the arrest, hearings before the high priest (plus Peter's denial?) and before Pilate, and crucifixion (empty grave and angel's message?) while the entry, cleansing of the temple, question about authority, death sentence, betrayal, Last Supper (with designation of the betrayer), and Gethsemane were added later but still before Mark. The first report is terse and sober, describing the ordeals neither heroically nor sentimentally, neither threatening the enemies with divine retribution nor stressing the exemplary faithfulness of Jesus. The Old Testament linguistic form in which the echoes of the suffering of the Righteous One are perceived may be pre-Markan also. In Mark there is only a general reference to the fulfillment of the scriptures (14:49), while the frequent adoption of Old Testament expressions (14:34, 38, 62; 15:23-29, 34-36) is not noted as such.

Certainty, however, cannot be achieved. Since the feeding of the five thousand, the crossing of the sea, and the seeking of signs in John 6:1-30, and the coming of the Spirit upon Jesus ("like a dove") in John 1:32 are also told in agreement with Mark, and John also may have used a "sign source" (see 29.1 below), there was conceivably even a pre-Markan minigospel, which might have contained Jesus' baptism, a few miracles (Peter's confession? transfiguration?), and the passion story with (the announcement of) the resurrection (by the angel), and which was known to Mark and John.[55] Others posit only a collection of Galilean disputes, a parable source, a compilation of pericopes that go into concrete community problems, a little apocalypse,[56] and perhaps also an arrangement of a few miracle stories as we find them now in Mark. Yet it has also been suggested that we see the whole second half of the Gospel, from Peter's confession on, as essentially already assembled very early on in Jerusalem.[57]

7.3 Q: Scope? The source Q, however, is theologically important (see 7.1 above). Setting its exact boundaries is admittedly difficult. Where Matthew and Luke follow Mark, there are only rare and very small agreements that are not identical with Mark. These differences can be explained in that the copy of Mark known to them did not entirely agree with the one that has come down to us, that oral tradition also had an influence, and/or that later copyists assimilated the Lukan text to the better-known Matthean. Where Mark is missing, however, the other two often agree almost word for word, for example, in Luke 10:21-22/Matt 11:25-27 (apart from the redactional introduction). Above all, however, the identical sequence of baptismal words, Jesus' baptism,[58] temptation, Sermon on the Mount/Plain (with the same order of the corresponding sayings of Jesus), and the healing of the centurion's servant in Matthew and Luke is no doubt a sure sign of a written model. If one takes the sequence Luke 3:16-17 (21-22); 4:1-13; 6:20-23, 27-49; 7:1-10, 18-35; 9:57-62; 10:1-15, 21-25; 11:9-26, 29-32 as original, then the rearrangements in Matthew (8:19-21; 10:7-16; 13:16-17) are easily explained (see 26.4 below), likewise the compilation in the Sermon on the Mount (e.g., 7:7-11) of isolated Q sayings that originally stood in various places (see 26.3 below). In the later sections the reference to Q is less sure, because the order and wording are often different (e.g., in the parable of the banquet, Luke 14:15-24/Matt 22:1-10). Behind these may lie another tradition, perhaps even a purely oral one.

7.4 Q: Different Strata? We must of course reckon with the possibility that the Q collection also grew. On the one hand, it may have acquired material that Matthew did not have before him and which we now, however, designate as special material of Luke (see 27.1, 3 below). Already at the level of what also lay before Matthew, stories such as the temptation of Jesus and the healing of the servant were linked with Q; the process could have continued up to the form of Q that lay before Luke. On the other hand, what lay before both evangelists was probably gathered together only gradually. Unfortunately, at this point we lack clear criteria for distinguishing earlier and later strata, even if in general we may assume that the assertions about Jesus as Christ were more and more precisely defined. Even if we place in a later stratum the confession of the Son of God (Luke 4:1-13) or of the "Son" in contrast to the "Father" (10:21-22) and of Jesus as the fulfillment of prophetic predictions (Luke 7:18-23), the difference from other collections of "sayings of the wise"[59] remains striking.

7.5 Q: Christology. The sayings of Jesus collected in Q are almost always an expression of a particular situation. That is fundamentally true of the parables (see 2.3-4 above). But it is also true of the fact that sayings, as sayings of *Jesus*, are expressly linked with his activity; that is, they are told as "apothegms," short stories that culminate in a saying of Jesus (see 2.2 above). That is particularly true of Jesus' statements that are incorporated into the story of the temptation and the healing of the servant, where it is clear that the dimension of the historical event is important for his sayings. It is likewise true of a saying that connects the presence of the kingdom of God with Jesus' exorcisms (Luke 11:20) and the call to discipleship (9:57-60; 14:26-27). The characteristic sign is the authoritative "(*Amen*) *I* tell you" with which his sayings are often introduced (7:9, 28; 10:12, 24; 11:51), in contrast to the "thus says the Lord" of the prophets and the "thus it is written" of the exegeting scribes. It is especially true of sayings that deal expressly with Jesus. He is at the very least the eschatological, all-fulfilling prophet (12:54-59; 16:16; etc.). Acceptance or rejection of his message will be decisive in the judgment

(10:12-15; 12:8-12). In him is more than Jonah, Solomon, and the Baptist (11:29-32; 7:28). He is the Son of man, now rejected (6:22?; 7:34; 9:58), but finally coming in glory (17:24-30, etc.), who is (and will be) addressed as "Lord" (6:46; 13:25). In his emissaries, listeners encounter him, and in him, God. Hence what is reported of his work goes far beyond symbolic prophetic actions: the call to discipleship, the sending of emissaries (9:57–10:2), the demonstration of the already inbreaking kingdom of God (10:8-15), healings and exorcisms (7:10; 11:14, 20), the struggle with Satan (4:1-13; 11:15-18), and the last judgment (3:16-17).

7.6 Q: The Community as the Renewed Israel. Q also seems to be familiar with the circle of the twelve. In the list of names in Matthew and Luke there are, in distinction to Mark, little agreements in the introduction ("his disciples," "apostles"—Matt 10:1-2/Luke 6:13) and in the attachment of Andrew to Peter, including the addition "his brother" (Matt 10:2/Luke 6:14). That still does not show, of course, that Q contained a particular list of disciples, since both of these agreements could be coincidental.[60] But the promise given the disciples that they would sit on twelve[61] thrones and judge the twelve tribes of Israel presupposes the circle of the twelve (Luke 22:30/Matt 19:28). Thus Jesus' typical vision of a renewed Israel (see 2.8 above), to which, of course, all peoples will stream (Luke 13:28-29), is also prominent here. The sending of the disciples proceeds entirely within the framework of Israel. In this way the presence of the kingdom of God is emphasized. Since the Baptist, the end events have begun, and the dominion of God is already alive in Jesus (16:16; 11:20; cf. the present tense in 6:20*b*). The secret of Jesus revealed to the "babes" might well be his position as Son of man, as which he will soon appear as judge (10:21-22; 11:29-30; 12:8-9; cf. 7:34; 9:58; etc.). Thus the report of Jesus' preaching as a teacher of wisdom is thoroughly linked with his being preached as the rejected Son of man, exalted by God and coming to the judgment, in whom the destiny of the prophets was finally completed.

7.7 Q: Cross and Resurrection. Q lacks the more radical statements of Jesus in criticism of the law and above all the reference to his cross and his resurrection. Yet the rejection of the Son of man by "this generation" is strongly emphasized (Luke 7:31-34; 9:58; 11:29-32, 49-51; cf. 10:12-15). Jesus will finally die the prophet's death in Jerusalem (Luke 13:34-35; cf. v. 33 and Matt 11:12). Apparently standing in the background is what the Old Testament and Judaism said about the wisdom of God. In Luke 7:34-35 the work of the Baptist like that of Jesus—both of whom were rejected—is expressly understood as that of wisdom. Perhaps also in the background in Luke 9:58 is the image of homeless wisdom that wanders around, accepted by no one (*I Enoch* 42).[62] Likewise, Jesus' exaltation is presupposed, at least everywhere that Jesus is equated with the coming Son of man (12:8-9;

17:24-30; etc.). Whether wisdom ideas are also at work at this point remains questionable. To be sure, *I Enoch* 42 tells of the return of wisdom to heaven, yet this is not exaltation. The Q sayings of Matt 11:25-30 are also clearly shaped by wisdom texts (Sir 51). Q comments on that in verse 27 to the effect that everything has already been delivered by the "Father" to Jesus, the "Son," yet that is still not said of wisdom.[63] Also, for Q what is essential is actually not the exaltation, but the function of the Son of man as future judge, before whom one's present way of life will be called into account.

The lack of statements about cross and resurrection reflects first of all the fact that Jesus himself, of course, knew of the struggle against him and presumably had also come to terms with his death, but in any case did not publicly speak of it any more than of the resurrection. So here again we can ascertain striking faithfulness to tradition. More important, however, is the theological side of this situation. A theory that solves the puzzle of Jesus' death is not offered. But his disciples will no doubt share his destiny as messenger of wisdom (Luke 7:35) in the hostilities of their environment (11:49), when, without special armament, poor, and in solidarity with all the poor and hungry, they work as bearers of the good news of the end time, like sheep in the midst of wolves (10:3-12). The saying that the Son of man is at home nowhere—less than the foxes and the birds—is said to the *follower* (9:58). Thus the sufferings of Jesus are described in a way that becomes effective in the life experiences of his church. The passion is supposed to be more lived than told and preached. Likewise the exaltation of the Son of man to future judge already places the life of his disciples in the light of one who will one day acknowledge them or deny them (Luke 12:8-9).

7.8 Q Christology and "Hymnic" Christology. In the otherwise very different Christologies of John 1:1-18 and Phil 2:6-11 we can also see curious affinities with Q.[64] They may in part be coincidental, in part may come from common roots in the Old Testament and Jewish wisdom theology, and in part may also be traceable to direct or indirect dependence. The hymns speak of a heavenly being who becomes human, and of the connection with the whole of humanity in mind—indeed, of the whole cosmos—while Q speaks of an earthly teacher of wisdom and of Israel as his aim. But Matthew had already expanded the view of Jesus as the messenger of wisdom, as John the Baptist was also (see 26.8 below). In Jesus the wisdom of God, which had already been embodied in the law of Moses, became a person, so that Matthew could have formulated, similar to John 1:14: "And wisdom became flesh," except that in this he is thinking first of all of Jesus as teacher and thus of the wisdom of God that meets us in Jesus' teaching. In John 1 as in Phil 2 the conclusion is expressly drawn that therefore the Logos (the "Word") or the Wisdom or the "Christ" (God in his loving openness toward us) already lived forever "preexistently" in "heaven," and thus before appearing in the man Jesus. In John's prologue, similar to Q, this revelation in the "flesh" (John 1:14; also I Tim 3:16) is related to Jesus' teaching, in which he makes God known to us (1:18), only here the unbreakable connection, indeed, the unity of Jesus with God himself is stressed. Thus already in the prologue the incarnation is the aim, and thus the genre of *gospel* is preprogrammed as a report of the incarnate one. As soon as the prologue is linked with the Gospel, however, the relationship to the person of Jesus becomes much more central. The "glory" radiating in that person (1:14) is now to be found in his whole activity, in his miracles (2:11), as seen by the "sign source" adopted by the evangelists (see 29.1 below), and paradoxically also in his "glorification" on the cross (12:23, 28; 13:31-32; cf. 21:19). It is described as the "lifting up" of the "Son of man" (3:14; 6:62), with the title also typical for Q, and includes the idea that to him, the "Son of man," judgment is given (5:21-22), as again Q also presents it. From the beginning everything in Phil 2 is directed toward this glorification, which on the one hand is tied to the message of the one who is resurrected and installed as "Lord" (see 5.2-3 above), and on the other hand also takes up the expectation, characteristic of Q, of the judge of the whole world, albeit in the image of the universal adoration of the "Lord." Here Paul—and probably also the hymn before him—thought of the Parousia. One *could,* nevertheless, also interpret the statements from the beginning in such a way that with the exaltation of the incarnate one in his "ascension" everything is already completed. That shows how near an even greater hellenization lies, in which everything, as in John, is concentrated on the already fulfilled present—admittedly in such a way that the dimension of the still delayed future does not fully disappear. Conversely, there are also Q sayings that explain that the future judgment is already decided now in one's attitude toward Jesus (Luke 12:8-9) and sayings that pledge the presence of the kingdom of God to those who can now already see it in the authority of Jesus (11:20; 17:20-21).

7.9 Q and the Message of Expiatory Death and Resurrection. In the hymns the express proclamation of Jesus' death and resurrection is missing (see 5.10, 13 above), and this shows that as much as they differ from Q, they are also rooted in a similar "world" of experience and thinking. Indeed, one could, precisely from the standpoint of wisdom experience and wisdom thinking, pursue an entirely different path. Wisdom 2-5 describes how the "wise man" (4:17), the "poor virtuous man" (2:10) is rejected and brought to "shameful death" (2:20), but then is taken up to God (4:10), will meet his enemies in the judgment (4:16; 5:1), and will be counted among the sons of God and live with the "saints" (5:5). Already at work here are motifs from the servant of God songs, above all from Isa 53. From that point on, then, the focus would be on the passion of Jesus, whether understood more as a protoevent that

45

repeats itself in the fate of the disciples or, with Isa 53, as the expiation for the many, and with it the resurrection and exaltation to God as Jesus' justification and as salvation for those who let themselves be taken along by him on his way. That is the line that prevails in many confessional formulas (see 5.4-6 above), but also in the pre-Markan passion story (see 4.4 above) and then in the synoptic Gospels. That can be summed up "kerygmatically" (as preaching) in short formulations, but can also be presented in narrative fashion, for example in the Gospel of Mark, just as the self-humiliation or incarnation of the preexistent one and his exaltation or glory are presented kerygmatically in concentrated form in hymns, for example, in Phil 2:6-11 and John 1:1-18, but also "narratively" in the story of the Fourth Gospel.

7.10 The Incorporation of Both Possibilities in the New Testament. Thus in Jesus one could see a teacher of wisdom (see 7.5 above). Outside of Q this is also to be found in the Letter of James (see 22.1 below) and perhaps also in the false teachers of the Johannine letters (see 30.2 below). One could gather his sayings like those of Jesus Ben Sirach or the writer of Proverbs. Of course, it already became clear in Q that everything here depended on the one who spoke these words, for he was the last, all-deciding messenger of wisdom (see 7.5 above). His instruction could go against the law of God without abolishing it (Matt 5:17-48), so that already in Matthew he was identified with the figure of wisdom (see 7.8 above). His rejection by humanity and the prophet's death that he finally died (Luke 13:34-35) could be understood in Q as the rejection of God (see 7.7 above). Thus, if in him the wisdom of God himself was at work, then we are only a step away from the assertion of his being with God even at the time of creation (see 7.8 above). Jesus is indeed nothing but the embodiment of the salvific presence of God, as it was already active in the creation and then in the proclamation through "wisdom," even if the majority of humankind did not recognize it. One could, however, also conceive it from the standpoint of the rejection of wisdom and its messenger and then take up all the statements about the suffering righteous one, including his expiatory death precisely proclaimed in Isa 53 (see 7.9 above).

In spite of the wholly different genres of the collection of Jesus' sayings in Q versus a christological confession in the hymns, the interesting thing about these similarities is the fact—still hardly reflected in the research of this field—that without any visible dependence there or here, we have a similarly structured conceptuality that in both cases, by Matthew and Luke there, by Paul here, is adopted and newly interpreted and refined through incorporation into the Gospels or the corpus of letters. In so doing, the sayings source begins with the earthly wisdom teacher Jesus but tries to establish his unique special nature by presenting it mythically; that is, it lets the wisdom, already dwelling with God from eternity, speak through him. By contrast, the Philippian hymn, like the prologue to John, begins with a heavenly figure presented in mythical categories as divine, and tries to describe the unique special nature in his degradation to the status of a slave. Thus in both cases the death is understood only as the end of life and the beginning of the exaltation to future judge and cosmic Lord. It is crucially significant, however, that neither Q nor the hymns were simply incorporated as such into the New Testament. They are woven into the context of a whole Gospel or an entire letter. In this process their assertions are reshaped: Jesus' death is now understood as death on the cross, and the resurrection from the dead as the beginning of the proclamation of the community. We would do well to ponder these things very seriously.

8. THE BIG QUESTION:
JESUS TRADITION AND/OR CHRIST CONFESSION?[65]

8.1 The Two Ways to Jesus Christ. On the one hand, in the tradition that led to our Gospels, Jesus' sayings were preserved and placed together, and reports about Jesus' work were gathered and also linked with Jesus' sayings. In the process they were also always commented on, expanded, and even in part newly created by the faith of the reporter; but all interest was concentrated on the work of the earthly Jesus. On the other hand, in the tradition that became visible above all in Paul, there developed in the early church certain expressions, faith formulas, and verses of hymns in which faith in the resurrected Christ was expressed. Here, resurrection could be understood as pointing to the second coming and the end of the world, or of God's seal on Jesus' vicarious death, or as his exaltation to lordship over the church (and the world). In this case, the incarnation could also be seen as descent, earthly existence as humiliation. Are those two completely different ways of faith that perhaps also go back to two or more separate points of origin? Is the first development to be located, for example, in Galilee, the second in Jerusalem and the missionary movement emanating from there? In the first tradition would be the collection of Jesus' sayings that Matthew and Luke have in common (see 7.1, 3 above), and in the second, Paul, in whose letters there is so little of the earthly Lord apart from Jesus' death on the cross. Would that first tradition not be for him even "a different gospel" (Gal 1:6)?[66]

8.2 Galilee and Jerusalem: Two Early Churches? Unfortunately, we know almost nothing about the time that lies between these beginnings and their reflection in Paul's letters on the one hand and in the Gospels on the other. Many things speak for separate origins. In Acts 9:2, 31 we hear about churches in Damascus and Galilee without any mention of a mission there. Should we consider a movement, analogous to 8:4, 40, going out from Jerusalem, or did groups live here who were nurtured by the imprint of the earthly activity of

Jesus, without being especially oriented toward his death and his resurrection? That would explain why in the sayings in Q, common to Matthew and Luke but missing in Mark, nothing is said of his cross and resurrection, but rather of his authority as the earthly one and the one coming in judgment (see 7.8-9 above). To be sure, this presupposes a knowledge of the death and resurrection (or exaltation to heaven), yet not an actual confessional interest. The former would be understood along the lines of the homeless Jesus (Matt 8:20; Luke 9:58), the latter as the rapture to be the heavenly Son of man who one day will act as chief witness or judge (Matt 24:27, 37, 39; Luke 12:8; 17:24, 26, 30). Likewise, it would be understandable why, for example, in the incident in Antioch when Peter no longer wanted to have table fellowship with the Gentile Christians, Paul did not refer back to Jesus' meals with tax collectors and sinners (Luke 7:34); why on the question of abstinence from certain foods, Paul did not point to Jesus' conviction that it is not what goes into the mouth that defiles a person (Mark 7:15); why on the sabbath problem, he did not point to Jesus' behavior (Mark 2:27; 3:1-6), but to faith in justification for all through faith in the crucified one (Gal 2:11-21; Rom 14:13-23; I Cor 8:7-13; Rom 14:6-9). Even according to the Acts of the Apostles, no reference is made at the apostolic council (Acts 15) to Jesus' actions or sayings, but to the grace of the Lord Jesus. Finally, it can be shown that in Paul in similar fashion his theological model, that is, his proclamation of Christ, on the one hand, became important above all in the letters of Paul's disciples (see chapter 3 below), but also in Ignatius, among others; on the other hand, his life was handed down in a completely separate tradition in the legends of the apocryphal acts of the apostles already shaped by Gnostic influence. Both streams of tradition ran independently of each other. Must one thus imagine at least two early churches, one in Galilee for whom the work of earthly Jesus was decisive, the other in Jerusalem, where death on the cross and resurrection stood at the center? In addition one could postulate a pre-Markan and a pre-Johannine community and separate the Aramaic-speaking Jerusalem community from the Hellenistic, so that four or five roots would become visible.

8.3 Jerusalem, the One Early Community. Yet the Acts of the Apostles knows only one community that was important for later development: the one in Jerusalem. This is, of course, Luke's intention, and the fact that during the persecution after the death of Stephen, the apostles could remain in Jerusalem unattacked (8:1) demonstrates that—contrary to what Luke would like us to believe—this persecution was only directed against the Greek-speaking church, which was obviously freer vis-à-vis the law than the "apostolic" group. Nonetheless, there are two groups in the same place, and the differences seem to concern more or less logical consequences of the question of the law, not the emphasis on the earthly activity of Jesus on the one hand and on the death and resurrection on the other. Above all, according to Gal 1:17-20; 2:1-2, Paul knows only *one* early church: that in Jerusalem. This is all the more striking since he was called near Damascus and brought together with the community of Jesus there and as its former opponent he had known only the churches outside Judea (Gal 1:17, 22). That shows that even for followers in Damascus the apostles in Jerusalem were the deciding authority. To be sure, according to Acts 18:24-25; 19:1-3 there were disciples who had experienced nothing of Pentecost; yet in both cases it is—contrary to the Lukan intention—no doubt a matter of Hellenistic Jews and those impressed by the Baptist, who did not become Christians until in Ephesus. If one then adds the fact that all apostles were Galileans who—if not everything is deceptive—had already accompanied Jesus during his earthly activity and had probably experienced the appearance of the resurrected one in Galilee, the thesis of two or more, widely separated early communities becomes very questionable.

8.4 Reciprocal Influence of Various Strands of Tradition. The three Letters of John do not mention the earthly activity of Jesus; nevertheless, they did not arise in a community tradition different from the Gospel of John; indeed, their author was familiar with it. In Acts there are only sporadic references to the earthly Jesus, twice in a mission sermon (2:22; 10:38), once in an ethical question (20:35) with a saying that is not in Luke's Gospel(!); yet they come from the same author. Paul presupposes a certain familiarity with the passion story (I Cor 11:23)—which was, no doubt, already a continuing arrangement of various individual stories, which is typical of the Gospels—further, the poverty of Jesus (II Cor 8:9), and a few sayings (I Cor 7:10; 9:14 [cf. 14:37; 15:3]; I Thess 4:15). In any case, that is more than we find in the Johannine Letters and is to be compared, say, with what is found in the Acts of the Apostles. More important is the fact that for Paul the return of Christ, which is also central in the collections of Jesus' sayings, remains essential. The connection between Ps 8:6 (which, like many sayings of Jesus, speaks of the Son of man) and Ps 110:1 (which also appears in the synoptic tradition) was no doubt already adopted by Paul (I Cor 15:25-27; cf. Eph 1:20-22), apparently from the same milieu from which the tradition of Jesus' sayings is drawn (cf. Mark 14:62, perhaps also the Greek text of Mark 12:36, influenced by Ps 8:6; later Heb 1:13 beside 2:6; Pol. *Phil.* 2:1 "glory"/"subjected" beside "throne on his right hand"). The *abba* cry is common to Mark 14:36 and Rom 8:15; Gal 4:6; the Son of God title to Matt 4:3/Luke 4:3 and Paul (often). One can presume that sayings such as Luke 10:4 led to attacks on Paul (I Cor 9:1-18, see 31.2 below),[67] and if we are not mistaken, prophets—perhaps even the itinerant prophets who held to the literal obedience of Jesus' missionary rules (see 3.9 above)—went out directly from Jerusalem (Acts 11:27-28; [13:1;] 15:22, 32; 21:9, 10). According to the Gospels, to be sure, Jesus' disputes took place in

Galilee as well as in Jerusalem. In the first three Gospels the miracles have settled almost entirely in Galilee, but is this a sign of a special Galilean tradition or of a Markan schema that concentrates the miracles before the confession of Peter? (Cf. nonetheless 10:52.) Above all, there must have been a tradition of the earthly Jesus which was at home in and oriented toward Jerusalem, as shown by John, who does report miracles in Jerusalem, and the related notes in Luke. Also the assembling of (only one!) feeding, crossing, sea walk (and demand for a sign in Mark 8:11-13; John 6:26-30?) seems to belong there, while the immediate reaction of the people is reported only in John 6:14-15. The report of the anointing in John 12:1-8 combines Markan and Lukan motifs. Since John could hardly have known one or more of the synoptic writers, this makes it still probable that in Galilee as in Judea, Jesus stories were collected with the sayings belonging to them. In particular, the passion story, which came from Jerusalem and is centrally oriented toward the death and resurrection of Jesus, is no doubt the oldest connected Jesus tradition (see 7.2 above). Finally, in the previous section it became clear how much the Q tradition also belongs with the hymnic assertions that are found in the letters, even if no direct dependencies can be demonstrated in detail.

8.5 Teaching and Telling. Even in the Judaism of that time a certain separation was observed between the areas of the teaching tradition, that is, the interpretation of the law, and the telling of the legends of the prophets and martyrs. Of course, teaching here meant clarification of moral questions—and thus precisely what is also typical of Jesus' sayings—while the narration conveyed the proclamation of salvation in the acts of God, as is also typical of Jesus stories. Still, we may presume that the same community that gathered sayings of Jesus and stories that mostly ended in a saying—but, naturally, did not yet concern death and resurrection—nonetheless also emphasized in its liturgy of the Lord's Supper, for example, the report of the passion and resurrection and their significance for faith. Yet this does not clarify the different interests of the Gospels and the letters.

However one weighs matters in particular, the first community in Jerusalem was, in any case, one that was hoping for the imminent inbreaking of the kingdom of God and also was a community shaped by prophets (see 3.2 above). For this reason the disciples resettled from Galilee to Jerusalem with their families and all their possessions. As certain as was the Easter experience, which also included the mission that already bore witness to the great turning point, the community no doubt still thought about a short time of preaching and of calling for repentance before the final fulfillment (see 3.3 above). Whether Jesus' resurrection was more important as the presupposition of his coming, the general resurrection, and the establishment of the kingdom of God, or as the entrance of his lordship over the church already living in the new world under

God's forgiveness, in the center, in any case, stood the resurrected one, not the earthly teacher and his example. The death on the cross, at first a puzzle and embarrassment, became understood in the light of scripture as the substitution and expiation for Israel's sin. Thus the preaching was first of all news of the coming salvation that was now already pledged to those who repent and believe. Jesus' sayings and stories presumably came into play in the gradually emerging ethical questions and in dealing with attacks. At first that remained a secondary movement but became more and more important. In many everyday questions it was not so simple to derive proper behavior if one was not a trained theologian like Paul. Yet even he, in I Cor 7:10; 9:14 and in content also Rom 12:14-17, appealed to Jesus' sayings, which appear beside Old Testament commandments (Rom 12:20; I Cor 9:9-10).

8.6 Easter Experience and Appeal to the Earthly Jesus. This development can be compared with that of the confessional formulas. If at first the whole weight lay on the resurrection of Jesus, which served as the beginning of his divine sonship (Rom 1:4; Acts 13:33) and lordship (Rom 10:9; Acts 2:36), later this time was transposed back into Jesus' life and finally to the day of his birth: Jesus' activity as Son of God began at his baptism (Mark 1:11; Acts 10:37-38); through his birth by the virgin he became God's Son (Luke 1:35). This development, of course, did not proceed in a straight line. Even before Paul resurrection and second coming, on the one hand, were linked (I Thess 1:10, without reference to Jesus' death, see 5.2 above), and on the other, mission and expiatory death of God's Son (Gal 4:4-5; Rom 8:3, see 5.2 above) or humiliation from a heavenly existence and exaltation to cosmic Lord (Phil 2:6-11, see 5.10 above). Conversely, neither Jesus' baptism nor birth appears as the basis of his rank in Paul; only his Davidic lineage is named in a formula cited by Paul in Rom 1:3 (see 5.3 above). Thus it is certain that very different later developments have proceeded beside each other. They all appear to be rooted in the Easter experience of an already immanent new world of God and at the same time in the high future expectation of the first community in Jerusalem, in which salvation was preached on the basis of the appearances of the resurrected one and the experience of the presence of God's Spirit, and the final establishment of the kingdom of God was expected.

8.7 Various Issues. Paul knows nothing of any other preaching (I Cor 15:11). He was called in Damascus and returned to this church, and perhaps also became acquainted with other churches in "Arabia," certainly with those in western Syria later on, whereas he remained at first unknown to the Judean churches (Gal 1:17, 24). If there had been preaching that excluded the death and resurrection, in just a few years after Jesus' death it must have merged with the preaching that originated in Jerusalem, at least everywhere Paul had gone.

As the Johannine Gospel and letters show, the difference is more likely to lie in the particular issue here and there. Where it is a question of fundamental testimony to the Christian faith, Jesus' resurrection and final coming are stressed (I Thess 1:10; 4:14); where it is a matter of individual questions such as the death of community members before this coming and the proper words of comfort in this situation, the sayings of Jesus (genuine or considered genuine) became important (I Thess 4:15-18). The pre-Markan as well as pre-Pauline form of the language of the Lord's Supper shows that from the beginning the interpretation of Jesus' death as salvation event and perhaps as pledge of his coming again was tied to the celebration, while it was not yet established whether the "for many" was to be interpreted as expiation, substitution, ransom, communion of suffering, or whatever (see 4.3, 5.4 above). Where the interest lay in didactic clarification, as in Paul, these interpretations became decisive and placed the focus on the initially incomprehensible crucifixion of Jesus: the very death cursed by God became salvation. Where the admonition was on accepting a life of humiliation, for example, in times of persecution or in life together with other community members, the stress was laid on the humility manifested in the whole life of Jesus, for which his death formed the climax. That is true for the sayings on the homelessness of the Son of man (Luke 9:58) as well as for the pre-Pauline hymn of Phil 2:8 (see 5.10 above) or Pauline assertions such as II Cor 8:9; Rom 8:17; 15:3. Here the tradition of Jesus' itinerant life must have become important, quite especially for those who sought to continue this form of preaching and who worked as itinerant prophets.

8.8 The Suffering Righteous One and Expiatory Death, Resurrection, and Exaltation. Where the main emphasis was laid on the future inbreaking of the kingdom of God, Jesus' sayings on the coming Son of man were repeated, together with the consequent admonitions to a life lived in preparedness for it and in responsible service in the meantime. Naturally, Jesus himself had not yet or hardly spoken of his death and his resurrection, but both were presupposed, since it was Jesus who as the Son of man would come to the judgment. The linguistic form in which that became understandable was the category of the righteous one who suffers and is then raised to God, as especially the early passion statements show. Where the main emphasis was laid on the salvation already granted to the believer, death and resurrection had to become the decisive turning point. Sentences from Isa 53 already reverberated in the Jewish texts that spoke of the suffering righteous one (see 7.9 above). Where the eschatological turning point was seen in Jesus' death, those sentences were used exclusively for the uniqueness of this event. That Jesus' resurrection was originally understood above all as exaltation (to the coming Son of man, as well as to Lord of the church and the world) is also shown by the fact that Paul equates without distinction the appearance of the resurrected one to him from heaven with the earlier experiences of the apostles before him (I Cor 15:5-8; Gal 1:15-17). Here too, of course, great shifts in emphasis can be ascertained, but hardly by separate early communities. Finally, common to the tradition leading to the Gospels as well as that leading to Paul is the anchoring in Jewish wisdom theology (see 7.8-10 above).

8.9 From the Kerygma to the Jesus Tradition and from the Jesus Tradition to the Kerygma. Thus, on the one hand, the starting point was the resurrection and the unique position of the exalted one evidenced by it, the one who would also come as Lord in the final establishment of the kingdom of God. In retrospect his teaching and his actions were examined when it was a question of ethical issues, problems of shaping the worship service or of the common life, and uncertainties about the future. On the other hand, there was interest in the teaching and example of the earthly one as instruction for concrete problems, an instruction that was based explicitly or implicitly on his unique authority. The fact that the witnesses of his work already asked themselves before Easter, who is this man who acts this way, and that many of them experienced God's coming in him, points forward to what was recognized after Easter. Certainly a large part of the Jesus tradition was collected in Galilee, but another part very likely in Jerusalem. Certainly the weight that was laid on it in the various churches was also different, but it remains very improbable that there were churches that lived only with this or only with the confession of Jesus' death and resurrection without knowledge of his earthly activity.

8.10 Gospels as Correction of a Pure Kerygmatization. There are, however, indeed signs that the Jesus tradition became important in a time in which the dogmatic anchoring of faith in the death and resurrection as the crucial salvation events was clearly assured. Matthew, in contrast to Mark, stresses in four places that it is a question of the gospel of the kingdom of God preached by Jesus, apparently because he saw the danger of a faith in the "gospel" (as Mark tersely calls it—see 6.2 above) that was no longer interested in the preaching of the earthly Jesus (4:23; 9:35; 24:14; 26:13). He also stressed that Jesus remained present with his church, especially in his commandments (28:20). The introductory formula to a Jesus saying, "remembering the words of the Lord Jesus, how he said . . ." (or something similar), appears in Acts 20:35; *I Clem.* 13:8-9; 46:7-8; Pol. *Phil.* 2:3.[68] The collection of Jesus' sayings in the so-called *Gospel of Thomas* seems to presuppose the first three Gospels, and for Papias in the middle of the second century the oral tradition of eyewitnesses and their immediate informants is more important than what is written in books.[69] The very late Second Letter of Peter (1:16-18) appeals to the story of the transfiguration of Jesus (Mark 9:2-8), in order to assure the certainty of the preaching. The danger of a later theology leading to Gnosticism (see 20.2 below)—which, it is true, held the message of grace and salvation to be important but no longer bound it to the history of Jesus—seems to have also influenced the beginnings of the Jesus tradition of the Gospels.

Mark, in the oldest of our Gospels, already knows such an interest in the earthly Jesus. He seems, namely, to be fighting an image that shows Jesus only as a miracle worker. Thus he, of course, recognizes the miracles of Jesus throughout as signs of his authority, but stresses that they cannot be properly understood until one also recognizes his way to the cross and follows him there (see 2.1 and note 13 above). In the development leading to Gnosticism, the miracles of Jesus are no longer told, only those of the exalted Lord who works in his apostles (see 2.1 above); in that view the heavenly ''Christ'' worked only from the baptism of Jesus until his last evening, but then left the man Jesus before the latter was crucified (see 30.2 below). In the oldest Gospel, by contrast, we see again the close linkage between the tradition of Jesus and the theology of the cross. It is precisely the kerygma of cross and resurrection that leaves a pervasive impression here on the gathering of the tradition of the earthly Jesus. Hence, Mark has remained faithful to what was characteristic of the proclamation from its very beginnings (see 25.8 below).

Paul

No one from the New Testament period is as well known to us as Paul. Not only is his work spoken of in detail in the Acts of the Apostles, but we also possess a number of his letters, whereas Jesus left nothing behind in writing. Nevertheless, there are many unanswered questions, not only concerning the dates of Paul's life, but also his message.

9. LIFE AND LETTERS

9.1 Dates. In connection with Paul's first stay in Corinth on the so-called second missionary journey, Acts 18:12 mentions Gallio as the Roman proconsul. He was in office from spring 51 to spring 52 (or perhaps one year later). This agrees with Suetonius's note (see 1.1 above) that the Jews—perhaps only the Jewish Christians and their fiery opponents—were driven out of Rome,[70] if that really happened in the year 49, as first determined around 400.[71] That could explain how Paul was received by Aquila and Priscilla, who had already become Christians in Rome (Acts 18:2; I Cor 16:19). According to Gal 1:18; 2:1 the time from Paul's calling until the apostolic conference (Acts 15; Gal 2:1-10; see 13.1 below) was fifteen to sixteen years, or perhaps only thirteen to fourteen if 2:1 is calculated, contrary to what seems normal, from the calling and not from the Jerusalem visit. In antiquity, as a rule, the first and last years were included in counting. Reckoning back from the stay in Corinth in 51/52, one would have to place the calling of Paul in, say, 32 or 35 at the latest; that would be only two to five years after Jesus' probable date of death in the year 30 (or 31—see 1.2 above).

According to Acts 13–14 the first missionary journey through Cilicia took place before the apostolic conference. Then followed the journey through all of Asia Minor and Macedonia to Athens and Corinth, where Paul remained a year and a half (18:11). It would be different if one were to assume that the information in Acts is in error or to be interpreted otherwise. One could place the apostolic conference of Gal 2:1-10 in Paul's second visit to Jerusalem in Acts 11:30/12:25, as indeed Gal 2:1 actually requires. Since Herod Agrippa died in A.D. 44 (12:23), one would in this case have to reckon back from there at least thirteen to fourteen years, so that the calling of Paul would have to be placed around A.D. 30.[72] Yet in Gal 2:1-10 the topic is the circumcision of Gentile Christians; that is discussed in Acts 15, not at the time of Acts 11–12. It is conceivable, to be sure, that after the incident of Gal 2:11-21 the question of table fellowship between Jewish and Gentile Christians was discussed, and that Acts 15:19-20, 29 refers to that; but Paul knows nothing of this arrangement. According to Acts 21:25 it was first communicated to him (in distinction to what is recounted in Acts 15) when he stayed in Jerusalem for the last time shortly before his arrest. Also, in Rom 14:13-23; I Cor 8:4-8; 10:25-34 Paul decides quite differently. To clarify: this discussion took place after the council (of Acts 15). It would be different again if one were to assume that Paul had taken the so-called second journey much earlier, before the apostolic conference, whereby, of course, the incident with Gallio would then have to be placed later, for example, during Paul's visit in Corinth from Ephesus (see 12.4 below). Then his first letter, to Thessalonica, would be set in, say, the year 41 (see 10.1 below).[73] Because Gal 1:21, however, mentions only Syria and Cilicia between the calling and the apostolic conference, this is improbable.

9.2 Biography. The assured facts are: persecution of communities of Christ by Paul, who was blameless as to righteousness under the law (Phil 3:6)—to be sure, not in Judea (Gal 1:22), and whether in Jerusalem (Acts 7:58; 8:1) remains uncertain; then his calling near Damascus (Gal 1:17; Acts 9:3; II Cor 11:32); two or three years in Arabia, which could mean the vicinity of Damascus, and entail early missionary activity; then a visit with Peter and the Lord's brother James; about thirteen years afterward (or alternatively after his calling?) the apostolic conference; then the quarrel with Peter, which presumably ended unfavorably for Paul, since he says nothing about his view having prevailed (Gal 1:13–2:20; see 13.2 below); finally, the suffering of Jewish and Roman persecutions during his missionary activity (II Cor 11:24-33). His vocation as tentmaker[74] and his growing up in Tarsus, including study as a Pharisee under Gamaliel in Jerusalem are mentioned only by Luke (Acts 18:3; 22:3; 26:5), but the other data fit (cf. I Cor 4:12; 9:12-15; I Thess 2:9; Phil 3:5). According to Gal 1:22 he was not in Judea (outside of Jerusalem?). According to Acts 19:8, 10, 22; 20:31 Paul remained two or three years in Ephesus on his last missionary journey. In agreement with this is the information in II Cor 12:14; 13:1 (cf. 2:1), according to which Paul once went from there to Corinth for a short visit—later, to be sure, than I Cor 16:1-9, where only *one* stay is mentioned. Since Paul worked a long time at least here and earlier in Corinth, and also made excursions from both places into other areas (Illyria [Rom 16:19] from Corinth?), and since, moreover, the break between the so-called second and third journeys in Acts 18:22-23 is not very well defined, one can speak of "journeys" only in the terms of an organizing overview of his activity (see note 73 above). According to Acts 28:30, after his arrest in Jerusalem (ca. A.D. 57?), court appearance, and journey to Rome (ca. 60?), Paul worked there for another two years unhindered. Apparently he was executed there (in the Neronian persecution of A.D. 64?), for the pastoral letters (see 20.1 below) attest no return to the East. His martyrdom, after he "had reached the extreme West" (Spain?—Rom 15:24), was mentioned in A.D. 95 in *I Clem.* 5.

9.3 Paul's Letters: Extent of the Collection. Paul no doubt dictated all of his letters (except the short one to Philemon) and only added the greeting himself (I Cor 16:21; also Gal 6:11 probably applies to the closing section[75]). Important things were written on parchment; short notes were scratched on clay shards. For letters one mostly used papyrus, the stalks of the plant being glued together to produce a raw, porous surface that is not easy to write on; wrapped around a stick and provided with the address, it was then dispatched. Paul often corrected himself during dictation (I Cor 1:16) and disrupted the sentence structure (Rom 2:17/21; 3:8; 5:6-8, 12/15; 9:22-24; Gal 2:4-6).

The thirteen letters ascribed to Paul and Hebrews, in which the naming of Timothy in 13:23 is perhaps intended to suggest Paul as the writer, are named according to their recipients; the seven "catholic" or "ecumenical" ones—that is, those intended for a larger circle of churches—are named for their writers. Among the Pauline letters, seven are generally recognized; seven (including the Letter to the Hebrews) are traced back to other authors (see 9.4 below). The first and third letters to Corinth (I Cor 5:9; II Cor 2:4; yet see 11.1 below) have been lost, and also the Laodicean letter mentioned in Col 4:16.

9.4 Are the Letters Genuine and Intact? Whether the letters handed down to us correspond exactly to the ones written by Paul or whether they were later reworked during the collecting, perhaps even so that two or three letters were combined into one (II Cor—see 12.1-3 below), cannot be decided with certainty. Parallel processes are hard to demonstrate. False and even consciously forged letters (e.g., of Plato) were relatively frequent in antiquity.[76] The Greek translation of the Old Testament contains a letter of Jeremiah that was certainly written much later. In the course of being handed down, many texts were modified or expanded. It is especially easy to show how verses of Homer and Hesiod were quoted, reshaped, even invented, and with the help of greater expansions presented as witnesses to the truth of Jewish faith.[77]

Christian additions to Jewish scriptures can be clearly recognized in the *Sibylline Oracles,* the *Testament of the Twelve Patriarchs,* and in Josephus. A model that is used by the *Didache,* a Syrian church discipline (end of first century A.D.?), or even the *Didache* itself, is freely adopted and developed in the *Letter of Barnabas,* in the *Shepherd of Hermas,* in the so-called *Apostolic Church Order,* and in the *Apostolic Constitutions.* Translations often differ in content from the original. The interesting titles "the person/the man" in *I Enoch* 89:1,9 are lacking, for example, in the Aramaic fragments of the original.[78]

Often it is assumed that in most of the extant Pauline letters several writings have been combined (see 10.1; 11.1; 12.1-3; 14.1 below), and apparently in the Second Letter to the Corinthians we must really deal with the combining of two letters. Nonetheless, it would be exaggerated to declare that the burden of proof in the individual case lay on the one asserting that a particular passage was added or corrected later, but on the whole it lies on the one who assumes the unity and integrity of one of Paul's letters.[79] To my knowledge there are no parallels to the idea that various letters were (broken up and) combined into one. Certainly, in the prophetic books of the Old Testament, sections from various times and various authors are put together, and the Gospels contain material from very different sources; but both cases are quite different, for there was no closed unity in the beginning, as in a letter of the apostle. It is also hardly imaginable how in a "Pauline school" letters would have been not only strung together but in part split up and recombined. Paul's letters were always considered more strongly as "Holy Writ" than other texts and certainly also more often copied. It would, of course, be possible that there are no traces of an original letter not yet broken up; the insertion of Rom 16:25-27 and I Cor 14:34-35 have left behind traces in the manuscripts, but not that of II Cor 6:14–7:1, which likewise scarcely belongs to the original letter. In any case, however, it is not to be simply expected. Real difficulties are presented only by the Second Letter to the Corinthians (see 12.1 below). So certainty is not to be had, and in the following we can only specify the reasons that speak for a possible division.

It is no doubt true, however, that II Thessalonians, Colossians, Ephesians, I and II Timothy, and Titus were almost certainly written by students of Paul. The Letter to the Hebrews was, in any case, ascribed to Paul only sporadically and very late. At that time students often put forth their writings in the name of their teacher in order to express the fact that they had learned everything from him. The concept of "intellectual property" as we understand it today did not exist. In addition to that, the community was convinced that in the power of the Holy Spirit the word of the apostle was still alive among them and spoke directly to their problems. When someone who had no recognized position wanted to fight in the name of Paul against a dangerous trend, he of course had to let Paul himself speak in order to be heard. That does not exclude the fact that remarks such as II Thess 3:17, where the genuineness of the signature is stressed, or the appendage of names of those staying with Paul, as in Eph 6:21; II Tim 4:19-21, are questionable means of lending the appearance of genuineness to the letter.[80]

9.5 The Character of a Letter. It is astonishing that of the twenty-seven New Testament writings twenty-one letters were accepted into the canon. They stand, to be sure, completely in second place behind the Gospels, which were the first to be designated as ''Scripture'' or ''the books'' (ca. A.D. 180), because in them the church found the foundation laid once and for all, in the person of Jesus Christ (I Cor 3:11). Even the fact of a collection of letters, however, shows that in the New Testament it was not simply a matter of information about past events (still alive in their influence), but of encouragement from what is told as good news in the concrete present. Thus one can get to the core of the New Testament, the message of Jesus Christ, in no other way than by listening to what it expresses of Jesus' relationship to God, to the world, and above all to the hearers and readers of the message. His relationship to God or to the world may stand in the foreground, but even so always including its meaning for the hearer and reader.

Even the form of the letter itself involves the devotion of the writer to the particular situation of the recipient (see 6.1 above), in such a way, though, that the decisive help is in the exhortation of what God has long since done, beyond the effort of the author or recipients. Therefore, what is at stake in the letters is the very concrete present, the quite particular situation for which they were written, even before the first Gospel was written (yet cf. 7.2 above), and precisely as such they concern the one event recounted by the Gospels. In them it becomes clear that ''the Word became flesh'' (John 1:14) and can only be heard when it goes into the particular human situation. Absolutely pure, distilled water, even water just melted from the snow in the mountains, does not quench thirst; it does so only when it has passed through the ground and absorbed the minerals—that is, in a certain sense, the dirt. So also, the message of the New Testament would bring no help if it had not entered the world at that time and been translated into the world of today.

Self-corrections (see 9.3 above) remind us how much the recipients, their situation, and their problems are involved when God wants to speak; and uncorrected sentence fragments indicate the difficulty of speaking appropriately in human language about that which no human word can truly comprehend. In these so historically conditioned writings—whose selection seems again to be historically ''accidental'' (see 9.3-4 above), and which are also in no way limited to *one* man of genius, Paul, but also give ample voice to his coworkers, disciples, and other witnesses (the Johannine letters) and critics

59

of Paul (James)—the church hears what Paul in I Thess 2:13 formulates as "the word of God which you heard from us."

9.6 Faith in Jesus. The theological significance of Paul lies in the fact that he, as no one else in the time after Easter, dealt with the question: What does it mean to proclaim Jesus now?[81] Even the churches that Paul had persecuted before his calling, and in which he began his life as a missionary, did not simply hand down the preaching of Jesus and cultivate the memory of his deeds, but rather proclaimed him as the crucified one, the resurrected one, and the one who will some day return as the consummating one (see 5 above). Thus from the very beginning Paul stands in the tradition of the churches of Christ in the Jewish Diaspora (Damascus, later Antioch) and also consciously incorporates that tradition into his formulations and some quotations. With extraordinary power, however, he reworked it theologically and thus gave direction to the preaching of the whole church over the centuries.

What does it mean in the time after Easter to preach Jesus as the one who still lives and indeed now lives more than ever? Paul speaks of faith "in Jesus" or faith "that Jesus" (died for us and was resurrected). That is a new formulation. As little as it is intended to designate a mere holding of certain statements or historical facts to be true, so much more does Paul also speak of "dying and being resurrected with Christ" and of "life in Christ," and yet it so clearly expresses that salvation lies in what God has done in Jesus' life, death, and resurrection. Thus it does not lie in our enthusiasm or effort, nor in the strength of our faith and the intensity of our experience of God. Certainly for Paul faith is new life through trusting in the God who graciously meets us in Jesus Christ. What Paul, however, understood about Jesus and underlined with unusual clarity is the message that the ups and downs of this life of faith do not decide our salvation. For that there is only *one* solid basis: Jesus Christ himself (I Cor 3:11). He wants to and will live in us, but we are not saved because we are perfect believers, but because we have become whole through his life, death, and resurrection, completely and forever. Therefore, he also works in us so that such trust and faith is reshaped ever anew for life in all its aspects.

9.7 Paul as Reflected by His Readers. That makes it understandable that Paul, already in his lifetime, was hotly disputed and remains so today. Probably as early as the beginning of the second century, Jewish Christians saw in him the great deceiver who, on the basis of a questionable vision, quarreled with the reliable message of Peter, who had lived with Jesus and heard his message (*Ps. Clem. Hom.* 17:14-19). Around that same time II Pet 3:15-16 recognized Paul, to be sure, as "beloved brother," but went on to explain that there is much that is hard to understand and hence is twisted by many. For Augustine Paul was crucial, and through Luther's study of the Letter to the Romans in 1515-16 came the actual breakthrough of the Reformation. Dialectical theology was launched with Karl Barth's interpretation of the Letter to the Romans in 1919 and 1922. If Friedrich Nietzsche perceived in Paul the "logician's cynicism of a rabbi" and thought that "on the heels of the 'good news' came the very worst: that of Paul," then today he is conversely reproached for having inaugurated a pagan, even byzantine lord-and-court theology with pagan nature myths, thereby betraying his Jewish heritage.[82] Others see Paul as completely Jewish, as long as one does not misunderstand him and interpret him from the standpoint of Augustine and Luther.[83] Whether Paul totally falsified Jesus, had to distance himself at least from a part of the Jesus tradition,[84] or was the only one to perceive him in his deepest meaning,[85] was and will continue to be fervently discussed.

10. THE FIRST LETTER TO THE THESSALONIANS

10.1 Unity, Place, Date. One could see in 1:2-5 and 2:13 two different epistolary openings and in 3:11-13 and 5:23-28 two different closings, all of which point to the two different situations in 2:17–3:4 and 3:6-10, and from this one could presume that a letter of recommendation given to Timothy (say, 2:1–3:4 [without 2:15-16]; 3:11–4:8) and a letter written after his return (say, 1:1-10; 3:6-10; 4:9–5:28 [without 4:18; 5:27])[86] were combined. That is possible, though hard to imagine (see 9.4 above).

According to 3:1-2, 6, Timothy, who had been sent by Paul from Athens to Thessalonica, came back to him (in Corinth?). No doubt that is the situation described in Acts 18:5, and thus we have here the oldest letter of Paul still available to us. This is true independently of whether one sets the date at ca. 50-52 or a good ten years earlier (see 9.1 above).

10.2 Pauline Missionary Preaching. Paul's missionary preaching is expressly summarized by 1:9-10 (see 5.2 above). Included are proclamation of the one God and thus detachment from idols. This is interesting because other than here the two scarcely appear in Paul's letters, but are simply presupposed there. Thus in a certain sense the presupposed but no longer expressed contents of the proclamation are often the most important. The letters have a different function from fundamental missionary preaching, and consistency in content is not to be expected. That could also be true for what Paul told and later presupposed about Jesus.[87] In addition, part of the first preaching was the announcement of the judgment, which Paul still expected in his lifetime (4:17). Neither, however, is simply general instruction about the unity of God and the goal of world history. God is proclaimed as the one who raised Jesus, and judgment as the place of meeting with the saving Jesus. Verse 4:14 speaks in formulaic language of Jesus' dying and rising (Paul himself would have formulated it "being crucified and raised"), and 5:10 of his dying "for us" (see 5.4-5 above). Thus the proclamation of the death (occurring "for us") and resurrection of Jesus is doubtless already here the foundation of Pauline preaching, as also attested in I Cor 15:3, according to which the preaching of Jesus' dying for us and of his being raised occurred "from the beginning" (or: "above all"?). Presumably, however, Paul did not expressly speak of the resurrection of the dead, although as a Pharisee he believed in it.[88] It is correct that the connection of the resurrection of the dead with that of Jesus did not become explicit until in the discussion with the Corinthians, whereas here (as in I Cor 15:51) the rapture is still the norm, which, however, does not necessarily require an early date (see 9.1 above).

10.3 Near Expectation of the Parousia. The expectation of the future, however, no doubt became a problem, because community members died, and the Thessalonians became unsure whether these had lost the hope of the return of Christ. Paul—who assumes that most of them, as he himself, would still experience this and then be taken away (4:15)—perhaps did not previously take deaths into account at all. His answer is important because it relativizes the still presupposed near expectation, for whether this is fulfilled in our lifetimes or after our death is beside the point, since life "in Christ" is not abolished by death, but leads for all to the final being "with Christ" (4:16-17; see 14.4 below). Also connected with this, Paul can still speak here of "spirit and soul and body" (5:23) and still has no thoughts on God's Spirit (also working in the believer), which, as it is then spelled out in I Cor 15:44-45, 50, stands in contrast to "flesh and blood"—indeed, to the soul (see 11.5 below).

10.4 Theological Center: "Sanctification." The actual thrust of the letter, however, is the "sanctification" of the community (4:3, 4, 7), the embodiment of the message heard, which was preached "not only in word, but also in power and in the Holy Spirit and with full conviction" (1:5) and had assumed a corresponding form in the community. Chapters 1–3 contain a look back at the recent first stay with the addressees; it is full of praise and thanksgiving that turn into intercession. In this they are similar to those earliest psalms of praise in the Bible, which to a certain extent are still reflected in the presence of the salvation event (Exod 15; Judg 5; etc.). They lead to the exhortation to mold life out of such joy. This joy is described in 1:6; 2:14 as imitation of the apostle or of the churches in Judea, and thus also of the Lord. Otherwise Paul is reserved in the use of this concept (only in I Cor 4:16; 11.1), because he did not want to abolish the fundamental otherness of Jesus (as the one who died and rose "for us"—5:10) or of the apostle, whose message is not the "word of men" but the "word of God which you heard from us" (2:13). Here, however, the actual theme is the formation of faith; therefore, Paul recalls his own behavior, because it can help the community to see how faith is lived. That too, of course, can finally be only the act of God himself (5:23), but the community, thankful and carefully judging, should make room for his Spirit and his word and let them work (5:18-22). The invective against a part(!) of the Jews in 2:14-16 is, naturally, not conditioned by racism, but is aimed against the hindering of the Gentile mission. If this is not a question of a non-Pauline gloss first inserted after the destruction of Jerusalem,[89] the idea that *now* God's wrath has turned against them is, in any case, not the last word of the apostle (see 12.5 and 16.4 below).

11. THE FIRST LETTER TO THE CORINTHIANS

11.1 Unity, Place, Date. For a long time now it has been presumed that parts of the previous letter mentioned in 5:9—or even the whole letter, apart from introduction and conclusion—were incorporated into our First Letter to the Corinthians. That is suggested here especially because the unity of the Second Letter to the Corinthians is, in any case, extremely difficult to defend (see 12.1 below). Mostly, one thinks of (5:1-8; 6:1-11) 6:12-20; 9:24–10:22; 11:2-34, but many different proposals have been put forward.[90] Although the division of the material into two, three, or even more letters is widely assumed today, certainty cannot be obtained (see 9.4 above and 12.3 below). At any rate, our First Letter to the Corinthians was written in Ephesus, where, according to 16:5, 8 (cf. Acts 19:21), Paul claims to have stayed until Pentecost in order then to travel through Macedonia to Greece. If Acts 20:3, 6 is correct in stating that shortly after Easter Paul left Greece again after a stay of three months, it was presumably not until fall when he left Ephesus. Aquila and Priscilla, whom he met on his first, year-and-a-half long visit in Corinth and with whom he worked (Acts 18:2-3, cf. 7), are now with him (I Cor 16:19). In due course they went with him to Ephesus, according to Acts 18:18. Paul heard something from "Chloe's people" (I Cor 1:11) and received a letter (7:1), which presumably Stephanas, Fortunatus, and Achaicus brought him (16:17) and which he now answers point for point (7:1, 25; 8:1; 12:1; cf. 16:1, 12). He has sent Timothy to Corinth, but he has apparently not yet arrived (4:17; 16:10). Apollos, who according to 3:6 and Acts 18:27–19:1 had already worked in Corinth, did not want to go along, despite the urging of the apostle (16:12).

In the church in Corinth, with its harbor region and pleasure areas, the great majority belong to the socially lower and also morally questionable classes (1:26-29; 6:9-11); yet those who are socially better off, are important for the congregation, for they make their houses and food available for the common meal (11:21-22; Rom 16:23).[91] Verse 11:5 presupposes that women also pray in public and preach in the worship service;[92] of course, that does not agree with 14:34-35, which states that they should be silent, but since this remark is placed after verse 40 in many manuscripts, it is probably a marginal note added later, which was incorporated by one copyist where it began in the margin, by another where it ended (but cf. 20.4 below).

11.2 Kerygma and Life. Scarcely any other letter shows as well as this one the penetration of the gospel into the concrete life of the community. Both points are crucial: (1) Paul does not formulate his preaching in timeless, situationless statements, but in sentences that are very practical and that thankfully declare, admonish, warn, and shape everything in life; *and* (2) these statements are never based only on their possible usefulness, on their agreement with custom, or on reasonable reflections, but always on the presentation of the central message of Jesus Christ, the crucified and resurrected one.[93] Now, one can certainly ask whether this always succeeds and whether individual decisions are always correct, but it is quite clear that what is at stake is this central proclamation and that in Paul's understanding it can only be comprehended when it penetrates into the concrete life of the community in all its uncertainty and manifold experiences. In 1:18–2:16 everything Paul has to say is concentrated on the crucified one; chapter 13 sees in unlimited love *the* way in which faith in him can be lived; and chapter 15 proclaims the resurrection of Jesus, and with it also the resurrection of the dead in general, as the event without which all faith is in vain. Here the statements about cross and resurrection are assertions that define the life of the community, and the exhortation to love is an exhortation to life "in" the crucified and resurrected Christ. In it one can find again the three-note chord of faith-love-hope of I Thess 1:3.

11.3 The Word of the Cross. The fundamental anchoring in the Christ event (3:11) becomes visible in 1:18–2:15 as the emphatic stress on the "word of the cross." This shameful death, unacceptable to Jews as well as Greeks, destroys the wisdom of this world (1:17; 2:6-7; 3:19). Those are not just reasonable reflections; they are also a penetration into the "depths of God" based on the gift of revelation (2:10). It is only the Spirit of God himself that reveals this very dying on the cross as the hidden mystery of God that is expected by no one (2:7-10).[94] Therefore, the appeal to human leaders (Paul, Apollos, Peter, perhaps also to an immediate connection with Christ,[95] 1:12), which calls forth factions played out against each other in the community, is impossible (1:10-17; 3:1-23), for everything they can communicate is a gift bestowed by God (4:7). Thus it is precisely the weakness and impotence of the messenger that witness to God's power (4:9-13). Presumably Alexandrian wisdom thinking penetrated into the community with Apollos, with whom Paul expressly deals in 3:1–4:6 (3:4-6; 4:6), yet without polemicizing against him (16:12), and against it Paul must place a certain counterweight. The idea that even if all of a person's works are reduced to ashes in the fire of judgment that person will be saved, albeit in a shameful way (3:15), expresses the opposition of human works and God's justification, which is formulated more radically in Galatians as a polemical thesis.

11.4 "All Things Are Lawful, But . . ." In what follows the slogan, "All things are lawful," basically accepted by Paul, is modified by the idea of the embodiment in the community of what happened through Jesus: "but not all things are helpful," precisely because people do not remain free when they let themselves be ruled by other powers (6:12). That is followed up in chapters 5–6 with respect to three concrete ethical questions.

Intercourse with prostitutes is clearly differentiated from the no longer to be feared contamination through food, for joining with a prostitute affects not only the "stomach" but the "body." By this Paul obviously means the person himself in his totality, his whole "self" (cf. 11.5 below on 15:42-49). Hence union with a prostitute is incompatible with the equally effective union with Christ in *his* body (6:13-17).[96] In especially sharp fashion sexual contact with one's stepmother is rejected, because even the pagans shy away from that (5:1).

This raises the problem of church discipline. Paul refines it to the extent that he demands no separation from the world, which is relegated to God's judgment, but separation from church members who live thus. Already in Israel the death of the paschal lamb led to the cleansing of the house of all impurities before the feast: how much more the death of Jesus to the cleansing of the church (5:1-13)! Renunciation of judicial processes within the community is based on the new standing of all community members, who participate in God's sovereignty (6:1-11). On the one hand, questions of love and marriage are discussed very soberly in chapter 7: the sexual need of the partner can be more important than my religious one (vv. 4-5)—"each has his own special gift from God" (v. 7)—marrying is better than being consumed with desire (v. 9); separation is allowed if the unbelieving partner desires it (vv. 15-16). On the other hand, the tie with Christ may not be hindered by other ties; everything worldly must thus be used in such a way that one can also leave it where necessary (vv. 29-31). Even the full freedom to eat meat originally offered to idols (chaps. 8, 10) is limited by the question whether it could lead astray another person, for whom Christ also died, and thus separate him or her from Christ (8:11-12). Such freedom and restriction was also experienced and practiced by Paul in his preaching (chap. 9; see 31.2 below).

The worship service as the shaping of the body of Christ defines chapters 11–14. Paul attempts (in dubious fashion) to have even the question of the head covering of a woman who prays and preaches in the worship service (see 11.1 above) based on the function of Christ (11:1-16). Above all, what is said in 8:11-12 applies all the more to the Lord's Supper (11:27). Where the poor and weak are shamed by the premature and immoderate eating of others,[97] the body of Christ cannot take shape (11:17-34). That can happen only in the rapt openness of each community member to the gift of Christ, and through each to all others (chaps. 12, 14). Paul knows people, to be sure, who devote themselves especially to the church and ought to be recognized for that (I Cor 16:15-18; Phil 2:29-30). Nowhere, however, does he address officeholders (e.g., in connection with the problem of incest or the Lord's Supper, I Cor 5:1-5; 11:17-34). Nowhere do elders appear, and the "bishops and deacons" of Phil 1:1 are presumably to be understood only as functional designations (but see 18.3 below, also 28.4 on Acts 14:23). Therefore, as in Rom 12:9, the exhortation to love in chapter 13 stands, here as hymnic praise, between the indication of the many kinds of gifts and the admonition to proper, helping devotion to others within and without the community (14:23-25), that is, to the "upbuilding" of the community. Because speaking in tongues is certainly an important experience for the speaker but does not directly build up the community, the more important gift is prophecy, preaching to the actual situation of the community, in which reason also plays a part (14:1-19). The simple comparison with a body breaks down in 12:12-13, where the body is plainly equated with Christ, who joins all together (see 17.7 below). The community is everything that sets it apart from the world only to the extent that it lives "in Christ" (1:30; see 29.6 below). Baptized into him, Jews and Greeks, slaves and free are the "body of Christ" (12:13, 27). The fact that, different from Gal 3:28, "male and female" is missing may mean that this goes without saying in Corinth or that Paul is more careful in his formulation.

11.5 Resurrection of Jesus and Resurrection of the Dead. According to 15:1-5 Paul based the community from the beginning on the tradition of the one who "died for our sins in accordance with the scriptures" and "was raised on the third day." In the list of witnesses to the resurrection, who have "seen Jesus our Lord" (9:1; 15:5-7), he includes himself (15:8). In this way the resurrection of Jesus is preached in fellowship and in unity (v. 11). The fact that the resurrection of the dead was called into question (v. 12) forces Paul to reflect on what (or who) human beings are. He can no longer naively talk of them as "spirit, soul, and body" (see 10.3 above). "Flesh and blood" belong to earthly existence and will one day die (15:50). But does that not also apply to the soul? It can lead a person to evil just as well as it can stimulate the doing of God's will when it adopts God's word—just as flesh and blood can sin or carry out God's will. Therefore Paul can also distinguish the dying "psychic" or "earthly" body from the future and imperishable "spiritual" or "heavenly" one (vv. 42-49). Even the Jewish philosopher Philo of Alexandria—an older contemporary of Jesus, who had learned with Plato to place the psychic, as the actually divine, over everything earthly—determined that in Gen 3:17 the "psyche" (or "soul") belongs to the earthly that is cursed by God.[98] In a similar way Jas 3:15 contrasts the wisdom that "comes down from above" with the psychic (see 22.3 below), and Jude 19 calls the people who are "devoid of the Spirit" (of God) psychic (see 20.2 below).

Nevertheless, for Paul the new, heavenly life is a bodily one. Thus it is precisely not a "mental" body that is contrasted with a "material" one, but the resurrection body—which one day will be led out whole and unhindered by God's Spirit—that is contrasted with the earthly one, which allows itself to be defined and ruled physically and psychically by all sorts of things. Hence, *body* for Paul means something like our "self" (see 11.4 above on 6:13-17), but understood completely as means of communication. My body is, to be sure, bounded by my skin and always to be found where I go or stay, but it also has, above all, eyes in order to see beyond myself, ears to hear, feet to go to others, hands to receive or to give. Therefore Paul emphasizes both: the fact of a bodily resurrection that transforms, but also preserves, my "self" *and* the totally different nature of the spiritual body, which goes beyond all our imaginings (15:35-50). Thus human beings remain those whom God has called by name and to whom he has pledged himself, even through death and beyond (cf. Mark 12:26-27); on the other hand, however, the history and victory of God in Christ's coming again are decisive, and hence perfection is not simply the blessedness of the pious individual soul, but fulfillment in the unanticipated openness for God and communion with his people (vv. 20-28, 51-58; see 14.4 below).

Following in chapter 16 are greetings, recommendations, and travel plans, which show how much a Pauline letter in itself draws congregations together and thus builds up the church.

11.6 Lived Faith. So what is new vis-à-vis the First Letter to the Thessalonians and also the Letter to the Galatians written shortly after I Corinthians? We can first answer that a number of practical difficulties in the community have forced Paul to consider how what is preached as faith can also be lived as faith. Since faith is lived not only with heart and mind, but also with hands and feet, stomach nerves and sexual desire, it can only become real in this way. Therefore in I Corinthians it is not merely a matter of supplementary moral admonitions. What appears in I Thess 4:14 and 5:10 as a traditional manner of speaking in order to console the community even in the face of death, in Galatians receives a whole new dimension in a crucial attack against a way of life that expects salvation from one's own work. By contrast, the crucified one, as the one who failed totally, is the antitype who makes that way impossible. In a different version the Galatian danger also appeared in Corinth. Here it is one's own wisdom, and hence a spiritual life, which thinks itself important and understands its freedom as boundless. To be sure, this is understood in a Christian way and presumably also promoted by the preaching of Apollos. Thus the word of the cross (1:18)—which says that it is precisely the weak, poor, insignificant, nontriumphant, and inferior that are the bearers of God's power—defines the fundamental exposition in chapters 1-4 as well as the discussion of various everyday problems, in which such faith must be practiced. It is the death of Jesus—which was suffered for the sisters and brothers just as for me (8:11-12; 11:27)—which determines behavior concerning the eating of meat offered to idols or in the communion of the Lord's Supper. It is being bound to the crucified one in the "body of Christ" (12:13) that shapes sexual behavior (chaps. 5–6), freedom, and commitment in marriage (chap. 7), as well as the ordering of the worship service, in which the gifts given to others are taken seriously (chaps. 12–14). Also included in this list is the new reflection on human beings and their resurrection, which Paul was perhaps the first to connect with Jesus' resurrection,[99] because it reminds us that the consummation is not here yet, but again is wholly an act of God, indeed, a Christ event.

12. THE SECOND LETTER TO THE CORINTHIANS

12.1 Unity? In 7:16 Paul writes: "I rejoice, because I have perfect confidence in you" (cf. vv. 11, 13). According to 9:13 the churches will glorify the Corinthians before God for their "obedience in acknowledging the gospel of Christ" and the purity of their communion with them and all others. In 11:3-4 we read: "I am afraid that . . . your thoughts will be led astray from a sincere and pure devotion to Christ," because "another Jesus" is preached, "a different spirit" is bestowed, "a different gospel" is proclaimed, and "you submit to it readily enough." At work among them are "false apostles, deceitful workmen," who like Satan disguise themselves (11:13-14). In 12:20 Paul writes: "I fear that perhaps I may come and find you not as I wish, and that you may find me not as you wish," so that hate and discord will arise. "Examine yourselves, to see whether you are holding to your faith" (13:5). That cannot have been written at the same time. One must at least assume that chapters 1–9, which in (9:12-14 and) 9:15 also have a certain conclusion, were left lying for some time, perhaps because the anticipated messenger could not travel then, and that after the arrival of new news (of which, admittedly, nothing is said) Paul wrote chapters 10–13, but also gave the previous letter to the messenger as a sign of his openness to reconciliation, which can also be seen in 13:6-13. That is not impossible. Chapters 1–9 have no actual closing and 10–13 no new opening. Also according to chapters 1–8 not all is in order in Corinth (e.g., 3:1; 6:12-13; 7:2), and chapters 10–13 are aimed against certain people (10:2), the "superlative apostles" (11:5), especially against one of them (10:11; 11:4). According to 11:22-23 the opponents emphasize that they are "Hebrews," "Israelites," and "servants of Christ." Presumably it is thus a matter of Jewish Christians, perhaps Jerusalemites who are related to Peter.

Nevertheless, that is hard to imagine. For 12:18 looks back to a visit of Titus and another brother in Corinth. According to 8:6 Paul is now sending Titus, who earlier had already begun[100] to organize a collection among them and is now supposed to bring it to a close. According to 2:13 and 7:5-9 he has just returned from Corinth and brought good news. Paul had waited for him uneasily in Macedonia, because he had sent (through Titus) a harshly written letter to Corinth and before the return of Titus did not know how the community had accepted it. He rejoices that they, of course, "were grieved" but "into repenting," and now all is well. Thus we may assume with certainty three trips for Titus to Corinth, the first for the first organization of a collection, the second with Paul's harsh letter, and now the third in order to bring the collection to a close. If the letter were unified, all of that would have been written by Paul in chapters 1–9. But before Titus departed, the apostle would have received new bad news and therefore written chapters 10–13 and sent them to Corinth with the rest, that is, with the request to bring the collection to a close. Afterward he would have traveled there himself and, as we learn in Rom 15:25-29, would, to his joy, have indeed received the collection in Achaia, whose most important center is Corinth, in order then to journey with it to Jerusalem. That is almost beyond comprehension.

12.2 Two (or Three) Letters? It is much simpler to assume that after the first visit of Titus to Corinth, to which 8:6 looks back, difficulties erupted, probably toward the end of Paul's first stay in Ephesus, since at the time of I Cor 16:1-11 everything was still in order. Paul then sent Titus there with the letter in chapters 10–13; in Macedonia he received good news and wrote chapters 1–9 as a sign of reconciliation and with the request to finish the collection. Also in other respects it is difficult to get around the assumption that different letters are assembled here. Chapters 8 and 9 deal with the same theme, the collection, and each writing seems to be, more or less, a self-contained unit, apart from the fact that chapter 9 begins with "for" (RSV: "now") and the "brethren" in verses 3 and 5 are not named. Was it supposed to be an appendix simultaneous with chapter 8 and intended, for example, for the churches in the country, or—perhaps more likely—the request for a collection given to Titus on his first visit? Then chapter 9 would have been brought over by Titus on the first visit, 10–13 on the second, and 1–8 on the third.[101] There is, however, a further difficulty. Apart from the word *Christ* (in verse 15), 6:14–7:2 is a Jewish admonition that is deceptively similar to the writings of the Jewish monks of the Dead Sea and which in four verses contains six expressions that otherwise never appear in the New Testament, as well as the totally un-Pauline formulation "defilement of body and spirit," and which, moreover, fits quite poorly into the context. Thus, it is very probable that a text known later in the churches was inserted here.

12.3 A Combination of Various Writings? How can we conceive that such letters were brought together? We can easily imagine that individual sections (here 6:14–7:2) were later inserted (see 9.4 and, on I Cor 14:34-35, 11.1 above). Placing different texts in a series has its parallel in the joining of second and third Isaiah to Isa 1-39, and no doubt also the appending of John 21 (see 29.3 below) to the Fourth Gospel.[102] After the death of the apostle his letters were no longer read as occasional writing for a particular time and in a particular situation, but as documents that were still more or less eternally valid, as we in fact also do in the worship service or in private Bible reading. Therefore one could also place documents on the same theme together (chaps. 8 and 9).[103] Chapters 10–13 could be placed at the end because the dangers envisioned there are also the dangers of the postapostolic age;[104] indeed, one could no longer know which was temporally the earlier letter and which the later. That is entirely conceivable, while it is much more difficult to assume that such an editor brought together as a completely new creation individual excerpts from various letters and to a certain extent interwove them—thus, for example, inserting 2:14–7:4 (or 6:13) from another letter into chapters 1–8, right in the middle of the travel report that begins in 2:13 and continues in 7:5 (cf. also 11.1; 14.1).[105]

12.4 Probable Order of Events. According to I Cor 16:10-11 Timothy has traveled to Corinth and is expected back again. Then Paul must have gone over once from Ephesus (see 9.1 above), for according to II Cor 12:14; 13:1-2 his coming visit is already the third, and 2:1 obviously has in mind the visit from Ephesus, where an encounter with an individual took place (2:5-7; 7:12). After his return Paul writes the Corinthians a harsh letter "with many tears" (2:4; 7:8), presumably the letter contained in chapters 10–13. He no doubt sends this letter with Titus, whom they already know from a first visit to get the collection started, and expects then to meet him in Troas (2:12). Originally he wanted to travel via Corinth to Macedonia and, on the way back from there to Jerusalem, to go by Corinth again (1:15-16), which, however, he was unable to do (1:23–2:2). Still in Asia—and thus probably in Ephesus—Paul comes into danger (1:8-9) and then travels (see 11.1 above) to Macedonia, where he meets Titus (2:12-13; 7:5-7). The Acts of the Apostles says nothing about all these complications. It reports only that Paul travels to Corinth, where he remains three months in order then to go, in the company of Timothy and others, by Macedonia to Jerusalem (20:2-5). That is confirmed by the Letter to the Romans, which must have been written in Corinth or its vicinity, because Cenchreae (Rom 16:1) is a Corinthian suburb. Since the letter presupposes a good relationship with the community, all difficulties have been cleared away (15:25-29, see 12.1 above).

70

12.5 Even Religious Experiences and Accomplishments Can Be "Flesh." There is probably no other letter in which almost all the central assertions of the apostle appear at least briefly and at the same time are said in a concrete situation with unusually personal involvement. Chapters 10–13, which were presumably written earlier, show the double character of the apostolic service, which corresponds to the Lord who "was crucified in weakness, but lives by the power of God" (13:4). It is, to be sure, practiced "in the flesh" but not "according to the flesh" (10:3). If it is Jesus Christ who is to shape the life of the apostle and then also of the community, then any life "according to the flesh," that is, any trust in all sorts of imaginable human merits, is impossible. If, therefore, I Cor 1:29 already excluded any personal boast, then the community made uncertain by such ambiguity now forces Paul to play the fool and speak of his suffering (11:23-33), his experiences of God (12:1-6), and miracles (12:12). Only because of this do we learn of the five synagogal punishments of thirty-nine lashes, from which many people died. That Paul subjected himself to them (though he could have denied being under the jurisdiction of the synagogue) is an even more impressive testimony than Rom 9–11 for the meaning that he ascribed to belonging to the "Israel according to the flesh" (I Cor 10:18). Of the three shipwrecks Acts tells nothing (27:41 is a later, fourth one). Only because of the criticism of the Corinthians do we also learn about astonishing visionary experiences of the apostle. What he formulates theoretically in I Cor 12:2-3 he carries out here in practice: even the most astonishing, "supernatural" form of an experience, a transport into the third heaven, into paradise (in which it is all the same to Paul whether it happens bodily or not!), in no way proves the presence of the Holy Spirit. On the contrary, the decisive point is only that "the Lord" speaks, and although Paul knows that his authority can also express itself in the signs of healing and similar mighty works (12:12; also Rom 15:19), it is the Lord who told him that his power comes to fulfillment in weakness (12:9-10) and therefore *not* in spectacular experiences. Thus the very opposition of the "superlative apostles" (11:5) enables the picture of Christ to gain sharper contours: the life of the resurrection comes out of human weakness, and Christ's power is thus to be experienced only in weakness (13:4).

12.6 Self-righteousness and God's Righteousness. Chapters 1–7 reflect in a positive way the service of the apostle. Still within the thanksgiving of 1:3-11 Paul understands the experience of threat of death as an aid to faith, that is, as liberation from reliance on one's own power as openness to the God who raises from the dead. The central difference between building on one's self and orientation toward the gift of God is greatly clarified in the personal experience of mortal danger. The reliability of God, which has proved itself in Christ as the "amen" to God's plan of salvation, also stands over the apostle's travel plans—not his own discretion, as the Corinthians think (1:12–2:13). In 2:14–7:4 his service is first described as that of the Spirit, excelling and in opposition to service under the letter of the law (chap. 3), then as the event of a new creation (4:1-6), whose whole treasure *must* lie in earthen vessels, so that the Lord himself, not his messenger, can prevail with his power. The "life of Jesus" thus proves itself in the "death of Jesus," which is manifested in the suffering of the apostle (4:7-18), for the body of glory belongs to the future (5:1-10; see 14.4 below), and the Spirit is merely the "guarantee" of future fulfillment (1:22; 5:5). Thus the service of reconciliation in the new creation (5:11-21) is demonstrated paradoxically in the very desperation and defeat of his messenger (6:1-13). The traditional fundamental assertion of the one who "died for our sins" (I Cor 15:3) was already formulated in I Cor 1:30 (cf. by 6:11) by the key word *righteousness,* and in the battle with the false teachers in Galatia Paul spoke all the more of the righteousness of Christ in opposition to righteousness out of the law (see 13.4, 14.5 below). In an almost puzzling way, II Cor 5:21 speaks of Christ as "made . . . to be sin . . . so that in him we might become the righteousness of God." With this the opposition of weakness and power is still more deeply anchored, as in Galatians and above all in Romans a short time later. It is not only a question of success or failure: it is a question of human existence before God. In the Second Letter to the Corinthians it becomes clear how little can be simply adopted as a formula to be accepted. On the one hand, it shapes the whole existence of the apostle, whose "inner nature is being renewed every day," while his "outer nature is wasting away" (4:16). On the other hand, it is seen in all community members in that "all have died" and now "live no longer for themselves but for him who for their sake died and was raised" (5:14-15). Faith is thus always a real-life appropriation that encompasses all of human existence. Verses 7:5-16 refer back to 2:5-13 and also understand Titus's message of the conversion of the Corinthians, in the light of what has been said, as God's comfort in human need.

Chapters 8 and 9 call for the completion of the "fellowship" as the collection is literally designated by Paul. Jesus' becoming poor, which makes us rich, will be implemented (8:9) when the unity of the church is lived in practice, in rendering help and in prayer (9:12-14); and this is always the "grace" and "gift" of God (8:1; 9:8-11, 15).

12.7 The Power of God in Weakness. The confrontation with opponents, who doubt his apostolic authority and perhaps are also superior to him in rhetorical and charismatic abilities (10:1-2, 10; 11:16–12:5), as well as Paul's dealing with his own dying, which has become very existential (1:8), let the message of the gospel take on a real-life shape for Paul himself. Only because he is compelled does he enter at all into his most unusual missionary activity, laying his life on the line more than once (11:16-33), and into his astonishing religious experiences (12:1-5), in order then *not* to rely on them, but rather to focus on his weakness (12:6-10; 1:4-9; 4:7-15). What is thought through in Galatians in the dispute with people who trust their righteousness, and in I Corinthians with those who build on their wisdom, now becomes very personally the dispute with the temptation to regard one's own missionary accomplishment and charismatic experiences as what is crucial and thus to repress one's own weakness or the threat of death and either forget all defeats or give in to resignation. The message of the one who "was crucified in weakness, but lives by the power of God" thus becomes the power of life. Paul is "weak in him" and will "live with him by the power of God"—also and especially "in dealing with you" (13:4). As he is "always carrying in [his] body the death of Jesus" (e.g., in quite visible scars from the lashes), the life of Jesus will also become manifest in his body, in such a way that while death may befall him, at the same time life goes out from him into the churches (4:10, 12). It *must* be that way, as Paul never tires of repeating, because only thus can Christ himself, the crucified and resurrected one, prevail and not, say, a speaker, healer, or heroic missionary admired by people (cf. the frequent "so that" in 12:9; 1:11; 4:7, 10-11, 15).

13. THE LETTER TO THE GALATIANS

13.1 Place and Date. According to 4:13 Paul was already with his readers twice. The Greek word translated "at first" means "the first time (of two)" though it can occasionally mean simply "before." According to I Cor 16:1 Paul had already organized the collection in Galatia. In all other churches, these arrangements were made on the third "journey." The letter to the Thessalonians written on the second "journey," shortly after the first visit there, betrays absolutely nothing of the fundamental assertions of the Galatian letter, and thus one can, in any case, hardly set it in this period, but must rather place it after the time of Acts 18:23. The Roman province of Galatia included the regions in the south that Paul visited on the so-called first missionary journey. Barnabas had also accompanied him there (Acts 13–14; Gal 2:1, 9). If the recipients of the letter were to be sought there,[106] the letter could have been written on the second "journey," for example, in Macedonia, and be even older than the Thessalonian letter. Paul can use the provincial names (Rom 15:26), but also the names that designate regions (Gal 1:21, where, by the way, Paul would have had to add "and to you" if the first visit had taken place before the apostolic council [Gal 2:1-10]). But since the province is designated only in abbreviated form as Galatia while otherwise officially all the individual regions are always listed, since by *Galatia* Acts means the country lying in the northern interior of Asia Minor, which Paul visited on the second and third "journeys" (16:6; 18:23), since this also seems to be true for I Pet 1:1, where it lies between

Pontus on the Black Sea and Cappadocia in the (eastern) interior of Asia Minor, and, finally, since Paul addresses his readers as "you Galatians," we must almost certainly think of the actual land of Galatia and its inhabitants, where an illness kept the apostle longer than he intended (Gal 4:13 = Acts 16:6?). In addition, 4:13 does not mention Barnabas, which fits in better with the second "journey," on which the latter no longer accompanied Paul (Acts 15:36-39; Gal 2:13), although I Cor 9:6 again speaks positively of him. Then the letter was presumably written during the long stay in Ephesus or, since Paul himself does not travel to Galatia, perhaps only on the further journey to Macedonia (after I/II Corinthians?). The "brethren who are with me" are named in Gal 1:2, but no churches. Naturally, Paul could have also written "so quickly" (1:6) after two or three years. The relationship with the Letter to the Romans (see 16.3 below) would speak for a dating after both Corinthian letters. According to I Cor 16:1, the collection seems to be causing no difficulties in Galatia. Thus either the Galatian letter (written before I Corinthians) has led to a reconciliation, or, more likely, Paul heard of the work of the opponents only after having written I Corinthians. One could even presume that the collection named there (which, according to Gal 2:10, is in any case familiar to the Galatians) was by that time brought to Jerusalem and had perhaps also initiated the countermovement to which the letter witnesses. This may even have led to the alterations in the apostle's plans (II Cor 1:15-16). Thus the Galatian letter more likely should be dated after I Corinthians at approximately the same time as the second Corinthian letter (or before, since Timothy is—in contrast to II Cor 1:1—not mentioned). From Ephesus Paul would presumably have traveled again to Galatia; from Macedonia that was scarcely possible. Nonetheless, the dating is in no way raised above all doubt, since a reconciliation in the two and a half to three years of the stay in Ephesus (see 9.2 above) would be quite possible if the Letter to the Galatians were placed at the beginning of the Ephesian stay. First Peter 1:1 and II Tim 4:10 perhaps show that Galatia was not totally alienated from Pauline influence. On the other hand, mention of a Galatian collection is missing in Acts 20:4 and especially in Rom 15:25-26, and many things suggest that no reconciliation was possible in Galatia (see 9.2 above and 16.2 below). Verses 7-8 in chapter 2 have been understood as a later addition, because elsewhere Paul always writes "Cephas" and never "Peter"; but it could also be a Pauline summary of the decision formulated thus at that time (which was admittedly difficult to carry out). For the rest, the letter is certainly of one piece.

13.2 The Situation in Galatia. After Paul's last visit missionaries came to Galatia who called his authority into question and required circumcision and the observation of special days, above all the sabbath, because only thus could one achieve full entrance into the cultic community of Israel and receive salvation (4:10; 5:2-4; 6:12). Certainly they were Christians who likewise claimed to preach a "gospel" (1:6), and the church is apparently ready to take it "more seriously" and to accomplish more for their faith.[107] Possibly they encountered a pagan, Pythagorean asceticism (see 17.4 below). This forces Paul to reflect fundamentally on his preaching. In itself, circumcision is possible, though I Cor 7:18 speaks only of those who were already circumcised when they were called. Yet it is not impossible for Paul to circumcise the son of a Jewish mother, who was also considered a Jew (Acts 16:1-3). "To the Jews I became as a Jew, in order to win Jews," says Paul (I Cor 9:20), and he knows of the privileges of Israel (Rom 3:1-4; 11:25-26). Fundamentally, circumcision is neither required nor essential. Why then is the requirement of the opponents impossible? First, they demand the circumcision also of Gentiles, who do not belong to Israel. The basis of Paul's resistance, however, lies even deeper. What is crucial is not the completion or noncompletion of a rite, but the basic attitude of life that is expressed in it. If salvation is made dependent on circumcision, then salvation follows a human deed and is accomplished only through human obedience. What became clear to Paul in Damascus, however, is the opposite: salvation comes *before* all human deeds that flow from it and thus does not depend on human beings and their actions. Therefore, it is also not simply the correctness of the Pauline message compared to other messages that is crucial, but the life that is shaped by it (see 13.5 below). For this reason, Paul begins with the description of his own way (1:10–2:21), which, however, was not a purely individual experience but a way in the church in agreement with the community in Jerusalem (2:1-10; cf. here 9.1 above). As the truth of the gospel was demonstrated there when a Gentile Christian was accepted as brother without circumcision (Gal 2:3), so also was it in danger when Peter withdrew from table fellowship with the uncircumcised in Antioch (who were not eating according to Jewish precept!) (2:11-21; see 16.2 below).

13.3 From Death to Life. It is not simply a question of finding a compromise here that makes a common life possible, as recommended in Acts 15:28-29 (a decision that, according to 21:25, is still unknown to Paul!). It is a question of a fundamental decision for or against a life in faith, that is, of one's relation to the law of Moses. Yet Paul also does not speak of this in the form of a doctrine that could be weighed against a different one and then regarded as better; he speaks rather of a "death" and a (new) "life." That is, of course, not simply a passive experience, as normal language usage might indicate, but a "dying to the law" and a "living to God," in short, something that changes our relationships to both, so that now everything goes from death to life and no longer vice versa. In 6:15 he calls this event a "new creation." So it is now not a matter of setting circumcising against not circumcising. Neither one helps, neither boasting about circumcision nor renouncing it, but only the recognition that with Jesus Christ a new world has begun in which neither circumcision nor uncircumcision, "neither Jew nor Greek . . . slave nor free . . . male nor female" is decisive (3:28), but only life in Christ, who joins all people together into a single person (3:28; see 16.3 below).

13.4 The Gift of Righteousness. From that standpoint Paul understands the Old Testament anew. The promise given to Abraham includes all peoples (3:8). This became true in Jesus Christ, in whom all are joined together (3:28). He is the "offspring" envisioned by the promise (as 3:16 determines with a very questionable interpretation), precisely because he has vicariously borne the curse laid by the law on death by crucifixion (3:13; 4:4-5). Therefore the law bestowed at Sinai, and with it the present, earthly Jerusalem, belongs on the side of the children Abraham had through the slave Hagar according to purely human considerations (*"according to* the flesh"). Isaac and his children, on the other hand, were born by the divine promise itself (*"through* promise"; see 16.5 below) for the freedom of the heavenly Jerusalem (4:21-28). If such an allegory appears curious, the step taken therein is crucial (see 16.3 below). What Paul calls "faith" is life in the new world that has come over humanity (3:23). In it an uncircumcised man can be accepted as brother, and a person not eating according to the law, as a table companion. The point here is precisely not that a special achievement would be completed, but that the "Spirit" or the "promise" itself effects the new life, as long as the believer does not hold back and take life into his or her own hands according to human standards and systems. While being righteous is designated in I Thess 2:10 without a more exact description as the right behavior of the apostle vis-à-vis the community, now, in view of the misunderstanding in Galatia, Paul asserts much more sharply that such righteousness is something the believer receives from Jesus Christ (2:16-17), not simply from human action according to the norms of the law (2:21). It is no longer Paul who lives, but Christ himself in him (2:20).

13.5 Life as Fruit of the Spirit. It is, nonetheless, a question of new *life* that Paul can describe admonishingly in 5:1–6:10, and which he designates in 6:2 with the catchphrase *law of Christ*. Now, according to the rhetorical schema in use at the time and taught in the schools, the whole letter can perhaps be divided first as a defense (as might be held before the court) into introduction (1:1-11), report (1:12–2:14), thesis (2:15-21), argumentation (3:1–4:31), epilogue (5:1–6:10), and summary (6:11-18).[108] In this very way, however, it becomes clear that this admonishing part in 5:1–6:10 actually does not fit into the schema but shifts into another genre, namely, into a deliberative talk, although in such a way that it is not a question of weighing something better against something worse, but of the only possible decision in view of this new creation[109] (see also 16.3 below).

Therefore, faith can be nothing other than the forming of Christ in us (4:19), that is, the working of love (5:6). In contrast to the multiplicity of plainly visible "works" of the flesh, this is the one "fruit" of the Spirit, which encompasses everything, even one's own and alien weaknesses and trespasses (5:19, 22; 6:1-4). One cannot believe in anything other than a living way, and living must likewise express itself in thinking and in doing, in feeling and in experiencing, in attentive listening and in dreaming. It has found its place as a wholeness in the new world of freedom created by Christ and can therefore not become the "launching pad of purely human behavior" (of the "flesh"—5:1, 13; see 22.4 below).

13.6 The Israel of God in the Hope of Eschatological Fulfillment. Thus the idea that God's gift becomes task (I Thess) is thoroughly thought out here in view of the demand for a return to the strict observation of the law and in the light o f the reproach of the Pauline proclamation that it leads one astray into ethical irresponsibility. This occurs in the sense of a radical opposition between humanly achieved and God-given righteousness, which, however, does not remain abstract but shapes itself into a life that no longer builds on one's own achievement and position and can therefore also understand one's own weaknesses positively as dependence on the power of God. At about the same time Paul has to think this through again in another version in his correspondence with the Corinthians in regard to those who place against Christ not their fulfillment of the law but their wisdom. Paul knows of faith formed by the Spirit as "fruit" and shaping all experience, feeling, thinking, and acting. But he also knows that this will become clearly visible only in God's final future: "Through the Spirit, by faith, we wait for the hope of righteousness" (5:5). Gal 5:17 corresponds to the strange twilight of impotence and power in which Paul's apostolic service is described, which can speak of his weakness as well as the glory of his service: "The desires of the flesh are against the Spirit, and the desires of the Spirit are against the flesh"; yet this sentence is enclosed between two others: "Walk in the Spirit and you will not fulfill the desires of the flesh," and "If you are led by the Spirit you are not under the law" (5:16, 18).

In all this, the Letter to the Galatians is written as a real letter. Its harshness comes from the fact that its author is again suffering "birth pains" over his readers (4:19). The assertions about human misconduct and God's righteousness are forged out of this most intimate participation in their way. With this the old idea that the Gentiles must first enter Israel in order to come to salvation (cf. Matt 8:11-12 etc.) is overcome. Along with Israel, they live only from God's good actions toward them. Thus are they the "Israel of God" (6:16).[110]

14. THE LETTER TO THE PHILIPPIANS

14.1 Unity? The section between 3:2 and 4:1 contains a sharp argument with Judaistic opponents. Independently of one another, various researchers have presumed that our letter was put together from three writings.[111] The assumption is that a short thank you was composed immediately after the receipt of the gift from Philippi (4:10-23).[112] After Epaphroditus recovered from his illness (2:25-30), Paul sent him back with a detailed report on his situation (1:1–3:1 + 4:4-7 [or 4:2-9?]) and held out the prospect of sending Timothy, who is supposed to bring him back a report from Philippi, and of coming later himself (2:19-24; everything together [in this order?] = the second letter). As Paul heard, probably after his release, that the fight that had broken out in Corinth and elsewhere had also reached Philippi, he wrote (as the third letter) 3:2–4:3, 8-9 (or only to 4:1?) to the community and perhaps also to the now present Timothy ("you . . . true yokefellow"—4:3). This would fit with Polycarp's remark (Pol. *Phil.* 3:2) about "letters," that Paul had written to them (which, of course, he could also have discerned from 3:1).

Again, this solution is possible and could clarify the different views of the community situation in 1:3-11; 2:17-18 on the one hand and 3:2-3, 17-19 on the other. Yet it is hardly imaginable that someone would assemble the new letter out of individual pieces woven together in this fashion. To avoid this, one could conceive of three short writings that were arranged one after the other, say, 1:1–3:1; 3:2–4:3; 4:4-23, although the similarity of 4:4, 8 to (2:18 and) 3:1 is striking. Nevertheless, according to 3:15-16; 4:1, Paul also feels quite positive about the majority of the community; and if the opponents of chapter 3 were not Jewish Christians but Jews,[113] then 1:28 could also refer to the same group. Therefore others have thought only of a longer interruption before 2:25 and again before 3:2,[114] or, on the basis of the rhetorical uniformity of the schema that corresponds to other Pauline letters, have assumed unity or at least a very conscious and well-defined final redaction.[115]

14.2 Place and Date. If three letters went to Philippi one right after another, only an incarceration in Ephesus (or vicinity) is conceivable. It is not mentioned by Acts, but II Cor 11:23 and 6:5 name various prison stays; in addition, shortly before the departure for Macedonia II Cor 1:8-11 speaks of the threat of death in Asia Minor—quite possibly in Ephesus (cf. also Rom 16:7, in case this chapter was sent to Ephesus; see 16.1 below). The comment on fighting with beasts in I Cor 15:32, on the other hand, is only to be understood metaphorically, since the listing of Paul's sufferings in II Cor 11:23-33 does not mention it. If one thinks of only *one* letter, one must assume at least two journeys there and back, for someone reported in Philippi about the place where Paul stayed and almost certainly about his arrest; then they sent Epaphroditus, whose illness someone had again reported to them, which Paul also had already learned. Besides Epaphroditus Paul also wants to send Timothy to Philippi and then through him expects a report on the church on his return (2:19-30). From Rome or Caesarea that is not impossible, but hardly conceivable. Furthermore, the announced visit of the apostle (1:25-27; 2:24) would be possible from Rome only by giving up the trip to Spain (Rom 15:28) from Caesarea only if Paul made allowance for a considerable detour for the trip to Rome and from there to Spain. Thus, Ephesus is, in any case, the most likely point of origin. Then the letter would be written, say, between the first and second Corinthian letters.

14.3 Personal Matters. Even if it is a question of two or three letters, they lie so close together temporally that they can be discussed together. Overall the tone is extraordinarily personal. This is true even of the polemical section, where Paul in 3:12-14 writes of his experience of Christ and in (3:15) 4:1 of his longing for the Philippians and his joy over them. He thanks them for their gift and all their loyalty already experienced over the years (4:10-20). He speaks of his imprisonment, his moods, and his experiences (1:19-26; 2:17-18). In all of this, however, the course of the gospel in the place of his arrest and in Philippi is much more important to him (1:12-18, 27-30; 2:12-16; 4:2-9). For this reason he calls them again and again to be joyful. For this same reason, however, he also reckons seriously with the possibility of execution and already looks forward to when he will "be with Christ" (1:23).

14.4 God's Future. Thus he no longer awaits with certainty the final coming of Christ before his death, as in I Thess 4:15. Even in I Cor 15:51 he no longer says that expressly, but still definitely assumes that a part of the community and perhaps even he himself will yet experience it. In II Cor 5:1-10 (after the experience of the threat of death? [1:8]) only the opposition of the present toilsome life and the future homecoming to the Lord are important, and here Paul is presumably not thinking at all about whether this will be the case before or at the coming of Christ. He hardly thinks, as verse 3 was already interpreted, that those who died earlier would have to wait in a bodiless state (which he hopes to avoid). Verse 3 no doubt only wards off this—for him horrible—ideal of his Hellenistic contemporaries: "Presupposing, at least, that after the taking off (of the mortal body) we will not be found naked (as the pagans expect)." Not until Phil 1:23 does he speak positively of a being "with Christ" immediately after his possible execution. Yet this in no way abolishes the expectation of the coming Christ, "who will change our lowly body to be like his glorious body" (3:21). That is not fundamentally different from I Thess 4, even if the emphases are placed differently according to the situation and Paul now reckons with the possibility that the fate of those who died in Thessalonica could also be his.

Therefore the "day of Christ" is also the actual horizon for the life of the community and thus its standard (1:6, 10; 2:16); the "resurrection of the dead" and the "upward call" are the goal toward which the apostle aims (3:11, 14). Here the coming lordship of Christ is clearly conceived as worldwide (2:10-11 [see 5.10 above]; 3:21). This takes up what is included in the parallels between Adam and Christ in I Cor 15:20-28 and then Rom 5:12-21 and formulated in I Cor 15:25-27 with Ps 110. It will increasingly become the theme in the letters to the Colossians and the Ephesians. There, as also in I Tim 3:16, it will be expressly linked with the mission to the Gentiles.

14.5 Righteousness from God. The establishment of the already reigning joy and hope for the consummation is crucial. In Galatians Paul sets himself apart from teachers (from Palestine?) who insist on circumcision and the fulfillment of the law; in I Corinthians, from people who build on their wisdom, that is, on "spiritual" gifts that prove themselves in authority of speech, visions, and revelations, and this becomes even clearer in the second letter to the same church. Paul also knows that the immoral, idolaters, etc., will not inherit the kingdom of God (I Cor 6:9-10). Because that is already said in the tradition, it does not have to be especially emphasized, but the other does: that precisely the righteous and the wise can miss the God who is revealed in the crucified one. In Philippians this receives even sharper contours. When others live to harm Paul, rejoice over his arrest, and make more difficulties for him, that is unimportant to him, as long as Christ is really proclaimed (1:15-18). Where, however, one's "own righteousness" competes with that "from God," as attempted by the opponents in Philippi (3:9-10), everything is at risk. While the Letter to the Galatians, to be sure (see 13.4 above), speaks of being justified "in Christ" and not "by works of the law" (2:16-17; cf. 3:11, 24; 5:4; and I Cor 6:11), also of "righteousness" not coming out of the law but attributed to faith (2:21; 3:6, 21; 5:5), the expression *righteousness of God* first appears in II Cor 5:21 (see 12.6 above) and is defined there very clearly as "righteousness from God," as the expression reads in Phil 3:9. It is no longer "my righteousness from the law," but "righteousness through faith in Christ" (see 16.4-5 below). Paul, certainly, is also circumcised, possesses all the privileges of a proper Israelite, is a Pharisee, and "as to righteousness under the law blameless" (Phil 3:5-6)—and precisely for that reason an opponent of God as long as he trusted in those things. In this very way he did not do the good that he would, but evil (Rom 7:19; see 16.4 below), and became a persecutor of the Jesus community. Thus Paul is astonishingly of the opinion that one can fulfill the law (to the letter) and nevertheless completely miss what God intended with the gift of the law; indeed, this failure is the real, "abounding" sin (Rom 5:20). The most dangerous enemy of God is thus not the godless person, the adulterer, or the thief—who can at least know their position before God—but the righteous and wise person who thinks God is no longer needed.

14.6 God's Solidarity with Humankind. In the hymn quoted in 2:6-11 (see 5.10 above) the accent shifts to the humiliation and exaltation of Jesus. Thus God exhibits solidarity with human beings, even to the last, unto death; this also means that everything human, joy and suffering, success and defeat, is taken up into God's world, into his control. Jesus' death is described not as atoning, not even as vicarious; his resurrection not as overcoming death. In this Phil 2:6-11 agrees with the message of Christ in the sayings source (Q) (see 5.10 and 7:8-9 above).

14.7 Dying and Rising with Christ. For Paul justification is a "being apprehended" (KJV) by Christ, in which his dying and rising more and more shape a person (3:10-12), until both completely define one's whole life (one's "body", II Cor 4:10). Already in I Thess 5:8-10 Paul maintains that Jesus dies for us so that now, already in faith, love, and hope, we may forever "live with him." In Gal 2:11-20 Paul describes his encounter with Peter in order to make visible how much life must be stamped by justification, for example, in table fellowship with the uncircumcised that is not according to Jewish dietary laws. This is illustrated in I Cor 6:15 in the statement that "bodily" belonging to Christ makes joining with a prostitute impossible. The Second Letter to the Corinthians shows in its chapters 11-12 and 4, by the example of the apostle and his service, how subjection to Christ becomes a living reality. Thus, just as the "foreign"—that is, God-given—righteousness and wisdom were ever more decisively to be distinguished from trusting in one's own righteousness and wisdom, so also in practical admonitions to the community it was necessary to deal with how this takes shape in the existence of the believer. Therefore, in Phil 2:1-11 Paul can quote the hymn as an example of how what is true for the community "in Christ" (theologically) must also prevail (practically) "among yourselves" in the common life of the community (2:5). Both will come to expression more fundamentally in the Letter to the Romans.

15. THE LETTER TO PHILEMON

15.1 Place and Date. Paul writes this private letter in a very personal style, plays with the name Onesimus ("useful"—v. 11), and signs, rather humorously, a promissory note to the one who is himself indebted to the apostle (v. 19). He pleads for the escaped slave but leaves various possibilities open to the recipient. He could restore him again without punishment or release him; he could keep him one way or the other for himself or—what Paul is clearly suggesting—place him at the disposal of the apostle. According to Col 4:9, 17 Onesimus and Archippus live in Colossae; except for the addressees Philemon and Apphia, all the named people also appear in Colossians. Paul writes both letters as a prisoner. Thus if both letters are written at about the same time (see 17.2 below), the Letter to Philemon also goes to Colossae or perhaps into the not far off Laodicea. Then the imprisonment in Ephesus, about 125 miles away, would be conceivable (see 14.2 above), although in Phil 2:24 Paul is considering, in case of his release, a trip to the northwest, not to the (south)east (Philem 22). If the Letter to the Colossians was written only later in assimilation to the Letter to Philemon, the connection with Colossae could be merely a presumption of the disciples of Paul, and one could also imagine, for example, Philemon residing in Pergamon,[116] where there were temple slaves, and which would lie on the route to Macedonia. Yet other imprisonments are also conceivable—even Rome—with Philemon living nearby.

15.2 Theology and Life. This short writing shows how much theology and life are united for Paul. Every practical question immediately reaches into depths to be plumbed theologically. This explains the detailed thanks to God at the beginning. Only in faith in Christ does life become real life (vv. 10, 19), and authority, even apostolic authority, can be lived only in love, that is, in readiness to renounce right and might on the part of Paul himself (vv. 8-9, 12-14), of Onesimus, who must give up his relative security and dare to return (vv. 10-12), and of Philemon, for whom it is crucial that he decide not under compulsion but in full freedom over his actions (v. 14)—whereby, of course, what is most obvious to the non-Christian, the severe punishment of the refugee, is excluded (vv. 15-17). Just as it was formulated in Phil 2:5, namely, that what is true "in Christ Jesus" must also be true in dealings with one another, so also is it formulated here in verse 16: what is true "in the Lord" must be lived "in the flesh."

15.3 House Churches. Philemon extends hospitality to a house church (v. 2). Also according to Acts 1:13; 2:46; 5:42; 12:12, the first Christians met "in the house" (of Mary, the mother of John Mark) or "in the houses." This was likewise true of the Pauline churches (18:7; 20:8; Rom 16:23), and in the same place there were also various house churches (Acts 20:20 for Ephesus; Rom 16:5, 14, 15).[117] The house church of Aquila and Priscilla is mentioned in Rom 16:5 (in Rome or Ephesus?—see 16.1 below) and in I Cor 16:19 in Ephesus; presumably already in Corinth a circle (of Jewish Christians?) gathered in their house (Acts 18:2, 6-7, 18). Also at that time pagan worship often took place in private houses, often sponsored by their owners and even under priestly direction. Above all, however, there were Jewish gatherings in houses, as long as no special synagogue had been built. Sometimes a room in the house could be reserved and furnished for these gatherings, such as in Dura Europus on the middle Euphrates, where a Christian house church from the time of A.D. 232/33, with a large meeting room of 650 square feet, has been excavated about a hundred yards from a Jewish one. That calls to mind the house church in Corinth next door to the synagogue (Acts

18:7). *House* can designate a building, but also a small or large family. Acts 2:46 and 20:8 show that all believers gather in *one* house; in Troas it is an upper chamber that is especially suitable for the reception of guests. The "one" place, in which, according to I Cor 11:20, the whole community came together for the meal and no doubt also for the worship service described in chapters 12 and 14, is probably located in the house of one of their members, for example, in that of Stephanas (16:15) or of Gaius (Rom 16:23). Perhaps we should think here of the atrium and the surrounding columned areas, but, in any case, scarcely of a room reserved or even especially built for such gatherings. Even so, one can hardly assume that more than a few dozen people met there. This shows that from the beginning relatively well-to-do people also belonged to the group of believers in Jesus, and without them the life of the community would scarcely have been conceivable; they also played an important role in spreading and caring for the faith (I Cor 16:15-18; Rom 16:3-5; Acts 18:26).[118]

16. THE LETTER TO THE ROMANS

16.1 Place, Date, Unity. The indication "in Rome" (1:7) is missing in some manuscripts; presumably they have omitted this in order to emphasize that this letter is valid for all Christians. According to 15:25-29 Paul is in the process of traveling with the collection to Jerusalem and from there via Rome to Spain. Acts 20:3–21:17 describes the journey from Corinth through Macedonia and Asia Minor to Jerusalem. According to Rom 16:1-2 Paul is writing from Corinth; Cenchreae is its harbor district. Chapter 16 is, to be sure, curious in many ways. Verses 25-27—inserted in a number of manuscripts after 14:23 or 15:33 instead of at the end of the letter, or missing altogether—certainly do not come from Paul. Vocabulary, style, and content are not Pauline (see 5.7 above). Verse 24 is also missing in many manuscripts. It, however, is almost identical with the closing of verse 20 and is found only where the verse 20 ending is left out or where verses 25-27 already stand after 14:23; thus it was presumably added in the course of tradition. Aside from this, however, one must ask how Paul knows so many people in Rome, where he has yet to go, and even designates them as his fellow workers and plainly calls a woman his "mother." In verses 21-23 he also sends them greetings from eight persons staying with him. And why are Priscilla and Aquila and their whole house church, who some two years before were still living in Ephesus (I Cor 16:19; Acts 18:19), now in Rome? Also the "first converted of Asia" (= Asia Minor) fits better in a letter to Ephesus than to Rome. Above all, verses 17-18 warn about false teachers, of whom there is no other mention in the whole letter. Finally, one could well imagine the benediction in 15:33 as the close of the letter.

Thus there is much to suggest that chapter 16 was directed at the church in Ephesus, perhaps because the Phoebe recommended in verses 1-2 was traveling with the Roman letter and the letter of greeting recommending her (ch. 16) on a sea route via Ephesus to Rome. The Letter to the Romans would then also be intended to be read aloud in Ephesus and was copied there and preserved with the supplementary greeting list. Chapter 16 alone is hardly conceivable as a full letter, and one would have to assume that 14:1–15:13, for example, also belonged to it, and conversely that 16:1-2 and/or 21-23 perhaps also belonged to the Letter to the Romans. But who would have torn two letters apart in that way and reassembled them? The other possibility, naturally, is that 16:1-23 (or 24) nevertheless belongs to Romans. The traffic from the capital into the province was heavy. Aquila and Priscilla, as well as perhaps a large number of others greeted by Paul, originally came from Rome (Acts 18:2) and presumably may have been able to return there again after the death of the emperor Claudius (A.D. 54).

On the other hand, it is difficult to understand the suggestion that 13:1-7, with its positive evaluation of civil power, no doubt adopted from Jewish tradition (see 31.5 below), is a later addition, in view of the strong vocabulary connections with the context ("the good/evil" in 12:2, 9, 17, 21; 13:3, 4, 10; "wrath," "vengeance" in 12:19; 13:4; "honor" in 12:10; 13:7) and the Pauline style.

16.2 Jewish Christians and Gentile Christians. As in Phil 1:1, the term *church* is missing in Rom 1:7. Must one, therefore, think about various house churches that flourish close to one another (see 15.3 above) like the Jewish synagogues, which in Rome were forbidden to organize? There was probably not an actual church founder; Christians came to Rome for business or personal reasons and won others there to their faith. It remains uncertain whether this happened primarily from Jerusalem, so that at first there were only Jewish Christians and not until they were driven out (see 9.1 above) was there a majority of, or almost exclusively, Gentile Christians,[119] or rather from Antioch, where both groups already lived together.[120] It is only clear that the majority of those addressed by Paul's letter are Gentile Christians (1:5-6, 13; 11:13; etc.). Reluctance in the eating of meat (not slaughtered according to the law, perhaps offered to idols) and the keeping of holy days is to be expected with Jewish Christians, but also with Gentiles who as "God fearers" had adopted not the observation of the whole law, but no doubt of certain main commandments[121] (14:2-3, 5-6). In any case, the question of Israel and its law played a large role, already in the expression "to the Jew first and also to the Greek" (1:16; 2:10; cf. 3:29; 4:12), but above all in chapters 9–11. In 4:1 Paul also joins himself to the Jewish Christians when he speaks of Abraham as "our forefather according to the flesh."

In Jerusalem the problems came to a head. Originally the Gentile Christians were probably considered "God fearers" who beyond their sympathy for Judaism also accepted Jesus as their Lord. One assumed that like the Jews they would hold themselves to the main commandments of the law, while it was conceded that they would not have to accept circumcision. It is entirely possible that the decisions made by the apostolic council in Jerusalem as a concession were understood by Paul as a vote for fundamental freedom from the law, so that the opposition between Peter and Paul in Antioch (Gal 2:11-20) was already preprogrammed. The quarrel between Paul and Barnabas (Acts 15:39) may have had the same basis, and since in Gal 2:11-20 Paul mentions nothing of the recognition of his viewpoint, and since the visit in Antioch, which is mentioned in Acts 18:22-23, is perhaps not historical (see n. 73 above), it is possible that he had lost his support in Antioch (cf., however, I Cor. 16:1 and 13.1 above). If the Letter to the Galatians had even become known in Jerusalem—and why would Paul's opponents not have sent a copy or a malicious summary there?—then it would indeed be easy to explain the attacks from the Jewish side, including a still totally unclear attitude of the Christians there, of whom Paul is afraid (Rom 15:30-31). In their view Paul is engaged in unfair competition and offering cheap salvation without obligation to God's law. Nevertheless, for the sake of the necessary unity of the church, Paul wants under all circumstances to resume the dialogue with the Lord's brother James[122] and the church in Jerusalem.[123] This is why Paul writes in such detail about his position on Israel and its law and about his understanding of God's way with Israel. Although he visits Rome only in order to have a base for his broader mission into Spain (15:28), it is clear to him not only that tensions in regard to the validity of the Jewish law are also present in Rome, but above all that his mission is possible only within a fundamental unity of the whole church.

16.3 Relationship to the Galatian Letter. The main part of the Letter to the Galatians has its parallels in the Letter to the Romans. It is true that the report on Paul's career (Gal 1:10–2:14) is missing; in its place are the praise of God missing in Gal 1, which also includes a short report on the apostle's travel plans (Rom 1:8-13), and above all the detailed laying out of everyone's guilt, the Gentiles as well as the Jews, in 1:18–3:20. The thesis, however, of justification by grace (Gal 2:15-21)—which is valid not only for Jews but also for Gentiles (3:6-29) because God sent his Son and through him has made us children (4:1-7)—clearly corresponds to Rom 3:19-28 (now with the catchphrase *God's righteousness*); 4; 8:1-16. Also in both letters the admonitions come toward the end, whereby the kinship between Gal 5:13-15 and Rom 13:8-10 is especially striking. Apart from personal passages (Gal 3:1-5 and especially 4:12-20), the Letter to the Romans lacks the tracing of the law back to angels (3:19-20); as well as the exegesis—questionable in form but outstanding in content—of the singular "Abraham's offspring" as a reference to the one Jesus Christ, who for his part takes up all believers and makes them "one" in himself (3:16, 28); and above all the Hagar-Sarah allegory, which greatly depreciates the "present Jerusalem" (4:21-31). They are replaced by a longer treatment that reflects on the positive role of the law in God's plan of salvation (5:12–7:25) and the presentation of God's treatment of Israel until the final fulfillment (chaps. 9–11). Each receives its importance in view of the dialogue soon to be resumed with Jerusalem and certain tensions and reservations expected in Rome, which Paul would like to eliminate.

If the Letter to the Galatians is really supposed to have been constructed according to a rhetorical plan for a letter (see 13.5 above), that must have been abandoned at least in the Letter to the Romans. Presumably it is enough to ascertain that in Romans Paul has combined the traditional missionary proclamation, which begins with the presentation of idol worship (now, of course, also extended to the Jews!) and continues with the conversion to the living God (I Thess 1:9-10), with the catechetical tradition, which starts with the proclamation of Jesus' death and resurrection, the "gospel," and closes with the resulting admonition.[124] Without doubt, in Romans Paul develops what he already presented in Galatians, whether because of their relationship we place the latter after I (and II?) Corinthians and draw it closer in time to Romans or, conversely, date it earlier because of certain later developments in the direction of greater openness vis-à-vis Israel and its law (see 13.1 above). Unambiguous in both letters is the sequence of (theological) proclamation of the gospel and (ethical) development in the admonitions, whereby the former expressly discusses already in Galatians—and this is then developed in Romans—the validity of the offer of salvation for the Gentiles beyond the border of Israel. The structure is determined by the attack on Pauline authority in Galatia and, in the case of Romans, by the traditional preordering of the topos of the position of human beings under the wrath of God.

16.4 Human Righteousness in Dispute with God's Righteousness. The letter is intended to prepare the way for the visit in Rome. At this time Rome is the hub of the empire, center of culture and barbarism, learning and military might. There the world lives, and it is the world that Paul wants to reach. About all this, however, Paul writes nothing. He bases his desire to go to Rome (1:15) on a chain of four *for* clauses (1:16-18) in which he confesses the gospel as the power of God for salvation, the revelation of the "righteousness of God" (see 14.5 above) for the believer, and the wrath of God for the ungodly. Here too Paul begins with the assertion of his authority and the characterization of his preaching (1:5-15). Nonetheless, the basis of this preaching, and with it the theme of the letter, is given in verses 17-18. When one recognizes the parallelism of the two sentences, " . . . for in it [the gospel] the righteousness of God is revealed" and " . . . for the wrath of God is revealed from heaven," one must ask whether verse 18 is not plainly supposed to be the other side of verse 17, that is, whether Paul does not mean to say that it is precisely the revelation of the justifying grace of God, and only it, that also discloses the wrath of God against all. Indeed, previously the Gentiles were convinced that they were wise (1:22), and the Jews that they could judge others (2:1). Yet precisely that is *the* sin in the deepest sense of the word. Be that as it may, the theme of verse 17 is, in any case: "He who through faith is righteous shall live." That means that no one, neither the worldly nor the pious, can in any other way really live. The wrath of God falls over all, Gentiles as well as Jews (precisely in the encounter with the gospel). Therefore no one is righteous of oneself (3:10). "For no human being will be justified in [God's] sight by works of the law" (3:20).

The second part (3:21–8:39) begins with the astonishing assertion that the very person who places himself or herself under the wrath of God begins to live from God's righteousness (3:21-31). This is illustrated—as in Gal 3—through Abraham, who lived "in hope . . . against hope" (4:18), that is, out of God's word and no longer out of trust in one's own abilities (chap. 4). If it is already clear here that faith lives on what is promised by God, 5:1-11 emphasizes that the already achieved *justification* leads to the final *salvation* yet to come. In connecting Adam, through whom sin and death came into the world, with Christ, through whom in a quite different way grace, righteousness, and life were given (5:12-21), Paul shows, in a surprising and shocking assertion, the special position of Israel, to whom the law is given, in that through the law "sin increased" and hence "grace abounded all the more" (5:20). If all cultures and religions know about people who are guilty before God—for example, murderers and adulterers—then in Israel even, and especially, the pious who want to serve God are far more seriously unveiled as sinners. This is only understandable because sin for Paul consists primarily in the fact that human beings assert themselves against God. The unity of his defense on both fronts, from I Thess 5:8-10 to Gal 2:5; 3:10-12 and Romans, consists in the fact that human beings can build just as much on their moral or philosophical perfection as on their money, the fulfillment of desires, and the carrying out of their aggressions. Therefore they are truly liberated from sin only where the freedom from the law given them in baptism binds them completely with Christ and thus shapes their whole life (6:1–7:6; see 17.6 below), whereas under the law it is precisely the person who wants to serve God entirely who revolts against him (7:7-25). In 8:1-27 the ideas of Gal 4:4-7 are taken up and developed. Only for those who allow Christ and his Spirit to give them a life of prayer and hope with the whole creation in continually threatening temptation and yet reaching toward the consummation (see 17.5 below), is nothing damning anymore. Nothing can separate them from Christ (8:28-39).

Chapters 9–11 describe the absolute superiority of the grace of God to Israel, which, in spite of its rejection of Christ, will recognize him one day. This has nothing to do with pro- or antisemitism, but rather with God's righteousness (3:1-5), which is stronger than all human resistance and disobedience (see 10.4 and 12.5 above, also 18.4-6 below). Chapters 12–15 deal with the spiritual worship of the community (12:1), which, as already said in Gal 5:14, fulfills the law in love (13:8-10), also in the pending questions (between Jewish and Gentile

Christians?) of holding fast to the dietary regulations and special days (14:1–15:13).

16.5 Law and Faith. The interpretation presented here is disputed, quite apart from the question of whether there is within the Pauline letters an evident development, for example, in eschatology or in the teaching of the law. We must admit that the traditional judgment statements of 2:6-11 are difficult, and that in Rom 6–7 Paul does not expressly make clear that the good that human beings want is the fulfillment of the law and eternal life, and the evil that results is the sin of the boastful person and spiritual death. Yet the words *boast* and *glory,* like the contrasting words *justify* and *righteousness,* are frequent and central in all Pauline letters except Philem and I Thess (where we have only the nonspecific evidence of the word root). The alternative would be to deny the apostle any uniform understanding and to explain that the function of the law in Gal 3:22-24; Rom. 3:20; 4:15; 5:20-21; and 7:7-13, 14-25 is different in each case and not to be harmonized with the others.[125] Even more fundamental is the related question of whether the believer is supposed to—indeed must—fulfill the law (of Moses), without the cultic aspect, of course, and supported by the Spirit of God that leads to love.[126] Paul certainly does not say that one cannot fulfill the law. He himself was "blameless as to righteousness under the law"—to be sure, before his calling by Christ (Phil 3:6)! He says, rather, that the "doing" of the law does not lead to life, because righteousness comes from "faith" (Gal 3:11-12), and that the whole law finds its fulfillment in loving one's neighbor (Gal 5:14; Rom 13:8-10). Paul can explain that "the just requirement of the law will be fulfilled in us" when we walk "according to the Spirit" (Rom 8:4). We should note here, however, that according to 8:13, as according to Gal 4:23; 5:18; Phil 3:3, human beings remain the subject where they live according to the norm of the flesh, but in the new life the "Spirit" or the "promise" of God becomes the actual subject (see 13.4 above). Thus the fulfillment of what the law, according to God's intention, wants in the life of the already justified person grows in the freedom bestowed by the Spirit and is no longer the precondition of righteousness. That is understandable only because for Paul life is always a unified whole either with all good or bad sides, all success or failure oriented toward God, his grace, and his gifts, as the one "good work" (see 18.5, 22.4 below; cf. 11.6 above)—or only oriented toward itself, which is *"the* sin" (the plural is found only in traditional expressions; see 16.6 below).

16.6 The Priority of Salvation. For us the Letter to the Romans is an unmistakable stroke of luck. It is true that here, too, Paul has in mind the concrete situation in (Jerusalem[127] and) Rome, but there are neither concrete inquiries into particular problems in the community nor direct attacks against Paul and his message that from the very beginning push him onto a certain path. Therefore the letter becomes something like the testament of the apostle. He wants to introduce himself to the community, but does that in such a way that he does not report, say, on his background, his studies, his calling, and his missionary successes, but only on his message, that is, on the proclamation of justification. Hence, in a way similar to Galatians, he begins with the righteousness given by God but without the direct confrontation with opponents. The reverse side is the wrath of God that hangs over every person. Paul radically preaches the God who brings justice to the ungodly, before whom even Abraham cannot boast because of works. Quite different from the Letter to the Galatians, here Paul has the freedom to reflect and to formulate for the Romans what is special about Israel as the people called by God. Their special situation consists in the fact that only under the law given to them are even the godly people (precisely in their perfect righteousness under the law) marked ungodly, because they do not do the good they intend, but evil, in that they also trust in the "flesh" instead of opening themselves fully to the Spirit of God. The prospect of the final consummation, alive since the First Letter to the Thessalonians, and an appropriate present life in the community, have by no means disappeared (see 17.6 below on Rom 6:3-9). The foundation on which both stand, however, is now revealed. For there is certainty of the coming salvation (it is already nearer than a few years ago—13:11!) only where it is entirely God's affair and not that of human beings, and there is life appropriate to him only where people let him and his Spirit work, without again erecting their own godly or ungodly moral structure and actively filling it. Only as human beings allow themselves to be fulfilled and shaped by God's gift do they live without sin (in the singular, namely, without a fundamentally false orientation of life with all its victories and defeats). In this way they fulfill the law because they have become free for love. They are not righteous before God because they have thus fulfilled the law; rather, they have fulfilled it because they have become righteous through God's decision. Therefore they never finish with their love either (13:8) and can thus never earn God's yes with it. Only out of such freedom, then, is there a real common life of the "strong" and the "weak." Only where salvation is not made dependent on whether feast days are kept or not kept, meat of questionable origin is eaten or not eaten, are these questions also no longer a reason for separation.

16.7 God Remains God. The great contribution of the Letter to the Romans to the whole message of the New Testament and its repeatedly demonstrated extraordinary effect on history consists in the fact that here God remains God unambiguously and radically. How could God be God without living as love, without taking his creatures seriously, rejoicing over their gratitude, suffering over their hardness of heart? Rom 9–11 and 12–15 speak especially of this. And how could God be God if God became dependent on human beings: on the morally perfect, whose perfection brought about God's reward, and on sinners, whose sin brought about God's punishment? Where then would be the freedom of God's love? This is discussed especially in Rom 1–8. The Letter to the Romans lets God be God. Before this all human possibilities have again and again become still.[128] And again and again God has been able to begin to live anew.

CHAPTER THREE

Paul's Disciples

With the exception of the Letter to the Romans, Paul always names fellow senders: Timothy (I Thess 1:1; II Cor 1:1; Phil 1:1; Philem 1), Sosthenes (I Cor 1:1), Silvanus (I Thess 1:1), "the brethren who are with me" (Gal 1:2). Yet it is quite probable that he wrote or dictated alone. Nonetheless, anyone thus mentioned never appears among those sending greetings; thus his co-responsibility for the letter is taken seriously: he is involved when Paul writes. It would be easy to imagine that when the apostle is hindered, his companion would, conversely, write in both names (see 17.2 below), because Paul is really decisively involved, just because the author has learned everything he writes from his teacher. This is, naturally, also conceivable after the death of Paul (see 9.4 above).

More important is the fact of the reformulation of the Pauline message in general. It means, on the one hand, that Paul still remains the valid foundation and norm, on the other, that one cannot simply preserve this and reapply it literally without formulating it anew. The greatest service rendered to us by the disciples of Paul is precisely that they provide a model for how one can hear and become obedient to the authority of the Pauline letters—thus, of "Scripture"—in one's own time and situation.

17. THE LETTER TO THE COLOSSIANS

17.1 The Question of Authorship. Paul does not know personally the Gentile-Christian church founded by Epaphras. It is threatened by a "philosophy" bearing Pythagorean characteristics. The mention of the imprisonment of Paul and the names of the greeters agree with the Letter to Philemon. In 1:23 and 4:18 Paul is named as author; in 1:1 he and Timothy as senders. Structure, certain expressions, and general attitude remind us of Paul.

A more exacting investigation of the style, however, shows—precisely in unstressed words, in sentence constructions, and train of thought—differences from Paul of a kind that make it impossible for the letter to be from him.[129] Even with all the dependence on Paul, the author argues in a totally different way from the apostle. That conclusion also agrees with the theologically essential differences, above all with the almost total absence of assertions about the Spirit of God.[130]

17.2 Various Possibilities. There are three possible answers. (1) Against a dangerous trend, a disciple of Paul later reaches back to the authority of Paul. When the opponents appeal to tradition (2:8, 22), the author must also, and not appear only in his own (perhaps totally unknown) name.[131] What is difficult is that in A.D. 61 Colossae, together with Laodicea, was destroyed by an earthquake. This is, to be sure, not absolutely certain; nonetheless, Colossae is, in any case, not attested again by coin artifacts until the middle of the second century.[132] The notes and greetings that agree with the Letter to Philemon appear in a different order and with new or different addenda. Tychicus and Nympha are new; the former is, however, the carrier of the letter (4:7) and hence is logically absent in Philem 23–24. Did someone later consider all of this and list the names in order to give the letter the appearance of genuineness? Was a Laodicean letter (4:16) known in his time but later lost? (2) Could a genuine letter have later been drastically reworked, for example, by the writer of Ephesians or by someone else on the basis of the latter letter?[133] The un-Pauline style and the theological peculiarities, however, are spread throughout the letter; only (3:18 or) 4:2-18 could then be reclaimed for Paul. (3) Most letters name in addition to Paul another sender (four name Timothy), although only Paul is in fact the author. In a period of stricter confinement, did Timothy, who like no other was "of the same spirit" with the apostle (2:20), perhaps write the common letter, which Paul only signed? "I, Paul" (Col 1:23) was necessary so that the calling of the apostle to the Gentiles and the astonishing assertion of 1:24 would not be related also to Timothy. In this case personal notes and greetings would be identical with what Paul himself would have written.[134]

17.3 The "Elements of the World" in Contemporary Hellenism. The continuing theological development is crucial. Before the middle of the second century A.D. the "elements of the world" (2:8, 20; RSV: "elemental spirits of the universe") were nothing more than earth, water, air, and fire (and perhaps the heavenly ether). They were neither gods nor demons, but powers, as also the law or any sort of passion can be. From the sixth century B.C. until the sixth century A.D. Greek culture was filled with anxiety over a battle of the elements with each other, which constantly threatened the world with earthquakes, floods, storms, and conflagrations. Hence even before Aristotle they were opposed by a coming or higher world, "heaven" or the "ether," to which the soul climbs after death, if after being redeemed from the material world it is pure enough to rise into the spiritual world. This goes back to Empedocles in the fifth century B.C., about whom Plutarch wrote ten books around A.D. 100. It can be demonstrated that these ideas were everywhere in the New Testament period. A first century B.C. description of the Pythagoreans tells how, according to them, the world is composed of four elements, whose balance, however—and thus the whole earthly sphere—is constantly threatened; that is why the ascent of the soul into the heavenly, divine element is so urgent, and only the pure souls succeed, while the others are pulled down again into the orbit of the elements. The whole air is full of (not yet fully perfected) souls, "heroes" (or "demons," equated three times by Philo with the angels of the Bible). To them also one must show honor, even if on a lower level than that befitting the gods, undertake purification baths, and abstain from certain foods as well as from sexual intercourse. Cicero describes the ascent of the soul through the elements physically; Ovid, the battle of the elements and the heavy lot of the souls that are again forced into human or animal bodies; Philo, the Jewish new year's festival as the conclusion of peace between the elements, the "members" of the universe, and the reestablishment of order, but also the ascent of the soul, which gives back to each element its own, whereas the impure cannot do that and are again pushed back into new bodies. Josephus presupposes for the Romans a faith in the ascent of the soul to the stars, from where it appears to its relatives as a helper. Plutarch describes the region of the moon as the boundary from which the impure souls are chased back and tormented for thousands of years, while the pure as "demons" or "heroes" become God's governors and serve those still on earth, before they ascend entirely into the world of the gods. Around A.D. 200 Hippolytus says that Marcion's asceticism (ca. A.D. 140) is based on these Empedoclesian ideas, which he cites in detail.[135]

17.4 A Pythagorean Background in Col 2:16-23 and Gal 4:3, 9? This corresponds largely with what is described in Col 2:16-23. Even before the birth of Christ, Judaism had already adopted a great deal from Pythagorean-ism.[136] The sabbath and new moon celebrations show Jewish components, but everything else can be explained as Pythagorean, as indicated by the designation "ordinances" used by them (Col 2:14, 20 [KJV]—never "law" or "commandments"!). Ascetic purification of the soul from the earthly elements is crucial in all the cited texts and in Col 2:20-23 is required of those who even now are not supposed to live "in the world." The worship of angels (2:18) applies to those helpers or saviors named in Alexander, Philo, Josephus, and Plutarch, who are the (almost) perfected souls that as demons, heroes, or angels (for Philo three designations for the same thing) fill the whole air.

Has the letter, however, not adopted the expression "elements of the world" from Gal 4:3, 9? Certainly in that letter there is an opposition that emphasizes the Jewish law. Nevertheless, it is hard to imagine how Paul could write of the "elements of the world" if he was not thinking of earth, water, air, and fire, which in Hellenism can be overcome through ascetic practice. In contrast to Colossians, slavery under the world elements in Gal 4:3, 9 is first related to the pre-Christian situation of the Galatians. Should Paul not know, as do Philo and Josephus, how much the whole Hellenistic world at that time was defined by the role of the "elements of the world"? Paul identifies in some way with the Galatians and in their present subjection to the law sees a throwback to this slavery. Now, it is precisely in Galatians, however, that *law* and *world* are interchangeable (6:13-14). Indeed, even Paul knows of the sighing under the load of the earthly tent, where one remains "away from the Lord" (II Cor 5:4, 6). Therefore he can equate the pagan enslavement under the universally feared "elements of the world," as it existed for the Galatians before they became Christians, with his own pre-Christian subjection under the law and designate the renewed Galatian observance of the law as a return to this slavery. Thus with the Galatians the Jewish component certainly plays a larger role than with the Colossians, but the similarity with the ascetic practices of the Pythagorean variety, which are supposed to purify the soul for its ascent through the elements, persists here also.[137]

17.5 Cosmic Christology? This raises the question of the cosmic significance of Christ. That the resurrected one reigns in heaven is not doubted, but how does that help in a world that lies in chaos and is subject to catastrophes at any time? And are human beings not so enslaved in this world that even after death their souls cannot get through to Christ at all, but are pulled back again into the elements of the world? The first question is answered by the hymn in 1:15-20 (see 5.11 above): Jesus Christ is not only the Savior of souls; in him God has also reclaimed creation as a whole for himself and placed it once again under his good government. That this can happen only when people reconciled to God learn to live in faith is stressed by the letter writer through his additions in verses 18 and 20, where he points to the church and its reconciliation through Jesus' death, but especially in verses 21-23. This also corresponds to the "schema of revelation" (see 5.7 above) in 1:24-29, according to which Jesus reaches all peoples through the Pauline proclamation and sets up his dominion over the world.

Thus, as in Rom 8:19-25 (see 16.4 above), the creation is also incorporated into the Christ event and awaits its final completion.[138] This is done, however, in such a way that the "new creation" (II Cor 5:17; Gal 6:15), which has now already become reality in the church believing in Christ, will one day also draw all living creatures into the glory that is promised the church. We must note that even in the original hymn it is the church that sings the hymn and thereby praises her Lord Christ as Lord of creation and the post-Easter new creation,

93

and this becomes even clearer in the context of the whole Letter to the Colossians. Although the whole created world is included in the eschatological promise, the movement is clearly from people—already called and one day finally to be redeemed—toward creation and not vice versa: that a Christ-power already at work in the creation will also effect the redemption of humanity.[139] Therefore Christ is also proclaimed at the same time in the house table (3:18–4:1; cf. Eph 5:22–6:9; also I Tim 2:1-15; Titus 2:2-10) as the one who reigns in the small and private realm of the (extended) family and thus intends to set up God's dominion in the individual house as well as among the nations.

17.6 Resurrection Life Today? The author answers the second question with the certainty of faith. Whoever really belongs to Christ is already "raised" with him (2:12; 3:1). Against the danger of an overenthusiastic faith that wants to live in heaven now and in the meantime forget the earth (I Cor 4:8), Paul clearly distinguishes in Rom 6:3-9 between a past burial with Christ and a future resurrection with him. Against the danger of scrupulous doubts in which many flee to ascetic practices, the author of Colossians emphasizes the certainty of the faith that Jesus as the Lord of the church and the whole world has basically already redeemed those who believe in him from the unholy state of the world. In order to avoid any misunderstanding that could lie precisely in the above mentioned priority of the church over the whole creation, however, he underlines that this new life is now still hidden and will not become apparent until the final coming of the Lord (3:3-4). Thus non-Christian speculation and ascetic practice forced reflection on the whole breadth of the Christ event, which also includes all of creation, so that it might not only be believed implicitly and praised in hymns (see 5.8 and 5.10-11 above), but also be openly expressed. In the process the faith of the church and the central meaning of the proclamation of the word are not at all forgotten. Indeed, only that faith can consciously live in the world made new through Christ's resurrection and also let itself be shaped by that event.

17.7 The Body of Christ. This includes a new understanding of the "body of Christ" (see 11.4 above). No longer is the individual local church now in the center, but the world as a whole, which has been led to Christ through the Gentile mission of Paul. Hellenistic statements, above all in Stoic philosophers, about the world as divine body receive here a completely new meaning. Not the cosmos as such, but the multitude of those in whom and through whom Christ establishes his beneficent, redeeming lordship in the world is the "body of Christ," which penetrates the whole world and offers to it salvation. Even this decisively corrects the Hellenistic equation of God and world.[140] More important, a second correction occurs precisely here, where we might be close to an overenthusiastic faith of those already resurrected with Christ and an identification of the church with the Christ who lives on in her on earth. While Paul regards the head simply as one of the many members, which serves with its special gift (I Cor 12:21), in Col 1:18, 24 and 2:19 Christ as the "head" is placed over against the church. Again, this corresponds in form to what is already asserted by Hellenism about "Zeus" or the "ether," by Hellenistic Judaism about "heaven" or the "logos" (i.e., the divine "word") as "head" of the cosmos.[141] In terms of content, however, the ordering of Christ over his church is thereby maintained. Thus both things now come to light: that the *world* is redeemed and called to salvation—that is, the preaching of the church knows no boundaries—and that this church is totally dependent on her *Lord* and is nothing without his grace and power.

18. THE LETTER TO THE EPHESIANS

18.1 Relationship to Colossians. In the oldest manuscripts "in Ephesus" (1:1) is missing. Marcion (middle of the second century) knew Ephesians as the Letter to the Laodiceans. Ephesus, where Paul worked many years, is impossible in terms of content (even if composed after the death of the apostle), since the letter is kept totally impersonal and contains no greetings. Perhaps the original address was for some reason deleted and then replaced by "Ephesus" (cf. II Tim 4:12) as the best known church or by "Laodicea" as the one mentioned in Col 4:16. Apart from the discussion of heresy, which is missing in Ephesians, there is much that agrees with Colossians in form (structure), content (Christ as head of the body, house table), and wording (even the information about sending Tychicus in 6:21-22), with Colossians showing the more original formulations. In place of the "saints" (Col 1:26) we find the "holy apostles and prophets" in Eph 3:5. Instead of the exhortation of the house table for the subordination of wives and for the love of husbands for their wives (Col 3:18-19), Eph 5:32 introduces an interpretation of this commandment in terms of the church and Christ (see 18.5 below). If in Col 3:22 slaves are exhorted to obedience of their masters for the sake of "fearing the Lord," Eph 6:5, 7 says that they should be obedient to them "as to the Lord." Of course, this does not prove that the Letter to the Colossians was written earlier, but makes it probable.

18.2 The Question of Authorship. The Letter to the Ephesians, however, can come neither from Paul nor from the writer of Colossians. His theological view (see 18.3-5 below) and his style, with long sentences and genitive constructions such as "the might of the power of his strength" (1:19) are too different from both. Expressions identical to those in Colossians are actually understood differently: *oikonomia* in Col 1:25 as in I Cor 9:17 is the "divine office" of the apostle; in Eph 1:10 and 3:9 it is God's "plan" of salvation in general; etc. The close relationship with the First Letter of Peter shows that both letters employ a common liturgical and catechetical tradition. Thus the letter was probably written by a disciple after the death of Paul.

18.3 The Church and Her Ministries. Theologically the concentration on the church stands out above everything. The body of Christ, as in Col 1:18, 24; 2:19 (see 17.7 above) is no longer the local church. Its foundation (Eph 2:20) is formed by the "holy" (3:15) apostles and prophets. This sequence, as well as 3:5 and 4:11, shows that the reference is to New Testament prophets. The view is different in I Cor 3:1-15: Paul, Apollos, and others build on the one foundation, Jesus Christ. Even when 4:7, like Rom 12:3, 6, speaks of the gift of grace given to all members, in verse 11, nevertheless, in addition to apostles and prophets (who are, of course, now the foundation that lies in the past) only "evangelists, pastors, and teachers" are named. Since neither elders nor bishops and deacons are mentioned, we cannot simply establish the transition from chrisma to office. We will, of course, presume that the three ministries named in 4:11 became the crucial ones. It is hard to decide[142] whether they are understood exemplarily as gifts—naturally occurring first to the author— within the various ministries of verse 7, because verse 13 also goes back again to the totality of all community members, or as "offices" exalted above these ministries.

18.4 The Church of Jews and Gentiles in the "Heavenly Places." The church as the joining together of Jews and Gentiles is especially emphasized. The schema of revelation (see 5.7 and 17.5 above) is thus elaborated, and indeed in such a way that with the revelation of the mystery to the apostles and prophets and the incorporation of Gentiles by Paul, the goal of God in the church that is still growing and will finally include all principalities and powers seems to have been reached—though within an ongoing history of salvation (3:1-13). In any case the reference to the final coming of Jesus (Col 3:4) is missing. In its place are the "heavenly places" (1:3 and elsewhere), into which the believers have already risen with the Christ who has ascended to heaven (2:6). Against them stands "this present darkness" with its "world rulers," the principalities and powers, who are at work as "spiritual hosts of wickedness in the heavenly places" (6:12 = "the air" according to 2:2). Therefore the church must be admonished to do battle against them (from 4:17 on, especially 6:10-20). Missing here is the express connection—typical for Paul and still found in Col 2:6, 20; 3:1-2—between the indicative pledge of salvation and the imperative challenge to let it become real in one's life.

18.5 The One Church, Bride of Christ. What is special about the Letter to the Ephesians is thus that the church in its totality has become the actual theme. In Colossians this occurs rather tangentially, conditioned in content by the doubts of a church unsure of its final salvation and in form by the Greek assertions about the cosmos as the body of God. Freed from that, it now becomes a message that is important in itself. Here, as in no other New Testament writing, the unity of the church becomes the central content of the proclamation (cf. also John 17:20-23), while at the same time its roots in Israel are maintained (2:11-22; cf. Rom 9-11 and 16.4 above). This also determines the emphasis on the foundation of the apostles and prophets that is uniform for the whole church, while for Gentile Christendom (that is, for the author and the addressees) Paul is *the* apostle and his Gentile mission the central salvation event (see 17.5 above). In 5:21-33—where, incidentally, the subordination of wives in the original text, different from Col 3:18, is only a special case of the subordination demanded of all in verse 21—the church is seen as the wife or bride of Christ. This is no longer mere comparison as in II Cor 11:2; Rom 7:2, 4. It is also less the founding of marital love on the love of Christ than emphasis on the "mystery" that Gen 2:24 is to be related to Christ and the church, which then, secondarily, is also supposed to color the marital life of the believers. Yet not to be overlooked is the ethical exhortation to "arise from the dead" (5:14), which is otherwise demanded only of new converts. Even "good works" are mentioned here (2:10), while Paul normally (only II Cor 9:8 is somewhat different) regards the whole life oriented toward Christ with all its ups and downs as the one "good work." Also part of this are the proper attitude toward Jewish Christians, who presumably have now become a distinct minority, and the recognition of one's own lostness without Christ (2:2-3, 12), which warns against any all too self-evident and overenthusiastic trust in one's new position as a child of God.

18.6 The Future as Growth. More clearly than in Paul, the theological interest in Ephesians as well as Colossians shifts from the local church to the universal church and, especially in the Colossian hymn, also to the world. In the process the hope of the final consummation on the day of Christ does not disappear, but it recedes. In its place are statements asserting the resurrection already achieved in Christ, and indeed the assumption into heaven. Certainly the future is not blanked out, but it lies within the history of the world, in the incessant growth of the church until it even reaches the cosmic principalities and powers (Eph 1:10; 2:21; 3:10; 4:15-16), without any word of the present hiddenness until the appearance of Christ (as still in Col 3:3-4). The danger of an ecclesiastical triumphalism is not to be overlooked. Already the faithful are "one flesh" with Christ (Eph 5:31-32); already they sit on God's right in heaven and look down on the "sons of disobedience" (2:2, 6); already Christ has subjugated everything, even the principalities and powers (1:20-23), and even "reconciled" them (Col 1:20—though corrected in vv. 21-23). Thus one can say that especially in Colossians the "vertical" unity of heaven and earth

97

has replaced the "horizontal" assertions oriented toward the final consummation. One must, however, immediately add that likewise in the "horizontal" dimension the winning of the Gentile world and, especially in Ephesians, the consequent uniting of Jews and Gentiles became essential.[143] In both cases the final consummation is seen more as the goal toward which what has already happened continues to grow.

18.7 Relationship to and Distinction from the Gnosis. In both letters Paul appears as the unimpeached authority, and the time before his calling becomes dimmer and dimmer and thus his calling more and more the sign of the divine miracle of forgiveness (see 20.4 below). Where, however, one regards people's guilt and their justification through Jesus Christ, which is central for Paul, and "with Christ" no longer as a freely given miracle of God's incomprehensible grace (Col 1:13-22; 2:13-14; Eph 1:4-7; 2:1-10; 5:25-26), but as something actually given to humans by nature, where it is thus no longer a matter of justification and reconciliation and hence also of ethical testing, but only of instruction about the proper understanding of human beings, there we would be standing in the middle of Gnosticism (see 20.2 below). The Second Letter to the Thessalonians on the one hand and the letters to Timothy and Titus on the other will demonstrate a completely different development from Paul into the early church.[144]

19. THE SECOND LETTER TO THE THESSALONIANS

19.1 The Question of Authorship. Throughout the whole letter, except in 2:1-12, the only section that contains anything new, whole parts of sentences are repeated almost word for word from the First Letter to the Thessalonians. Thus if the letter came from Paul, it would have to have been written almost at the same time. In contrast to I Thess 4:17, however, he fights against those who expect the coming of Christ in the immediate future and therefore have stopped working (3:10-12; cf. I Thess 4:11). They do that on the basis of forged letters of Paul (2:2; 3:17). This is hardly imaginable shortly after Paul's first visit, nor is the quite different viewpoint of the apostle, who anticipates here the coming of a kind of antichrist before the end (2:3-4, 8-12). According to 2:5 he is supposed to have already presented this in his first preaching, yet it is totally absent from the first letter. Besides, 2:6-7 speaks of "one" (neuter in v. 6, masculine in v. 7) who (or which) still restrains the coming of Christ, without it becoming clear whether an angel, the Roman state or emperor, or someone else is intended. In 1:6-10 the punitive judgment against nonbelievers, as readily happens in times of persecution, is described in detail. In 2:16 and 3:16 "the Lord (Jesus Christ)" appears beside or in place of "God" in the similar sounding sentences of I Thess 3:11; 5:23. In 1:12 Jesus is, strictly speaking, designated as God ("of our God and Lord Jesus Christ" with only one article), but it could be a matter of careless formulation. In any case everything points to the idea that someone, who was already familiar with false Pauline letters and enthusiasts who appealed to Paul, later wrote against his misinterpretation [145] in the name of the apostle and even with reference to his genuine signature (see 9.4 above).

19.2 Enthusiasts Expecting an Imminent Parousia in Times of Persecution. The writing gives an impression of the dangers threatening early Christendom. Toward the end of the first century, when for the first time official persecution by the state led to prison and executions, prophets moved by the Spirit again took up the hope of the imminent final coming of Jesus to judge and to establish the eternal kingdom of God (cf. 1:3-10). During this period the Revelation to John (see 31.1 below) was written. Now, I Thess 4:13–5:11 (see 10.3 above) speaks especially clearly of the coming of Jesus. This was made current by our letter, probably at the end of the first century. The statement in 2:2 actually means that the day is already here, but what follows shows that an immediate future event is intended, not, say, a purely spiritually conceived return of Christ in the church. With Paul we discovered that the very orientation toward a turning point expected totally from God also makes the present become new. In the coming world there will be no oppression of the poor and weak by the rich and strong; therefore such oppression simply no longer has a place in the community that is already living for that time. Here, however, this has a different result. The expectation of the imminent end of the world encouraged a faith that out of overabundant spirituality pushed aside this earth and its everyday work and now lived in the near expectation of the glorious future. In contrast to this the soberness with which the apostle himself is drawn on as an example of taking seriously the earthly tasks, such as the earning of a living, is thoroughly Pauline even if the argumentation with the antichrist and the one who still restrains him remains questionable. But the idea that the consummation on the "day of the Lord" is not written off, but is maintained as God's aim with his world, is central to the New Testament.

20. THE "PASTORAL LETTERS" TO TIMOTHY AND TITUS

20.1 The Question of Authorship. The special message of these letters can be truly perceived only if one realizes that the writer here is not Paul but some one later in a totally different situation. As long as one compares them to the Pauline letters, one can only ascertain that everything is paler and sounds weaker than with Paul and not nearly as creative and progressive. The message is repeated in "orthodox" fashion, but it is no longer discussed with those who reject it; they are simply dismissed. The "faith" becomes ("sound") doctrine

(I Tim 1:10 [cf. 4:6]; II Tim 4:3; Titus 1:9, 13; 2:1-2). What Paul meant by "faith" is now designated rather as (sound) "godliness," which, linked with "contentment," is "great gain" (I Tim 6:6). Pauline concepts are missing and are replaced by new ones: instead of the "return" (Parousia), the "appearance" of Jesus is announced, which can also designate his incarnation (e.g., II Tim 1:10; 4:1). Above all the style, even in small, unstressed words (*with, for, as*), is completely different from that of Paul.

In the life of Paul, as known to us, there is no situation in which one could place the letters. Admittedly, we do not know whether he was again released from imprisonment in Rome and instead of going to Spain (Rom 15:28), or after a trip to Spain he again went into the East, though there are no indications of this. Even if that were true, however, it is hardly conceivable that Paul would write in such a general way in a letter to Ephesus (I Tim 1:3), where he worked so long. Also the presupposition of believing children of an elder to be appointed is hardly to be expected in areas newly won for Christ (Titus 1:5-6). In addition, the heresy predicted for the future in II Tim 3:1-5 is already there according to verses 6-9 and will make no more progress. Further, would Paul have written to the one who is of the same soul and genuine like no other (Phil 2:20): "Shun youthful passions," and "I was appointed a preacher and apostle (I am telling the truth, I am not lying), a teacher of the Gentiles in faith and truth" (II Tim 2:22; I Tim 2:7)? Also the idea that Paul wants to come to Ephesus soon himself and yet, in case he cannot come, gives such detailed instructions for the structure of the church (I Tim 3:14-15) is conceivable, but seems rather artificial.[146]

20.2 The Opposition to Gnosis. Thus if we compare the pastoral letters only with Paul himself, we are like a church congregation examining the new pastor as to what he or she says and does like the old one and what he or she does not. If, however, we read them without such comparisons on the basis of their own situation and their own concerns, we discover that in many ways they are closer to us than the Pauline letters are. The church has grown and has gone beyond the point where one can still leave everything to spontaneous regulation. Without a certain order chaos threatens. The church has also established itself in the world. It no longer expects the final coming of Jesus within a few years. Charismatic gifts such as speaking in tongues, prophecy, and healings are receding. Everyday questions, as they are posed in marriage, in the working world, and in common life with fellow citizens, are moving into the foreground. In addition there is the danger of "what is falsely called knowledge" (= gnosis) (I Tim 6:20). It is well possible, even if not certain, that this refers to the Gnostic movement strongly rooted in Jewish thought, which especially in the second and third centuries had laid hold of large parts of the Christian and pagan world. It is conditioned by the Platonic depreciation of the material world. Therefore the God of the Old Testament, as Creator of the earthly world, becomes antigod, and his angels evil powers. The real god is Man, the primeval human himself, and whoever has recognized that he is divine in his innermost being when he has liberated himself from everything earthly, from the "body" as well as the "soul" (see 11.5 above), that person has found his real identity and has become "spiritual." This event can be understood as "resurrection" to divine life (II Tim 2:17-18). Hymenaeus (cf. I Tim 1:20) and Philetus, who speak of this, were presumably Gnostic teachers at the time of the pastoral letters. The (Gnostically influenced) Gospel of Thomas writes similarly: "This (world) on which you wait has already come, but you do not recognize it" (51); and the letter to Reginus explains that whoever carries God inside has gone through death and is then "drawn by him up to heaven, like the rays of the sun, and nothing can hold us back; that is the spiritual resurrection; it swallows the soul as well as the body."[147] Where we find God in ourselves, faith becomes the recognition to which we can certainly adapt ourselves meditatively and understand ourselves as gift and revelation. For this, however, Jesus, his death, and his resurrection are only evocative example and symbol, as other myths of dying and rising gods can also be. We can then in one respect justify everything human, without distinguishing good and evil (II Tim 3:2-5; Titus 1:16),[148] or even more recommend asceticism (I Tim 4:3), so that the innermost divine being would no longer be bound by worldly (good or evil) everyday things. All of this is on the author's mind and burdens him. Against this flood of problems he cannot prevail. Only Paul himself can. What does he say to this age?

20.3 The Authority of Paul also for Church Order. For the author and no doubt also for the church in which he lives, Paul is the only apostle; that was somewhat different in Eph 2:20; 3:5; 4:11 (see 18.3 and 7 above). In his Gentile mission Jesus Christ himself moves through the world. Hence, this mission, like Jesus' resurrection and exaltation, belongs among the events of salvation (see 5.7 and 5.12 above). The central statements of Paul about salvation in Christ are therefore cited as fixed guidelines (Titus 3:4-8a; cf. 2:13-14; I Tim 1:15; II Tim 2:11), though their relevance for immediate current issues is no longer developed as with Paul. The formula that introduces them, "the saying is sure," is related in I Tim 4:9 to the hope of eternal life, in I Tim 3:1 also to the understanding of the bishop's office. In this way even the order of the church is traced back to Paul. The fact that he sent Timothy, as someone completely of the same mind, into churches that he himself could not visit (Phil 2:19-20) is now interpreted as a kind of ordination to the ministry of preaching (II Tim 1:6). In I Tim 4:14 we can still see that during the author's time, ordination is (or should be?) accomplished by a group of elders, and indeed only after previous prophetic utterances, as is astonishingly still emphasized (also I Tim 1:18).

Apparently the recipients of the letter are thus the models for church leaders, and the commission of Paul to them is a model for their installation. We can even wonder whether Timothy and Titus are not considered representatives of a leadership office—already known or to be created—for a larger district. In addition to the deacons, and deaconesses—if verse 11 does not designate only their wives (I Tim 3:8-13)—5:3-16 mentions the widows, no doubt especially in regard to their support by the church; yet even their ministry of intercession is taken seriously. For the leadership a majority of elders is presupposed, of whom, however, not all "labor in preaching and teaching" (5:17). *Bishop* is presumably their functional designation, while *elder* is the title of the office. Titus 1:5-9 makes it apparent that the same ministry is intended. That *bishop* here and in I Tim 3:1-7 is in the singular is probably due to the fact that something like a paragon of a bishop is cited, similar to the way we could say: "Install blameless people as ministers, for the pastor must be (thus and so)." Thus, ordered ministries are doubtless presupposed. The fact that the word for *office* throughout the whole New Testament remains reserved for Christ and the whole church, for Jewish priests and secular officials,[149] shows, of course, that the latter are basically not to be distinguished from the other ministries.

Beside the scripture (I Tim 5:18; II Tim 3:15-16) comes the doctrine and order established by Paul (see 28.6 below). On the basis of such "tradition" (*parathēkē, depositum*), passed by Paul to Timothy and by him to reliable people who themselves teach others (I Tim 6:20; II Tim 1:12-14; 2:2), the church is the "pillar and bulwark of the truth" (I Tim 3:15). That is certainly not at all the only New Testament model of church order for the future (see 30.4 below).

20.4 The Significance of the Pastoral Letters in Their (More Modern?) Situation. With respect to (Gnostic?) speculations (I Tim 1:3-7) the summons back to the tasks in the family and the working world (I Tim 5:1-16; 6:1-2; Titus 2:1-10) is necessary and helpful. The sometimes trite admonitions and teachings are nonetheless an expression of the fact that the necessarily inconspicuous ministries can be just as big or bigger before God than the performances of ministry visible to all. That is doubtless also one side of the Pauline proclamation of justification. The assertion of the salvation intended for "all men, especially [but not only] those who believe" (I Tim 4:10) also belongs here. The admonition of intercessions for the governors who make it possible for the church to have a "quiet and peaceable life" (I Tim 2:1-2) struggles against a fundamental turning into devils of all rulers (Rev 13, see 31.5 below). The much more questionable slighting of woman, including the curious interpretation of Gen 3 in I Tim 2:8-15, is to be seen against the background of Gnostic successes among women (I Tim 4:7; II Tim 3:6), even if it cannot be thereby justified. The difference from the genuine Pauline letters, which include the involvement of women in worship (see 11.1 above) and in apostolic missionary preaching (Phil 4:2-3), and indeed probably even female apostles (Rom 16:7), is unmistakable. Jewish Christians have disappeared from the scene and with them the thorn of their joy in the law. That may be related to the fact that the Gnostics understood the books of Moses as the document of their myths (I Tim 1:7; cf. Titus 1:10, 14). Following this in I Tim 1:8-11 is a reminder of Paul's serious discussions of the question of the law, which, however, are already far in the past, and are now presumably interpreted as fighting Gnostic misuse. The statement that "the law is not laid down for the just" (cf. also Titus 3:9) is actually only correct if one sees the much more differentiated statements of Paul behind it. Paul could hardly speak even as II Tim 1:5; 3:15 do (cf. Acts 16:1) about the continuity of Jewish pre-Christian and Christian piety.[150] It is important that Paul is the model not only in his teaching but no less through his life (e.g., as early as I Thess 1:5-6; I Cor 11:1). This is now above all also true of his calling, which in exemplary fashion became his lot as "the foremost of sinners" (I Tim 1:15-16), similar to Eph 3:8: "the very least of all the saints," not just "the least of the apostles" (I Cor 15:9). But even the fact that he can be satisfied with a cloak as cover and his books (no doubt the holy Scriptures—II Tim 4:13) is instructive for the church, as is the admonition to Timothy not to let ascetic tendencies keep him from also enjoying a little wine for the sake of his stomach ailments (I Tim 5:23). In a church that no longer knows the zeal for the law and for the strict ordering of obedience to the law before salvation which marked its pre-Christian period, even insisting on "good works" can in no way be anti-Pauline, even if Paul would have formulated it with greater differentiation.

20.5 The Situation-dependent Nature of the Gospel. In these letters it becomes especially clear that the word of scripture is never understandable without the situation in which it is spoken. Thus we can understand it only when we also let it shed light on our own situation. Just as Timothy was advised to drink a little wine, but the alcoholic would have to be warned against it (I Tim 5:23; 3:8; cf. Titus 2:3; I Pet 4:3), so must doctrine and order be impressed upon the church in danger of individualization and disintegration, but the freedom of charisma on one that is stifled by bureaucracy. Thus there are also situations in which justification without the works of the law must be emphasized and others in which good works must be stressed. Therefore no part of the New Testament can stand without the others (see 32.2 below).

CHAPTER FOUR

The Remaining Letters

If one does not count the Letter to the Hebrews, which is held to be Pauline, there are seven letters that give no addressees or are aimed at a larger circle of churches, in addition to twice seven Pauline letters (including Hebrews and those whose genuineness is questionable). In the third century they were designated as *catholic* writings, that is, ecumenical, intended for the whole church. They were only gradually recognized (see 32.1 below): in the second century only I Peter and I John. They testify to the fact that the church does not just gather around *one* genius (Paul), but is founded on the message of various witnesses. The issues of Romans and Galatians have been fought through and except for James 2:14-26 no longer play a role. Detachment from at least the Jewish ritual law has become the accepted foundation. Because of this, of course, the Pauline opposition of faith and works of the law has also faded theologically. Essentially what is at stake now is perseverance in everyday life, in part even in suffering (and persecution), and in the upbuilding and life of the church.

21. THE LETTER TO THE HEBREWS

21.1 Place, Date, Author. What Heb 7:3 says of Melchizedek, "He is without father or mother or genealogy," could also apply to this letter.[151] Neither writer nor addressees are named. Without 13:19, 22-25 one would not consider this a letter, but theological meditations.[152] These verses report a release from prison for Timothy, no doubt the well-known companion of Paul, greet "all the saints," and send greetings from "those who come from Italy" (possibly inexact for: "the Italians"). Thus if these verses were not inserted later as a cryptic reference to Pauline authorship, which is unlikely, the letter was presumably not written in Italy, but elsewhere, and sent there, most likely to Rome.[153] That is also where it is first attested, probably in the First Letter of Clement (A.D. 96) and the Shepherd of Hermas (a few decades later?). The idea that according to 6:1 "faith toward God" is among the initial bases of instruction leads us to think of Gentile Christians; the strong emphasis on cult, on the other hand, suggests Jewish Christians. Thus one will most likely have to imagine a mixed congregation, and here we should forget neither how many shadings of Jewish Christians existed, from the "false brethren" of Gal 2:4 through the more or less liberal James, Peter, and Paul to the radicals who regarded the building of the Temple as backsliding (Acts 7:47-51),[154] nor the variety of Gentile Christians, from the former "God fearers," who had adopted parts of the Jewish law, to the gnosticizing fighters of the Old Testament God. Because of the description of the Jewish worship service in its current form and the lack of a reference to the Temple destruction, one could date the letter before A.D. 70.[155] Such seemingly contemporary description, however, is also found in Josephus and in I Clement. The description is not at all that of the Jerusalem Temple, in which the Ark of the Covenant, already lost in the exile, no longer stands, and there is no smoking altar in the holy of holies,[156] but rather of the tabernacle of the wilderness period represented in Exod 25–26. Since 2:3 presupposes the second or third generation of Christians, and according to 13:7 the deaths of the most important preachers of the word seem already to lie some time in the past (cf. 10:32), a later time must be assumed, yet before the First Letter of Clement and the severe persecutions suffered shortly before then.[157] The author is an independent teacher and writer of outstanding Greek, who like Apollos (Acts 18:24) and the Jewish philosopher Philo betrays an Alexandrian education. Harnack's supposition that the name was deleted because it was that of a woman, namely, Priscilla (Acts 18:26), is improbable because of the masculine form in 11:32, unless one assumes a correction there too. Because of the completely different style and content, it was certainly not Paul.

21.2 The High Priest in Heaven. Typical of the Letter to the Hebrews is the image of Christ as the high priest who "has passed through the heavens" and thereby opened the access to God for human beings (4:14-16; 6:19-20; 9:11-12; 10:19-21). As the "Son" he is superior to all the angels; he is "God" (1:8) and created earth and heaven. Thus, strickly speaking, he is the Creator (1:10—unique in the New Testament), not just the mediator of creation (1:2), and all enemies will be subject to him (1:5-13; cf. 2:5-9). The assertion of Christ as the Lord of the world in Col 1:16-17 (see 17.5 above) who reunites heaven and earth (I Tim 3:16 [see 5.12 above]; cf. 5.8) appears here in a strange new way. By contrast, here it is precisely the earthly life of Jesus and his atoning death on the cross that is the basis of this position and the actual salvation event. With his self-sacrifice Christ, as eschatological high priest, has entered the holy of holies and thus opened heaven. Perhaps behind this are

Jewish concepts according to which tabernacle or Temple as God's dwelling is the symbol of the universe. With its powers and principalities, heaven, separated from the earth by the "curtain" of the firmament, represents the "Holy Place," in the middle of which the throne of God, veiled by a "second curtain" (9:3), stands as the place of his mysterious presence in the "holy of holies."[158]

That the one exalted to the right hand of God is also a priest "after the order of Melchizedek" could already be read in Ps 110:1, 4 (Heb 7:21). While with Moses, who already suffered abuse for Christ (11:26), with Joshua, and all the more with the levitical high priests, it was stressed that they are only precursors, and Christ partakes of far greater glory and honor (3:1-6; 4:8; 5:1-4; 7:23-28), that is not the case with Melchizedek. He has "neither beginning of days nor end of life," is "without father or mother or genealogy," and "continues a priest for ever," "separated from sinners" (7:3, 26). Since this is in any case not correct for the earthly Jesus, whose function is especially stressed in Hebrews, and particularly because according to Ps 110:4 (in distinction to the Melchizedek of Gen 14:18-20) his very installation as a priest after the order of Melchizedek is important (8:3-6; cf. 5:1-10; 7:15), here too traditional ideas are to be presumed. In a fragment of the Jewish monks of the Dead Sea (11QMelch) Melchizedek appears as an eschatological, saving high priest figure and is perhaps(!) even called "God." Also, the Hasmonian priest-kings of Israel, ruling since 141 B.C., were designated with terms from Gen 14 and Ps 110. Thus in Hebrews Melchizedek is hardly conceived only from the Old Testament standpoint as an earthly manifestation of the heavenly prototype of Christ,[159] and there is no direct dependence on the named Jewish texts. Also, the preexistence of Christ (see 5.6 above) is nowhere stressed, but clearly presupposed. As the final Word of God (1:1-2; 2:2-3) he is "the same yesterday and today and for ever" (13:8), and the "kingdom that cannot be shaken" that is given to us (12:28) is probably his and not only God's kingdom.

21.3 Good Friday, Easter, Ascension as One Event. In an ingenious way that brings John to mind (see 29.7 below), the image of the high priest, who brings his self-sacrifice through the curtain into the holy of holies, into the presence of God, and thereby opens access to him, summarizes Good Friday, Easter, and ascension in a single event.[160] Crucial is his heavenly position of power, which he has assumed and in which he, on God's right hand, intercedes for his own (7:25; 8:1; 10:12; 12:2; cf. Rom 8:34). This also explains why the resurrection of Jesus, hinted at only in 13:20, is not central, but only the entrance into the heavenly world of the "forerunner" (6:20) who will finally pave the way. On the one hand, this describes picturesquely the certainty and world-encompassing magnitude of salvation and, on the other, gives the initial steps for discipleship (see 21.5 below).

21.4 Typology. Jesus is thus installed in this new priesthood (see 21.2 above), whose authority was acknowledged by Abraham and in him the whole priesthood of the Levites coming from him (7:4-6). This is not asserted of Melchizedek in Gen 14:18-20, but it is important because it accomplishes the transition from the "old" to the "new covenant." Here for the first time in the New Testament the important passage Jer 31:31-34 is expressly cited (8:8-13). The new covenant is mentioned in the sayings of the last supper (Mark 14:24; I Cor 11:25) and above all in Paul (II Cor 3:6; cf. Gal 4:24), but the theological orientation is different in the Letter to the Hebrews. The law as the requirement of works no longer disturbs the church. The formulation of "dead works" (6:1; 9:14), which brings Paul to mind, seems to be meant for pagans (cf. Rom 6:11; 8:10). In contrast to Paul's thinking, therefore, Abraham the believer is not the one central figure of salvation, although in 11:8-19, naturally, he appears among the Old Testament witnesses to faith, and Christ is the perfecter of Moses, not his antitype (Rom 10:4-8; II Cor 3:13-17; Heb 3:1-6). The time of Israel is regarded completely positively. The high priest also has his honor (5:4), but all priesthood in the tabernacle according to the law (7:16; 8:4-6; 9:22) is only a "copy and shadow" of the "heavenly things" (8:5; 9:23; 10:1; cf. Col 2:17). It is only that, yet it does not stand in opposition to the priesthood of Christ, but is merely relatively smaller than the "better," "greater and more perfect" (7:22; 9:10-14). Therefore it is not allegorized as, for example, in Gal 4:21-31, as if the sacrifice of the Old Testament should only represent the sacrifice of Christ, or even as the Letter of Barnabas (chap. 10) does later, according to which the prohibition of pig flesh is interpreted only as the prohibition of dealing with people who behave like pigs. The Letter to the Hebrews thinks typologically: whatever at that time had happened or had been commanded was in Christ brought to completion by God in a different way, superior to the old.[161] In this way the letter takes up the problem of the cult in the old covenant and of cultlessness or of a cult achieved by Christ himself in the new covenant, which otherwise is raised nowhere in the New Testament.

21.5 Discipleship. Likewise, the importance of ethical admonitions is clear. In the figure of the high priest the assertion of the sacrificial death "for us" is connected with that of his going on "before us" (see 21.3 above). This excludes both a sacrifice theory that leaves the individual completely passive, and the misunderstanding of the high priest as a mere model that we must imitate. A shift in interpretation of "discipleship" (in the sense of "following") to an emphasis on "imitation" of a model has been abetted by the fact that Latin and French and English, but not the Greek of the New Testament, all have a word that means both "following" and "imitating Jesus." Yet the Letter to the Hebrews, with its typological view of the Old Testament, already presupposes a path that God has traveled with his people to

Christ. This path continues in the church until the last "coming" of "the Day drawing near" and of its judge (= God or Christ?—10:25, 37, cf. 12:23; 12:1-3, 12-16). Naturally, one can argue whether the writer is thinking primarily apocalyptically in temporal categories of the coming down of the heavenly Jerusalem at the end of the ages or is speaking Hellenistically in spacial concepts of the final entry into the world already existing above. If the idea in the first case is more that of a "waiting" people of God, then in the second it is that of the heavenward journey of the soul through the earthly, which is a mere copy of the real heavenly world, and thus of the underlying idea of "the wandering people of God" (Ernst Käsemann), even if it is not directly the theme, but no doubt "the secret basis" of the Letter to the Hebrews.[162] Certainly the church has already come to God and to his angels, to the heavenly Jerusalem and the festal gathering of the elect (12:22-23), which again reminds us of John (see 29.7 below); but their faith (no longer in opposition to works of the law as in Paul) must prove itself as steadfastness, loyalty, and perseverance in persecutions (11:1–12:1). Falling away is a danger, and there is no repentance for it (12:16-17; 6:4-6). Naturally this does not mean ecclesiastical jurisdiction over church members who have fallen away and are rejected when wanting to return.[163] Such prohibition, seen from the standpoint of the whole New Testament, is also clearly restricted by Jesus' attitude toward Peter (Luke 22:31-34; John 21:15-19).

21.6 Christ, End of the Cult. What Paul does for the question of the Old Testament law, the Letter to the Hebrews does for the question of the Old Testament cult, which is fulfilled in the sacrifice of Jesus Christ completed "once for all" (7:27; 9:12, 28; 10:10, 14). In place of faith in the Christ who died for us and has risen, which sets aside works as a precondition of salvation, in Hebrews we have faith in the self-sacrificing and heaven-entering high priest Christ, which sets aside cultic ritual as a precondition of salvation (7:18; 8:13; 10:9). More than with Paul, the emphatic proclamation of the sacrificial death also includes the whole earthly activity of Jesus (2:9-18; 4:15; 5:7-9).

As clear as that is, it tells us little about what the author sees as a danger for the readers and what, in the face of it, he wants to stress. Is there in the church or a part of it the temptation to introduce a Christian cult corresponding to the Jewish one? If so, the author emphasizes the uniqueness and finality of the cult perfected by Christ and valid for all people and all times, and hence also the cultless adoration of God in the worship service of the church. Is the crucial problem of the church its fatigue and resignation or, even more, its fear of suffering? Then the most important thing for the author is his admonition to his readers—repeatedly mixed with statements about Christ and his salvation—to persevere and take seriously their transformation in Christ, and these statements are based on the proclamation of what Christ has already accomplished. Does the author have in mind a group of enthusiasts within the church (in distinction to "all," who are greeted in 13:24-25) who, similar to the Corinthians, think that everything is already completed? If so, chapter 8 contains their viewpoint, and the view of Christ as the heavenly high priest, who has already bound heaven and earth, has become for them the very temptation of a "triumphant church," which already lives in heaven, has left the earthly things behind, and no longer has to bother about them. In contrast to this the author emphasizes in chapters 9–10 the importance of Jesus' earthly service, his atoning death, and at the same time the ethical demands of the way that continues on to the last day. Thus in this case the author corrects an all too "Johannine" theology, which has the suffering and death disappearing behind the victorious exaltation of Jesus, and at the same time lets the still awaited future pale before the salvation-filled present.[164]

Nowhere is the attempt to reintroduce cultic activity mentioned directly, but the mere fatigue of the church cannot have brought forth the whole presentation of the high priest Christ. Likewise it remains very questionable whether one can really separate what was already tradition from what the author introduces, for example, in chapters 8–10. However one regards the situation and separates the redaction from the tradition that was definitely already there, it is certain that the new view of Christ, either from tradition and/or newly created by the author, is an answer—not otherwise to be found in this way in the New Testament—to the general question that was called forth by what at that time was the unique worship of the church without an image of God, temple, or priest, that is, without holy objects, places, or persons.

22. THE LETTER OF JAMES

22.1 Character of the Writing. Only 1:1 bears any similarity to a letter, and even here those addressed as recipients are "the twelve tribes in the dispersion," that is, the whole of God's people scattered in the world (see 23.1 below). In terms of content it is more a matter of a collection of wisdom sayings, above all on the theme of the law and right living according to it. In 108 verses there are 54 imperatives. Although the name of Jesus Christ appears only in 1:1 and 2:1 and much of the letter could thus also be said by a non-Christian Jew, the following catalogue of features clearly points to a Christian author: confession of sins, intercession of the elders, and forgiveness of sins (5:14-15), the expectation of the coming of the Lord ("Parousia," 5:7), the mentioning of the new birth (1:18) and the speaking of the "honorable name" (in baptism, 2:7), the prohibition of swearing (5:12, like Matt 5:34), and perhaps also the formulation "poor in the world . . . rich in faith" (2:5). Above all, 2:14-16 is scarcely conceivable without Paul, especially because the author argues with the only Old Testament statement that actually speaks against the view of the Letter of James but was greatly stressed by Paul (2:23: "Abraham believed God, and it was reckoned to him as righteousness" = Gen 15:6). The word *synagōgē* (2:2) is also used in quite similar fashion in Heb 10:25 for the Christian assembly.

22.2 Author and Date. The style is an educated Greek, the Greek translation of the Old Testament is quoted, and the cultic law—for example, concerning circumcision, food regulations prohibitions, and sacrifice—no longer plays any role. Therefore the author cannot be the brother of Jesus, the leader of the Jerusalem church (Gal 2:9; Acts 12:17; 21:18), who, despite his faithfulness to the Jewish law and the energetic support of the Pharisees for him, died a martyr in A.D. 62.[165] James is presumably named because he is recognized by the author and readers as an authority, and while no Jamesian school exists, there is still a certain connection with the tradition about James.[166]

The date of the letter is hard to ascertain. The author could have already heard of Pauline theology by rumor at a very early date. Nevertheless, the argument with Gen 15:6 is hardly conceivable before the discussions in Galatia; in any case we hear nothing yet of such difficulties in I Thess. There are also already teachers and elders in the church (3:1; 5:14), and indeed in apparently desirable positions; on the other hand, healing is not expected from charismatics, but from prayer of the elders (5:14). Nothing is said of false teachers, and there is no appealing to authorities for right doctrine. Nothing of the general persecutions of the nineties is detectable. Thus one also cannot place the letter too late, especially because the significance of the Jewish Christians and thus the discussion about the Mosaic law recedes more and more, although I Tim 1:7 still presupposes debates about the law, but presumably within discussion of (Gnostic?) speculations (see 20.4 above). Thus, without being sure, one could posit A.D. 80-90 as the best guess.[167] The letter was also first attested by Origen (185-254) and even then not yet recognized everywhere.

22.3 Faith and Works. Paul dismisses as foolish the question of whether one should do something plainly evil so that the effectiveness of grace alone can become all the more prominent (Rom 3:8). Here, however, that is felt as a problem: apparently there were fools who drew such conclusions. Paul himself knows that faith works through love and the law is fulfilled in love (Gal 5:6, 14). He can say that we are called to "every good work" and are judged according to our works (Rom 2:8; II Cor 9:8; 11:15). The concept of a faith that is merely a world view, that is, only an idea, is the farthest thing from Paul's mind. Vis-à-vis such misunderstandings it is doubtless correct to remember that there is no faith apart from works (2:18). Yet this does not touch Paul's crucial

110

assertion. The love that fulfills the law is central for Paul precisely because one never gets finished with it, but rather always remains obligated (Rom 13:8-10). Now, James also speaks of the "royal law" of love of neighbor (2:8) and of the "law of liberty" (1:25; 2:12), indeed, of the "implanted word" of the law (1:21-22). He knows that "we all make many mistakes" (3:2), but that the deed of mercy, that is, love of one's neighbor, triumphs over the law (2:13). Above all, in spite of the warning of 2:10 that "whoever keeps the whole law but fails in one point has become guilty of all of it," there is no indication that one must hold to all the ritual commandments. Thus one can say that the actual foundation is a wisdom theology such as that which, for example, underlies the Sermon on the Mount, but also stands in the background for Paul. It not only provides the basis for the ethical demand, but also describes the basis of salvation that makes new life possible to start with. For wisdom is the gift of God "from above," and is not earthly, psychic, devilish (3:15; see 11.5 above).

22.4 Christ as the New Lawgiver? In distinction to Paul, however, James asserts that a person "is justified by works" (2:24) and that faith works together with works (2:22). Paul understands faith as total trust in God's grace, which alone justifies, and love as the way in which such faith lives. Therefore, except where he adopts traditional formulas, Paul almost always uses the singular *work* when he speaks of expressions of faith. Naturally, there is no life that does not express itself in action as well as in feeling and thinking and suffering. The life of faith, with all its ups and downs, has become for him a oneness oriented as a whole, toward God. It is no longer divisible into individual expressions that can be measured and added up according to the letter of the law (see 11.5-6, 16.5 above). One can and must point to individual practices that cannot be brought into congruence with the basic position of faith, but one cannot conversely add up positive expressions in order to be justified before God. One can do nothing but repeatedly call people back to the true faith that justifies. Yet in the second century the other view prevailed for some time: Jesus became the one who gives the law, "our new lawgiver," indeed, "the eternal and final law" himself.[168]

22.5 Warning about Cheap Grace. It would be wrong if the correction of the Letter of James, which is understandable in a particular situation though not sufficient to solve the problem,[169] were to become the actual foundation of theology. Here, more than in other New Testament writings, we have only a particular excerpt of the proclamation. Jesus Christ is teacher and judge. Jesus' sayings appear perhaps in 1:5-6 (Matt 7:7; Mark 11:23); 1:22 (Matt 7:21); 2:5 (Luke 6:20); 3:18 (Matt 5:9); and above all in 5:12, where presumably an even more original form is retained than in Matt 5:34-37. Jesus' final coming is the basis of all these admonitions (5:7-8). We never hear of Jesus' preexistence, incarnation, earthly life, death, and resurrection, or exaltation. The examples for Christian piety are selected only from the Old Testament (Abraham in 2:21-23; Rahab in 2:25; the prophets and Job in 5:10-11; Elijah in 5:17-18; cf. Heb 11). To be sure, 2:1 speaks of the "faith of our Lord Jesus Christ, the Lord of glory," but 2:19 states this precisely: "You believe that God is one."

If one recognizes these limits, then the warning against a cheap grace that makes faith impossible even in the Pauline sense can definitely be heard. Here, it is precisely everyday sins that are exposed: evil gossip (3:1-12; 4:11-12), bowing before the rich and despising the poor (2:1-9), the social thoughtlessness that severely oppresses the worker (5:1-6), the way one automatically forges plans without prefacing them with, "If the Lord wills and we are alive" (4:13-16), and the simple failure to do good (4:17). That reminds us in a sober and very pointed way what faith is. And its character of gift ("from above") and its liberating effect ("law of liberty") are not thereby forgotten.

23. THE FIRST LETTER OF PETER

23.1 Author, Date, Place. The characteristics of a letter are clearer here than in the Letter of James. Admittedly almost all parts of Asia Minor except the southern boundary areas (see 13.1 above) are named as the homes of the recipients. The "elected strangers of the diaspora" (1:1) are Gentile Christians according to 1:14, 18; 2:9-10; 4:3-4. Election is thus to the church of Jesus, which is distinct from its Gentile environment (2:11-12). This is also true of James 1:1 and Rev 7:4, where the twelve tribes of Israel are mentioned (see 2.8 above). Thus behind this view stands a tradition that understood the formation of Jesus' community of disciples as the collection of the twelve scattered tribes in a reconstituted Israel[170] (see 7.6 above), but this is now reinterpreted to mean the primarily Gentile-Christian church. The good Greek and the use of the Greek translation of the Old Testament eliminate Peter as author. Nor could they very well be attributed only to Silvanus as Peter's secretary (5:12). Nowhere is there a reference to the earthly Jesus. Furthermore, the general persecution (4:12-19) presupposed at least in Asia Minor if not worldwide (cf. 5.9), for which no doubt just being a Christian was sufficient (4:16), is hardly conceivable before the death of Peter. He probably was active in Corinth (I Cor 1:12; 9:5), but a letter from him to the Pauline churches with so many Pauline thoughts is not easily imaginable, even though not impossible. Moreover, Paul knows no elders (5:1-4) in the churches founded by him. Thus we will imagine a later author writing in Peter's name, perhaps at the beginning of the persecutions in the nineties. It has already been assumed that the letter was originally composed in Paul's name. Silvanus and Mark, who are mentioned in 5:12-13 fit in with this. The former is, according to I Thess 1:1; II Cor 1:19

Paul's coworker, no doubt identical with Silas, who according to Acts 15:(27) 40–18:5 accompanied Paul on his second journey. The latter is probably the Mark named in Philem 24; Col 4:10, and the designation as "my son" is to be understood spiritually, as in Philem 10. Not until later, then, was the author's name changed, perhaps because the abbreviation PLS was misread as PTS.[171] Since, however, the idea of the apostle pair Peter and Paul and their deaths as martyrs (in Rome) was so well known in the nineties (for example, in *I Clem* 5), it is entirely possible in a time when Pauline theology threatened to fade that it could have been proclaimed anew in the name of the chief apostle. Intrachurch battles between followers of Peter and those of Paul are out of the question, since (except in 1:1) neither of the two apostles is mentioned or clearly characterized. "Babylon" (5:13) designates Rome, as in Rev 18:2-3 and Jewish writings.

23.2 Unity. The new beginning in 4:12 is curious because, in spite of 1:6-7, one does not get the impression earlier that suffering for the sake of the faith has already begun. The reference in 2:20-21 is limited to slaves, and 2:13-14 looks positively on the representatives of the state. Yet this view is taken from the tradition (Rom 13:1-5; I Tim 2:1-2; Titus 3:1) and simply shows that persecutions are only just beginning (4:17). In any case they have not stirred the author to the reaction of Rev 12:17–13:18 (see 31.5 below). Thus one will think neither of two originally independent writings nor of a later expanded baptismal address (1:3–4:11) nor even a baptismal worship service (with baptism between 1:22 and 23), after which a general closing worship followed (4:12–5:11).[172] Praise and *amen* (4:11) are also found elsewhere within a letter (Rom 11:36; cf. 1:25; 9:5; Gal 1:5; I Tim 1:17; cf. Rev 1:6).

23.3 The Pauline Connection of Grace and Sanctification. The letter shows what Paul signifies in this period when he is taken seriously. The double assertion in 1:2 of the complete gracefulness of the salvation achieved through Jesus' blood (also 1:19, cf. 2:24; 3:18; see 5.4 above) *and* its expression in obedience and sanctification (also 1:22) is Pauline. In terms of form and content, the continuation in an introductory thanksgiving (1:3-12) is also Pauline. Here faith, in distinction to future vision (as in II Cor 5:7) is described in a twofold fashion. On the one hand, its content is the already accomplished fulfillment of Old Testament hopes (cf. I Cor 10:11); on the other, faith still remains as hope for the final perfection that will transform the present sufferings into joy (cf. Rom 8:24). Already presupposed in Paul (II Cor 5:17; Gal 4:19; Philem 10) and typical of post-Pauline (Titus 3:5) and Johannine writings (John 3:3, 5) is the idea of a new birth (1:3, 23; 2:1-2). Finally, the expectation "that we might die to sin and live to righteousness" (2:24; Rom 6:18) is also Pauline.

23.4 Ascended into the Realm of the Dead. We are again reminded of Paul by the contrast of "being put to death in the flesh but made alive in [or: through] the spirit" (3:18, of Jesus). Of course, this does not mean the typical Pauline opposition of human, fleshly resistance against God and his Spirit, but the distinction between earthly and heavenly life, as it was adopted by Paul in Rom 1:3-4, no doubt out of the tradition, but also formulated by him somewhat differently in 9:5. This statement of death and resurrection is connected in I Pet 3:19-20 with the assertion, characteristic of this letter, of the preaching of the resurrected one to the "spirits in prison." Certainly the author does not have hell in mind, but rather the abode of the "dead" to whom "the gospel was preached," so that "judged in the flesh like human beings [or in the human world?], they might live in [through?] the spirit like God [in God's sight or world?]" (4:6). Also, the place of the dead should probably not be regarded as below, but as in Hellenism (see 17.3 above) and also in Eph 2:2; 6:12 in the air, through which Christ passes in the ascension. According to 3:20 this concerns the generation of the Flood but is probably extended generally to all who died during the period of the Old Testament. The naming of the time of Noah may even indicate that all peoples, even the heathen, are included. According to 3:20-22 the saving of Noah and his family "through water" is finally fulfilled in those who are being saved "through water" (now understood instrumentally as baptism), in that they are thereby associated with the one who has ascended to heaven and sits at God's right hand, the one to whom all authorities and powers are already subject. What happens now in baptism has thus in a certain way also been fulfilled universally.

Though this is naive and is expressed in the cosmic concepts of that period, it describes theologically the significance of the Christ event that reaches beyond the boundaries of both space and time. It is valid for all people, even those who never heard anything about the gospel.

23.5 The Priesthood of All Believers. The second, special contribution of the letter consists in the new view of the church as the temple and people of God, for whom the Old Testament promises are valid. Here too Paul has already provided the model. In I Cor 3:16 the church is designated as God's temple, and the quotation of the "no people" who become God's people and the unloved who become the loved (2:10) is also found in Rom 9:25 and, of course, as in I Pet 2:6-8, is connected with a combination of Isa 28:16 and 8:14 (Rom 9:32-33). Thus both passages seem to go back to pre-Pauline "scribal" reflections of the church.

In 2:1-6, twice we read in participial style of the crucial experience of turning away from the old and turning toward the new (vv. 1 and 3b-4). This is followed by imperatives that exhort the reader to realize their new status as "newborn babes" and "living stones" (2a and 5a). Then with a final phrase

114

("that . . ." and "to . . .") the goal is given (2b and 5b), and the passage finally closes with the substantiation of this whole movement through Christ's deed of love (3 and 6). This is repeated in similar fashion in vv. 7-10, where the separation from the nonbelievers (7-8), the exhortation of the new character as "a chosen race, a royal priesthood, a holy nation, God's own people" (9a), and the stating of its goal ("that you may declare . . ."—9b) is again substantiated by God's deed in Christ, which has made them "God's people" and loved ones (v. 10). Thus the predicates of the Old Testament that were valid for Israel are transferred to the church of Jesus. In the process the writer has chosen the only statement in the Old Testament that grants to the whole people priestly honor and holiness.[173] As developed in 2:11–3:17, the concern is not intrachurch tasks, but the proclamation of the Gospel among the Gentile (and Jewish) world with which each church member is gifted and commissioned. This in no way prevents there being various charismata within the church (4:10-11, only still divided according to proclamation of the word and *diakonia*) and also ordered ministries of "elders" (5:1-4), without officeholders thereby being separated from laity.[174]

23.6 The Church in Suffering—for the World.

This gift of the general priesthood vis-à-vis the world takes up anew the election of Israel to salvation of the *world*. Paul understood the life of the apostle above all as participation in Christ's suffering (I Cor 4:9-13; II Cor 4:7-18; Col 1:24), even if it is also true for the church that suffering with Christ leads to being glorified with him (Rom 5:3-5; 8:17). This is clearly adopted in the First Letter of Peter as both a commission and a promise for the whole church, and was presumably greatly conditioned by the experience of general persecution (4:16; see 23.1 above and 31.1, 31.5 below). Just as Jesus' passion is also his way to the resurrection and heavenly glory (1:11; 3:18-22), so also is this true for the church (1:6-9; 4:13-14; 5:10), which precisely in its suffering fulfills its mission to the world. This is said so soberly and so far from any glorification of martyrs that even wives' silent bearing of marital distress and especially the suffering of slaves under the whims of their masters (as certainly as that must also be critically examined today) are connected directly to Christ's suffering on the cross and are seen as an opportunity for the preaching of the gospel (3:1-2; 2:18-25).

23.7 The Pilgrimage of the Nations to Zion—the Church for the World.

The first confessions of faith were centered on the one who died for us and was resurrected. Forgiveness of sins, deliverance from the last judgment, and eternal salvation are primarily granted to the individual. The Jewish-Christian, pre-Pauline statement of Rom 1:3-4 already places the sovereignty of the earthly one and all the more of the resurrected one over his people in the center. The hymns praise Christ as the heavenly Lord. In I Tim 3:16 and especially in the revelation schema this lordship is also happening on earth in the Gentile mission of Paul (see 5 above). In the First Letter of Peter this comes to a notable further development. What is really crucial is not what the church knows theoretically about the exaltation of Christ to the right hand of God, or what in an already heroic past has played itself out in the triumphal procession of the great apostle to the Gentiles, but what is realized in the distress of marriages and in the everyday life of slaves, and more and more also in the prisons and at places of execution. *That* is where Jesus wants to establish his lordship.

To a certain extent the prophetic hope of the pilgrimage of all nations to Zion at the end time (Isa 2:2-3) is thus also adopted and reshaped. It still clearly defines Matt 8:11-12 and also echoes in Paul (cf. Rom 15:16 with Isa 66:20). For him too God's action with Israel remains the rootstock into which the people are grafted like wild branches. According to Rom 11:11-32, however, the commission to them consists in the idea that the Gentile Christians must now entice the Jews who do not yet believe in Christ until someday these also are added to the multitude of the Gentiles. In Eph 2:11-22 Israel remains the people originally belonging to God, but the two groups of Jewish and Gentile Christians stand beside each other as equals, united in "*one* body" as a consequence of the broken-down wall of hostility. In I Pet the changed historical situation is seen even more clearly. Neither Jewish Christians nor Jews play a role. The threat comes exclusively from the Gentiles, and to them the message must be directed through the obedience of the church. The danger that threatens the later, post-New Testament development is that Judaism as well as paganism will become forgotten entities, over against which Christianity will then appear as a "third race." In I Pet the antidote is obvious: in no event can the church rest on its laurels. As the priesthood encompassing all members, it can and must proclaim the great deeds of God, and in so doing it knows how much it is in this very way called into the inheritance of Israel (1:1; see 23.1 above) and into the graceful action of God toward Israel.

24. THE LETTER OF JUDE AND THE SECOND LETTER OF PETER

24.1 The Letter of Jude. In the Letter of Jude we see how the early church deals with the problem of erroneous faith. In its midst live people who indeed take part in the love feast (v. 12), which presumably is not yet distinguished from the Lord's Supper,[175] but whose teaching is so different that the author can only recommend total separation if they will not let themselves be led back on the right paths (v. 23). Normally Christian Gnostics (see 20.2 above) or their precursors spring to mind here. Yet the distinction between the psychic and the spiritual (v. 19) was already known before Gnosticism (see 11.5 above). If that already indicates a relationship to James 3:15, then the appeal to "grace" (v. 4) and perhaps even the threat of "judgment" (v. 15) points to Rom 3:8, that is, to the problems of faith and works, also treated in James 2:14-16.[176] In a certain sense "Jude" would therefore also be, theologically speaking, "the brother of James." Of theological importance is the fact that here we have finally left the age of the apostles (v. 17) and entered the period of church history. The apostles have "once for all delivered" (v. 3) the "most holy faith" (v. 20). This is also connected with the schematization of the false teachers who, as in the later heresy struggles of the church, are designated as types who were already observed in Judaism (and emerge again and again).[177]

At the end of the first Christian century the Old Testament canon was effectively set; here, however, are quotations from Jewish writings that are not included therein, especially from *I Enoch* (v. 14). Verse 9 probably also comes from such a writing, perhaps from the lost ending of the *Testament of Moses*. On the one hand, the false teachers are characterized as visionaries and "dreamers," who apparently also do not respect the boundary between human beings and angels or even God (v. 8; cf. also 6-7), and therefore speak haughty words (v. 16) and revile everything (v. 10). On the other hand, they are painted as libertines who exercise questionable sexual practices (vv. 4, 7, 8, 16, 18, 23). Heavily emphasized is judgment with "eternal fire" and eternal darkness (vv. 7, 13).

Quite apart from a rather good Greek style, all of this shows that the author cannot be the brother of Jesus and of James (Mark 6:3). Is "Jude" selected because the letter clearly stands in the Jewish-Christian tradition, and it was already known that James suffered martyrdom in A.D. 62? Somewhat later, perhaps even after the final Jewish defeat by Rome in A.D. 135, the Second Letter of Peter again appealed to the apostle Peter, because the author lived in the world of Gentile Christianity that also owed its existence to Peter (I Cor 9:5; *1 Clem.* 5; see 23.1 above).[178] Naturally, it could also be possible that a later Jude also had a brother named James, since both names are common. The praise of God (vv. 24-25) that appears in place of a letter's conclusion is beautiful.

24.2 The Second Letter of Peter: Author. Second Peter 2 incorporates a large part of Jude as a kind of insert. Since the letter serves as Peter's testament (1:14-15), but the false teachers do not come until long after his death, their coming (unlike in Jude 4) is only foretold (2:1-3; 3:3). In 2:10-22, to be sure, where the writer follows his model more closely, he speaks of them again in the present tense. This alone shows that the Letter of Jude is not conversely a—hardly comprehensible—abbreviation of II Peter. This is demonstrated even more clearly by the short references in 2:4 and 11, which cannot really be understood except through Jude 6 and 9. It is easy to understand why quotations from and allusions to non-Jewish writings have been stricken from II Peter; only the holy Scripture is supposed to have value. While Jude 5-11 names the wilderness generation, the fall of the angels (Gen 6:1-4), Sodom and Gomorrah, Cain, Balaam, and Korah as examples of divine punishment, in II Pet 2:4-7 the fall of the angels, the generation of the Flood, Sodom and Gomorrah, and Balaam follow in correct temporal order. By the change of *one* letter in the Greek, the remark that the false teachers participate in "your love feasts" (Jude 12) becomes "in their dissipation" (II Pet 2:13), because church love feasts are apparently no longer thinkable with them.

The letter is expressly designated the second one (3:1). The writer's status as an eye witness of Jesus' transfiguration (or resurrection?) is stressed (1:16-18), and Paul is named "our beloved brother" (3:15). In contrast to I Pet 1:1, II Pet 1:1 now has "Simon Peter" instead of "Peter," "servant [Rom 1:1; Phil 1:1; Jude 1] and apostle" instead of "apostle," and instead of addressing only Christendom in Asia Minor, now all Christians everywhere are addressed. Thus the letter clearly claims to be a letter of the apostle Peter.

In terms of content and style it is completely different from I Peter. Until the end of the second century the letter was unknown and even at that time still almost universally contested, as it was in Italy until around 400, when it was still not known in Syria. Thus it definitely comes from a later writer and is probably the latest piece of writing in the New Testament. The letters of Paul, in addition to others, count as "scriptures" (3:15-16)—of which the Letter of Jude still says nothing—and the problem of their interpretation is already at stake. Thus, in the writer's judgment, Paul's assertions have apparently been misused by opponents. The "holy prophets" are those of the Old Testament and stand next to "your apostles" (3:2; different still in Eph 3:5). The first generation, the "fathers," have already fallen asleep (3:4), which also does not quite fit with Peter, who probably died in A.D. 64 as a martyr (cf. 23.1 above).

24.3 Apostolic Guarantee—Divine Nature? The letter is not easy to evaluate because its intention is ambiguous. On the one hand, it certainly no longer speaks of the "most holy faith" (Jude 20), yet it sees faith as a possession that one obtains (1:1). It is above all "knowledge" (1:3, 8; 3:18; cf. 1:16, literally: "brought to your knowledge"; 3:15). The apostle is no longer primarily the one who is entrusted with the proclamation, that is, the insight into what happened for the church and the world in Jesus' life, death, and resurrection, let alone with a proclamation that is to be translated into an encounter with the individual hearers and readers, their questions, possibilities, and temptations, in order to make their lives new. He seems to assure correct faith by being the guarantor of miraculous events, for example, the transfiguration of Jesus (1:16-18). More questionable is the idea that through such knowledge the church becomes "partakers of the divine nature" and thus escapes the evil world (1:4). Though in 3:16 the writer knows about the phenomenon of the false interpretation of the apostolic witness, he does not attempt to justify anew the correct understanding, for example, on the basis of other Pauline statements, but only maintains that the opponents are "ignorant" and "twist" everything. Verse 1:20 could even be a prohibition of any interpretation of one's own that is not sanctioned by the church, but it probably only means that no prophet speaks out of his own interpretation.

All of this may sound like Hellenistic cults and miracle workers or Gnostic prizing of knowledge that reveals a natural divine essence of humanity. Yet knowledge and salvation are unambiguously bound to the apostolic witness that attests God's activity as occurring in history, as accomplished in Jesus Christ. In addition, 1:16 does not choose the normal word for "eye witness," but one used in Hellenistic mysteries, which designates the "observer" who perceives the presence of God in an event.[179] Thus not only is the apostle eye witness to facts, but at the same time he is given the knowledge of *God's* activity in them. Therefore he also not only knows of a divine nature inherent in humanity, but clearly sees in it God's gift of grace, which comes to human beings through the gospel and also distinguishes them ethically from the world.

24.4 The View of the Future. The situation is similar regarding what is said about the future. The mocking of the delayed return of Jesus (3:4) marks a time in which the immediate expectation of the last judgment is fading and the expectation of the future action of God is disappearing or is restricted to the salvation of the individual. This is certainly typical of the Hellenistic understanding of time. One could even ask whether the talk of the "eternal kingdom of . . . Jesus Christ" (1:11) or of the "day" that is supposed to dawn "in our hearts" (1:19) does not demonstrate quite similar thinking in II Peter as well.[180] Above all we must ask whether behind this may stand the correct perception that in Jesus something of the final future of God has in fact broken into our presence. This was, in any case, the way it was seen by Ephesians (see 18.4 and 6 above) and above all by the Gospel of John (see 29.7 below). Moreover, one would have to ask whether the adoption of the Stoics' vivid pictures of the end of the world and its "elements" (see 17.3 above) in worldwide conflagration (3:10, 12) really helps, especially when one notices that the writer not only speaks with Jude 10 of the "irrational animals,"[181] but also characterizes them as "born to be caught and killed" (2:12), and thus seems really to be interested only in the fate of the human creature, who in Stoicism is also singled out as the being blessed with reason.

And yet on the other hand one must thankfully recognize that the writer upholds the early Christian and Old Testament prophetic hope of "new heavens and a new earth in which righteousness dwells" (3:13; Isa 65:17; 66:22) and at the same time also, against all Gnostic tendencies, holds to the creation and maintenance of the world through God's word (3:4-5). In this way the character of promise of God's word, which also points prophetically into God's future, is upheld (1:19-20; 3:13; cf. 3:2, 17). The expected Parousia may be prominent as the demonstration of power and the day of judgment for the ungodly (1:16; 2:3, 9; 3:7), yet it serves directly the exhortation of the church itself to ethical obedience, in which again in good Hellenistic fashion virtue, knowledge, self-control, steadfastness, godliness, and brotherly affection are included between the Christian duo, faith and love (1:5-7). The warning that the day of the Lord will come like a thief (I Thess 5:2) is, therefore, not at all in contradiction with the assertion that for God a day is as a thousand years and thus he still grants time for repentance, and that the godliness of the church, as the rabbis also say, can even hasten the coming of the day (3:8-12). That is, to be sure, not the Pauline hope that one day "God may be everything to every one" (I Cor 15:28), but it holds fast to the central biblical viewpoints in a time that is scarcely receptive to them anymore. In this II Peter resembles the pastoral letters (see 20.2 above).

24.5 The Historiccal Nature of the Gospel Versus Gnostic Timelessness. We are probably dealing here with not only the latest but also the most questionable letter in the New Testament,[182] at least when it is seen outside the special situation of its time. This is shared to a large extent with the writings treated in sections 18–22. Faced with the coming assault of Gnosticism (see 20.2 above) and the danger that the Old Testament and early Christian hope, which understands history as the way of God toward a goal and not as only the chaotic jumble of human delusion, could fade into an ahistorical, timeless philosophy, this clear recall was essential. That faith and love also include the ethical demands that apply in the world, as far as they can be connected with these demands, is essential for the ongoing life of the community of Jesus and is also prescribed in Phil 4:8. Of the threefold authority of early Catholicism at the end of the second century, Scripture, dogma, and office (see 28.6 below), only the first is clearly laid down as the foundation (1:19-21; 3:16), while dogma is in any case not yet formulated—even if one presupposes that faith is above all doctrine passed down—and office, apart from the authority of the two decisive apostles, is still nowhere to be seen. The struggle for the meaning of the narrated history of God, in the past of the Christ event and in the future of God promised in the word, made possible the grounding of the later church in the Scripture, even though a great deal must be said differently in other times and situations.

For the Johannine letters, see section 30 below.

CHAPTER FIVE

The First Three Gospels and the Acts of the Apostles

Confessional formulas and early Christian hymns (see 5 above) certainly presuppose a man named Jesus and can also mention his death or his incarnation, but they aim at the statement of God's action in him and through him; that is, they describe above all the "dimension" in which his life and death are to be seen. Hence the events that "frame" his life are the crucial ones: his life with God already at the creation, his incarnation, his resurrection and exaltation, his activity in the mission to the nations and in the last judgment. Confessional formulas and hymns answer the question of who Jesus is, and what he means for the life, death, and resurrection of the church is developed in the letters. Thus the emphasis is on Jesus as the *Christ* of God. In addition there are at the same time and presumably in the same churches (see 8.3 above) sayings of Jesus, traditions about his passion, probably also about his relationship with the Baptist and his baptism, and reports of healings and disputes that are handed down orally, perhaps also in some cases already preserved in written form (see 6.3 above). Certainly this was the case in Q (see 7.1-3 above). The emphasis here became *Jesus* as the Christ of God. After the death of Paul, say, at the same time as the earlier level of post- and extra-Pauline letters, the first full Gospel was written. At that time the word still meant "proclamation of salvation" and designated a happening, not a book (see 25.3 below). Thus, strictly speaking, one can only speak of the "Gospel according to Mark," of the proclamation of salvation as it appears in the book of Mark.

25. THE GOSPEL ACCORDING TO MARK

25.1 Author, Date. The name of the author of the first extant Gospel (see 7.1 above) does not appear until a title was added later. The note by Papias[183] that Mark was Peter's companion and his translator is hardly correct. In any case he cannot be the one mentioned in Acts 12:12, 25; 13:5, 13; 15:37 (the same as Philem 24?) because, first of all, he does not seem to know the geography of Palestine very well (5:1; 7:31; 8:10, 13, 22; 10:1; 11:1). The name, however, is rather common, and thus a Mark otherwise unknown to us could be the author. Or his naming could go back to the same tradition as that in I Pet 5:13 (see 23.1 above). The Gospel was probably written shortly before the destruction of Jerusalem or perhaps shortly afterward as a "postwar phenomenon."[184] Mark 13:2, 7, 14 point to an especially dire time for Jerusalem and its Temple. Omens of the Temple destruction (similar to the tearing of the Temple curtain in Mark 15:38) are also told in Judaism, and indeed after the occurrence of the catastrophe. That these events mean that "the end is not yet" (13:7) is important to Mark, because it warns the church against seeing the fall of Jerusalem triumphantly as the sign of the imminent victorious return of Jesus. The fact that the author can hardly also be a direct eyewitness of the time that Jesus was in Jerusalem is shown first by the fact that he picks up and combines very different pieces of tradition.[185] Thus we are most likely dealing with composition shortly after 70 by a Christian unknown to us, who is writing for a (predominantly) Gentile-Christian readership for whom he must explain Jewish customs (7:3-4; cf. 5:41; 7:35; 15:34).

25.2 Structure. If we attempt to gain an overview of the Gospel,[186] the story of the last days in Jerusalem (chaps. 11–12 and 13), the death of Jesus (14–15), and the message of his resurrection (16) prove to be a special part, more comprehensive and more emphasized in comparison with the rest. In the introduction in 1:1-13 what is subsequently to be told is described from the beginning as the definitive action of God. The only passage from the Old Testament quoted by Mark himself in 1:2-3 shows that in Jesus prophetic prediction is fulfilled. In 1:4-8 he is announced by the Baptist as God's ultimate envoy. God himself acknowledges him as his Son (1:9-11), and Satan is conquered because Jesus resists the temptation not withstood by Adam, who according to contemporary Jewish tradition still lived in paradise with the animals and was served by the angels (1:12-13). The activity of Jesus between this beginning and his end in Jerusalem is divided into two parts by the confession of Peter (8:27-30). Though this confession is not rejected by Jesus, it is but also not especially welcomed (8:30). Actually, the demons in 3:11 have already recognized him as the Son of God much better than Peter does in his confession of the Christ—not until Matt 16:16 is the *Son of God* title also added to the story. For Mark what is truly essential is "the word" that Jesus "said . . . plainly" (8:32), after previously only having spoken the word "with many . . . parables . . . as they were able to hear it" (4:33): namely, the announcement of his suffering, his rejection, his being killed, and his resurrection. This twice repeated announcement divides the second half of his activity before the entry into Jerusalem, each time followed by the total misunderstanding of his disciples (8:31-33; 9:31-34; 10:32-37), followed by Jesus' renewed call to true discipleship. But the first half is also divided into three parts. Each section begins with a summary description of Jesus' activity (1:14-15; 3:7-12; 6:6), immediately followed by the calling, selecting, and sending of the disciples (1:16-20; 3:13-19; 6:7-13), and ends with the rejection of Jesus by the Pharisees, his fellow citizens, and the disciples themselves (3:6; 6:1-6a; 8:16-21). Immediately before Peter's confession and before the entry into Jerusalem, that is, before the beginning of the passion story, the healing of a blind man is told (8:22-26; 10:46-52), apparently showing symbolically that only God's power itself can open a person's eyes. Therefore 10:52 also ends with the line " . . . and followed him on the road," which picks up on 10:32: "And they were on the road, going up to Jerusalem . . . and those who followed were afraid."

25.3 Jesus' Power and Impotence. The real problem is the relationship of the authority of Jesus to the impotence in his death. On the one hand he proves to be a miracle worker, not, of course, in the sense of a Hellenistic "divine man," but of the Old Testament "man of God."[187] On the other hand, it is precisely in the ordering of the material, which goes back to Mark himself, that the rejection of Jesus, the misunderstanding of his disciples, and the way to the cross are emphasized and the miracles are restricted to the time before Peter's confession; afterward we have only the healing of the epileptic, in which, however, the decisive point is the discussion about the nature of faith (9:23-24, 28-29), the purely symbolic healing of the blind man in Jericho (see 25.2 above), and the prophetic sign of the withered fig tree (11:20). Finally, 15:39 shows that the recognition of Jesus as the Son of God occurs under the cross, where nothing is to be seen but the end of a criminal who dies with a loud cry; the tearing of the Temple curtain is not visible there. Then comes the problem of the conclusion of the Gospel, for 16:9-20 were certainly written later and appended. It is missing in the oldest manuscripts and already presupposes the Matthean, Lukan, and Johannine Easter stories. Presumably the original ending was lost, for the promise that Jesus will go before the disciples to Galilee (14:28) is, according to 16:7, already fulfilled—what was promised there in the future tense is now expressed in the present tense—but that they "will see him" remains to be fulfilled. That can only refer to the meeting with the resurrected one, since the resurrection was announced in 8:31; 9:9, 31; 10:34 and plainly proclaimed in 16:6. The second coming, by contrast, may require decades of waiting (13:7-10), so that it is necessary to write a Gospel around the year 70, when at least Peter and James (Acts 12:2) are no longer living. In addition it would be hard to explain the abrupt ending in 16:8—the last word of the original text is the conjunction *for*. If that, however, were nevertheless the original ending, the reference in 16:6-7 to the content of the confessional formula cited in I Cor 15:3-5[188] would be even more striking: Jesus is the one "crucified" ("for many" according to 10:45 and 14:24), whose grave is indicated, who "was raised," and whom his disciples and Peter "will see" (the same word that in the passive is usually translated "he appeared"). One could then even ask whether the whole book is not consciously designed with this Easter proclamation in mind; it would then be according to 1:1 the "beginning of the gospel," the proclamation that continues after Easter (see 6.2 above), as it is briefly summarized in I Cor 15:3-5.[189]

25.4 Jesus' Absence after Easter? Mark never speaks of the work of the resurrected one in the community,[190] although chapter 13 describes the period between Easter and the second coming. It is the time "when the bridegroom is taken away" (2:19-20) and the servants must be prepared for a long absence of the master in a foreign land, as the reshaping (by Mark?) of the parable of Luke 12:36 asserts (Mark 13:34-37; see 3.5 above). Is Mark plainly polemicizing against the twelve, who according to 16:8 never received Jesus' message and thus remained blind? They would then represent the church in Jerusalem and with it the (Jewish-Christian) development of the proclamation of Christ that went out from there. One possibility of understanding Mark would then be that he laid every emphasis on the earthly work of Jesus, for example, that he even transformed the story of the appearance of the resurrected one into the episode of the transfiguration of the earthly Jesus. Even the crucifixion would then be interpreted as the victory that finishes everything, and the final cry as Jesus' shout of triumph.

The other possibility would be to understand Mark in very apocalyptic fashion as only a summons to wait for the second coming of Jesus, or at least to see in chapter 13 (second coming) and 14–16 (passion) two equal climaxes of the gospel. The promise that the disciples are to "see" Jesus in Galilee (16:7) would then be related to the appearance of the one coming again in judgment or even already reinterpreted as his coming in the eschatological mission to the Gentiles beginning in Galilee. Such an interpretation of 16:7, however, is impossible at least for the evangelist himself (see 25.3 above), whether an Easter appearance was originally told or there was only a reference to a confessional formula in which the resurrection was asserted in accordance with faith. Admittedly, that Jesus is the coming Son-of-man/judge is essential to Mark, but especially for ethical admonition. Outside of the incorporation of chapter 13 (with its ethical summons at the end) and 14:62 from the tradition,[191] this is mentioned only once and only in this connection (8:38–9:1). It is Mark who emphatically expands and thereby reshapes the traditional concept of the coming Son-of-man/judge through the proclamation of the suffering Son of man (8:31; 9:12, 31; 10:33, 45; 14:21, 41), whether this was already present before Mark or was first done by him. But even the first suggestion, the limitation to the earthly Jesus, is not justifiable, for according to 8:32 (see 25.2 above) the fundamental proclamation, which no longer occurs in veiled fashion, is precisely that of the passion and resurrection. In general the polemic against the twelve and thus against the Jewish-Christian community is very unlikely. The secret of the kingdom of God is entrusted to the twelve (4:11). Jesus explains all parables to them (4:34) and then only through their tradition also to the readers of the Gospel. They have become Jesus' authorized preachers (6:7-13) and will continue to be so (13:9-13). As participants in the last supper, they have passed it on to the church (14:22-25). Certainly they remain uncomprehending up to their flight in Gethsemane, but that is true for all people and only stresses God's grace as the exclusive basis of all knowledge of Jesus (see 25.2 above).

Finally, according to Mark Jesus is not just the absent one in the time of Mark's community. He is present in his "name" and in the "Spirit," as he also is in the view of the Acts of the Apostles (see 28.3 below). The baptism by Jesus with the Spirit, announced in 1:8, occurs according to 13:11, 13 in the proclamation of his name after Easter, and 9:37-40 likewise speaks of this time, because the discussion concerns community with the disciples, not with Jesus. That the title *kyrios* is presupposed for the one sitting at God's right hand (12:36-37) should perhaps not be overly stressed, since it does not expressly include Jesus' lordship over the church but no doubt does include the rank of one who will some day come again (14:62). On the other hand, healings and stories of discipleship presuppose that such things still happen in the post-Easter community (11:22-24; 10:28-30). Thus one can only formulate that for Mark Jesus is the one who is active on earth but reaches his goal in the cross and resurrection and will one day come again as judge, but who is already at work in his "name" and in the effective preaching of his church.

25.5 The Messianic Secret. In Mark the whole description of the earthly activity of Jesus acquires another "dimension" through what one usually calls his "messianic secret." This term, however, is understood in different ways: (1) the prohibition against telling others about miraculous healings, (2) the emphasis on the language of parables as speech that is understandable only to initiates, (3) the prohibition to the demons against calling out that Jesus is the Son of God, and (4) the disciples lack of understanding.

(1) The secretiveness of miracles—for example, the withdrawal into the house with very few or no witnesses indicated—may belong to traditional style (II Kings 4:33-35). Miracles are certainly important to Mark. The fact that the prohibition against propagation is often violated shows how little Jesus' divine authority can be hidden. Redactionally, however, Mark stresses the *teaching* of Jesus, which is mentioned twenty times and, apart from 6:30 where in a

different linguistic form it is related to the disciples, it is always said of Jesus himself. Mark also mentions Jesus' retreat in the face of miracle mania (1:38) and the lack of understanding of friends and enemies in regard to miracles (3:6; 6:5-6; 8:8-21). Thus for Mark miracles can only be misunderstood as long as cross and resurrection are not understood and accepted by followers (8:31-37).

(2) The understanding of parables as a secret language is pre-Markan. Mark also stresses the secret of the kingdom of God, which is revealed only to those whom Jesus himself instructs (4:34) and whose eyes God himself opens (8:22-26; 10:46-52). But he can no longer separate those outside from those inside, as is still done in 4:11-12, a passage that he no doubt adopted from the tradition, and also in the writings of the Jewish monks of the Dead Sea. According to Mark the disciples also belong to those who do not understand (4:13; see 2.5 above), and in the end it is a Gentile who can "see," whereas the disciples have left Jesus (15:39; 14:50). If a reader can understand who Jesus is, then he should know that he owes it to a miracle of God.

(3) The supernatural knowledge of the demons is likewise a traditional trait. Mark uses it to alert the reader to that something extra of Jesus vis-à-vis contemporary, but also Old Testament-prophetic miracle workers (1:24; 3:11); but true faith in the Son of God will be given only by God's own voice in the words of Jesus (9:7; cf. 1:11).

(4) The blindness of the disciples is the means of asserting that faith and discipleship are totally a gift of God, an event of his grace.[192]

25.6 Theology of the Cross. Mark is so variously interpreted because he in fact combines such varied traditions; above all, miracle stories and an apocalyptic view of the future (chap. 13) are connected with the story of the passion. Jesus' authority for cleansing the Temple and cursing the fig tree (11:12-28) is thus also reported within the passion story and located in Jerusalem, and the mention of the one to come is already connected with the first announcement of passion and resurrection and the appended summons to discipleship in this way (8:31-38). Quite apart from the question of whether these different tendencies originally derived from different communities or continued side by side in the same community (see 8 above), such an overall view is also a theologically essential accomplishment. The special Markan accent consists in the fact that Jesus reveals himself more and more clearly as who he is—which the reader has known since 1:1 or at least 1:11—as the Son of God, who according to 1:2-3 fulfills the Old Testament (see 25.2 above). He does this, however, precisely not through greater and greater miraculous deeds, which at best convince only the demons. God's voice at the baptism, which was only for Jesus himself (1:11) and also drove him immediately into the wilderness and the struggle with Satan, is also heard at the transfiguration by the disciples, who only briefly see his actual position and are immediately

126

referred to his word (9:7). But the revelation that makes possible for the first time the human confession of the Son of God is his death on the cross (15:39). That this must be told at the end of the Gospel is, of course, historically predetermined. It is already announced in 3:6, however, and in a certain sense is also already indicated by the arrest of the Baptist in 1:14 as a heading for all that is about to be told.

25.7 Contrast with the Confessional Formulas and Hymns and with Paul. A bridge to the concept of a Son who eternally dwells with God and who comes to earth is, of course, not provided—actually even less than in Q (see 7.8 above). One cannot, however, maintain that Mark consciously suppressed such ideas or even merely excluded them. Jesus' sayings such as 2:17; 10:45 ("I came not to call the righteous" or "to be served"); 9:19 ("O faithless generation, how long am I to be with you?"); 13:32 (". . . not even the angels in heaven, nor the Son, but only the Father"); and the sending of the son in the parable of 12:6-8 are not protected from such an interpretation, although they would also be possible on the lips of an eschatological prophet. In other ways, too, Mark's theology of the cross is certainly not identical with Pauline theology. In Mark the "epiphany" of Jesus' authority is seen completely positively in his miraculous deeds, although it still remains "secret" and can even lead astray unless one follows the crucified and resurrected one. Different from Paul, Mark also sees the danger to his readers less in boasting, against which the justification of the godless is to be proclaimed, than in the shortcomings of discipleship, for which a renewed exhortation is made. This occurs on the one hand with the image of Jesus' way, on the other with the prospect of the second coming. Jesus' whole life is confirmed by the resurrection—just as the suffering righteous one, according to Wis 2:10-20; 5:1-5, is confirmed by his exaltation to God (see 7.9 above)—and will evoke followers. His resurrection brings the expectation of his final coming at the end of the ages and thus substantiates the urgency of discipleship. It always stands under the sign of the one who once went to the cross in order "to serve and to give his life as a ransom for many" (10:45; 14:24), who came "not to call the righteous, but sinners" (2:17).

25.8 Proclamation as Narrative. It is a crucial theological act that Mark wrote a gospel at all, and thus took seriously the idea that narrative represents a form of proclamation of God's action that is just as necessary as the formulation of confessions and the call to a decision to believe and to live out of faith. This act is preconditioned by the Old Testament. There, alongside the confessions that praise God and the commandments that describe a life founded on them, the history of God with Israel is handed down in narrative fashion. Both can appear mixed together beside and within each other in the same psalm or prophetic book. Mark's undertaking was essential; it resolutely recorded the beginnings of the narrative tradition, above all against the danger of a pure ideology, that is, a faith that lives from statements such as those of justification of the godless, forgiveness of sins, and the necessity of holding the right truths, without basing all of that on God's historical action in Jesus of Nazareth. One could then see Jesus as the first representative or even as the symbol of this correct way of thinking—just as one can say Plato was the first representative of Platonic philosophy or as the myth of Attis symbolically portrays what repeatedly takes place in the human soul, without knowing more about Plato's life or even believing in a real Attis living on earth. Jesus would then remain at best a teacher and perhaps also a model of such faith. For Paul the fact that the Messiah had to die the death on the cross cursed by God (Gal 3:13) was such a scandal that the rooting of his faith in this shocking history of Jesus remained central for him and was never for a moment called into question. That changed, however, around the year 70. For the Gentile-Christian church this story, which had been played out in a distant corner of the Roman Empire, was moving farther and farther away and threatened to fade away entirely. It was precisely the decision to take it up in narrative form, in which its significance was not simply fixed "ideologically" but always had to be newly perceived and believed, that preserved the church in the following centuries from becoming simply one more religiously tinted ideology among others. That, quite apart from the content, is still the foremost contribution of Mark, and in part also of his predecessors, to the overall message of the New Testament.[193]

26. THE GOSPEL ACCORDING TO MATTHEW

26.1 Author, Date, Place. Since Matthew presupposes the Gospel of Mark (see 7.1 above), a date around the year 80 is suggested for the writing of this Gospel. A Gentile-Christian author has been proposed or, conversely, a Jew who still belongs to the synagogue and struggles there against the rejection of Jesus.[194] Speaking against both extremes are, on the one hand, the rooting in Israel with the strict attitude toward the law (see 26.7-8 below) and, on the other, the sharp rejection of the Jews (see 26.6 below). Thus we may think of a Jewish Christian and particularly of a Jewish-Christian scribe as described in 13:52. Yet James, the brother of Jesus and later leader of the Jerusalem church, plays no role, while Peter is the church's crucial bearer of Jesus' teachings. This suggests Syria as the location more than Palestine itself, where James took over the leadership after Peter's departure (Acts 12:17; 21:18; first named in Galatians in 2:9 in contrast to 1:18-19). In Antioch Peter also plays an important role according to Gal 2:11 (cf. 9.2 above). In Matt 9:9 the tax collector called by Jesus is named Matthew (in Mark 2:14 Levi). The author, however, is not an eyewitness of Jesus' life, as shown already by the use of Mark's Gospel. It is conceivable that someone traced the Q collection of Jesus' sayings (see 7.3 above) back to a Matthew, which then prompted the change of name (see the Papias testimony in 7.1 and n. 54 above). The extent to which Papias still had reliable information is, of course, uncertain; he also supplies fantastic stories, and his note is hardly applicable to the whole Gospel if he is really speaking only of the sayings of Jesus that Matthew gathered together in Hebrew. Our Gospel is no translation: it was written in Greek. Some of the Old Testament quotations also agree only with the text of the Greek translation of the Old Testament (e.g., *virgin* in 1:23).

26.2 Relationship to Mark and Q. The fact that Matthew wrote his book shows that for him Mark was not sufficient, though he incorporated Mark almost entirely, with occasional abbreviations. Only the parable of the seed growing by itself is omitted without substitution, perhaps because it represents human beings as totally passive (Mark 4:26-29), as is the introduction in Mark 3:20-21, according to which Jesus' family thinks he is crazy, which, naturally, is shocking. Both are also missing in Luke; were these already deleted from the copies of Mark that they used? In addition, Matthew also omitted Mark 1:22-28 and 12:41-44: the first because the confession of the demons was suspect, the second because Matt 24:1 ("Jesus left the temple") was supposed to follow directly as fulfillment of 23:38-39 ("Behold, your house is forsaken and desolate. For I tell you, you will not see me again, until . . ."').

Beyond Mark, our attention is first drawn to the framework of the Gospel. Chapters 1–2 describe Jesus' birth and earliest childhood, and 28:11-20 the guarding of the grave and the appearance of the resurrected one to the women and the eleven disciples in Galilee. The latter could have originally been in Mark. Both additions demonstrate the unique, all-fulfilling act of God in Jesus. Therefore the book even begins with a genealogy that in three times fourteen (i.e., twice seven) generations runs from Abraham to David, from David (counted again) to the last king before the exile, and from the first king afterward to Jesus (1:1-17). Therefore the book also ends with the promise of Jesus' presence in his church till the end of the world (28:20). There are also four Gentile women at the beginning (1:3, 5, 6) and "all nations" (i.e., Gentiles) at the end (28:19). Moreover, Matthew took Jesus' sayings from Q and inserted them in large blocks: in the Sermon on the Mount (chaps. 5–7), at the sending out of the disciples (chap. 10, where Mark 6:7-13 is much shorter), in the sayings about the Baptist (chap. 11), in the talk of parables (chap. 13, which greatly enlarges Mark 4), in "church order" (chap. 18 as an addition to Mark 9:33-50), in the series of woes to the Pharisees (chap. 23, only briefly indicated in Mark 12:37-40), and in the eschatological speech (chaps. 24 [par. Mark 13] and 25). They usually close with the formula, "And when Jesus finished these sayings . . . " (7:28; 11:1; 13:53; 19:1; 26:1).

26.3 Jesus' Authentication Through Word and Deed. In chapters 3–4 and then again starting in chapter 12, Matthew adopts Mark's order, while repeatedly inserting additional material.[195] In chapters 5–7 he gathers into the great "Sermon on the Mount" sayings of Jesus that are found in various places in Luke, in chapters 8–9 deeds of Jesus that appear in different places in Mark (and Luke), and in some cases only in Luke (Q). Why he does this is clear: in 9:27-34 he tells of the healings of two blind men and of one deaf and dumb, which are found neither in Mark nor Luke, and to a certain extent represent a doubling up of what is told in 20:29-34 and 12:22-24. Why? According to 11:4 the messengers of the Baptist "hear and see" what Jesus has them report to John: "The blind receive their sight and the lame walk, lepers are cleansed and the deaf hear, and the dead are raised up, and the poor have good news preached to them" (11:5). With the expansion in 9:27-34 Matthew succeeds in already having all these miracles narrated in chapters 8–9. The preaching of the good news to the poor happened previously in the Sermon on the Mount (chaps. 5–7), which begins with the sentence, "Blessed are the poor . . ." Thus all of what Jesus claims in his communication to the Baptist has already happened. Behind this is a theological decision that is also revealed in the fact that Matthew took Mark 1:22, "And they were astonished at his teaching, for he taught them as one who had authority, and not as the scribes," and moved it to the end of the Sermon on the Mount (7:28-29). This means that for him it is no longer enough simply to announce like Mark, on the basis of what the disciples perceived after Easter, that the authority of God has been revealed in the teachings of the earthly Jesus. Essential for Matthew is *what* the earthly Jesus taught with such authority. On the basis of his teaching the reader is supposed to form his or her judgment about the divine authority of Jesus. Hence it is similar to Jesus' deeds, which Matthew relates before he, on the basis of these deeds, announces the beginning of the end time. Mark 1:23 and 3:11 are missing: the fact that supernatural, if also "unclean," beings know Jesus' secret and reveal him as the Son of God is not satisfactory to Matthew. The reader is supposed to judge for herself or himself. Only the prophetic word of scripture, which Jesus himself announces as fulfilled, is for him an aid in interpreting these deeds of Jesus as what they really are (11:5). Thus one is not supposed to "believe" on the basis of the evangelist's message that in Jesus God himself has definitively encountered the world, and that this is true already for the earthly as well as for the resurrected and exalted Jesus, without inquiring into such faith. For this would again be a regression into ideology (see 25.8 above). Criteria are indeed given for faith and make possible a judgment that substantiates it, although Matthew also knows that words and deeds are never unambiguous and can likewise lead to lack of faith and opposition (12:14, explained theologically by 12:15-21). Yet even if there is no proof for faith, Jesus still gives us a basis for certainty in his words and deeds, which come to life in us.

26.4 Jesus' Life in His Band of Disciples. It is likewise theologically important that chapter 10 stands between the collections of Jesus' words and deeds (chaps. 5–7, 8–9) and his saying about the fulfillment of time in 11:5, at which these are aimed. Before Jesus speaks the clarifying word, the band of disciples comes to our attention. What is said in 9:35 about Jesus "healing every disease and every infirmity" is literally granted to the disciples four verses later (10:1). Jesus' typical twin activities of proclamation of the kingdom of God and healing of the sick, raising of the dead, cleansing of lepers, casting out of demons is likewise transferred to them (10:7-8). According to 9:36-38 it is not only the twelve, but the "workers in the harvest" of all times who are supposed to teach Israel's "sheep without a shepherd"; Mark 6:34 says this only of Jesus himself. Thus Jesus is also the one who lives on in the authority turned over to his disciples. As much as these disciples are those who were sent out in Jesus' time, to which the evangelist looks back, they are nonetheless transparent to later church members. That is seen already in 9:8, where at the close of the story of the healing of the paralytic the crowd is astonished at what authority has been given "to men" (not just to the Son of man in v. 6, = Mark 2:10). That this means not only the authority to heal but also to forgive sins is seen in 18:21-35 (see 26.5 below) and in the addition to the word over the cup, "poured out for many for the forgiveness of sins" (26:28). The disciples also participate in Jesus' suffering. The story of the storm on the sea (= Mark 4:35-41) begins with 8:18, but Matthew inserts two sayings about discipleship in verses 19-22 and modifies verse 23 so that the disciples "followed" Jesus into the boat and hence into the storm. Thus Matthew sees symbolized in this the little ship of the church and its fate.[196] Therefore he also removes the announcement of persecution and suffering as witness for the world from the eschatological speech (Mark 13:9-13) and places it in the mission speech of Matt 10:17-25, where already in verses 7-16 he has incorporated much of the mission speech from Q (Luke 10:2-12). The saying about bearing one's cross after Jesus, which in Mark 8:34-35 does not come until after Peter's confession, likewise appears in Matt 10:38-39 (and 16:24-25). Even at his baptism by John, Jesus explains in Matthew that it is necessary "for *us* to fulfil all righteousness," thus including his future disciples (3:15). Matt 26:29, 38, 40 also add to the Markan text that Jesus will drink the wine of the feast "with" the disciples in the kingdom of God and that therefore they should now watch "with" him.

In Matthew the disciples are no longer uncomprehending and unbelieving; throughout they are "of little faith" (8:26; 14:31; 16:8). The idea that they have no faith (Mark 4:40) and are blind and deaf like those standing outside (Mark 8:18) has been stricken. In 13:16-17 the disciples are even blessed in contrast to the blind and deaf, because they see and hear what even the prophets and righteous could not see and hear (Luke 10:23-24 Q), while Mark 4:13 almost equates the two. Thus the disciples also symbolize the coming church, which is not blind to Jesus' messiahship, but their faith is not sufficient to hold out against the assaults of earthly life. Already in 14:33, that is, before Peter's confession, the disciples praise Jesus as the true Son of God. This is not hidden from them, but the fact that he is this in all humility goes against everything within them. Therefore even the hard reproach of Peter, who cannot understand the way of suffering, is not softened (16:23), in spite of the immediately preceding blessing.

26.5 The Special Position of Peter. Among the disciples Peter is even more prominent here than in Mark. The blessing given to him stands in the middle of the Gospel (16:17). This does not exclude his also belonging to those "of little faith," indeed to those who think only in human terms (14:31; 16:23). Curiously missing is the appearance of the resurrected one first to Peter (Luke 24:34; I Cor 15:5). The first witnesses according to Matt 28:9 (cf. John 20:14-18) are the women, and Peter is not even especially named as in Mark 16:7 as recipient of the angel's message. He is, however, newly introduced in 15:15; 17:24-27; 18:21, and always in connection with a question of ethical behavior that is important for the community and in such a way that he speaks in the name of all the disciples (cf. 15:15-16; 18:21, 35; also 16:20, 21, 24; 19:27; 26:35). The structure of the special blessing of Peter in 16:17-19 also shows curious parallels to the blessing of all disciples of Jesus in 5:12-16,[197] where they are seen in the category of the prophets (5:12; cf. 10:41). After the words of encouragement, "Blessed are you (pl.)" (with which direct address begins in 5:12) and "Blessed are you (sing.)" (addressed to Peter in 16:17), comes their new definition with "you are" and a symbolic saying ("the salt of the earth," "the rock"), which ends in a promise: the city on the hill cannot remain hidden, the church built on a rock will not be destroyed (cf. also the same terms "loose" and "kingdom of heaven" in 5:19-20 [RSV: "relax"] and 16:19). Moreover, the authority to "bind" and "loose" is given to all church members according to 18:18. As with the rabbis, this means that again and again in newly emerging problems they determine what is obligatory and what is not—for example, in the sabbath or food commandments—and thereby also free either people from guilt or hold them to it. In this the first may fall above all to Peter, the second to the church. This is shown by the continuation in the parable of the servant who was forgiven a fantastically high debt (see 26.9 below), but who oppressed his fellow servant because of a relatively tiny sum. The presence of Jesus at the prayer of the two or three (18:19-20) thus provides the basis of the authority to forgive. Even if we take 16:19 to refer rather to the binding or loosing doctrinal decisions, this is designated with exactly the same words. What Peter and Christian scribes do is distinguished only by the accent from what is promised to all church members. Within the band of all the disciples

Peter is in a special way the guarantor of the tradition and interpretation of Jesus' commandments (28:20). Therefore 16:18 is not the founding of the church but a promise issued in the future tense that through the ongoing tradition of his words, entrusted above all to Peter, Jesus will build his church, the people of God.

26.6 Israel and the Jesus Community. In Matthew this people of God is Israel. The Gentile regions named in Mark 3:8 and 7:31 are omitted. With the possible exception of 15:21, Jesus remains within the borders of Israel. While Mark 7:27 explains that the bread goes first to the children (Israel), then to the dogs (Gentiles), Jesus states in Matt 15:24 that he was sent only to Israel, and he expressly sends his disciples only on a mission to Israel (10:5-6, 23). Jesus is emphatically the "son of David." Also missing is the promise that a house of prayer for all nations will replace the Jewish Temple (Mark 11:17). Not until the eschatological speech is the worldwide proclamation of the gospel foretold, and then only as precondition to the coming final judgment (Matt 24:14; as in Mark 13:10). And only after Israel has finally rejected Jesus (27:25) is the way open for the Gentiles after Easter (28:19). Naturally, this can never support the superiority of a church that in Matthew's time was already strongly characterized by Gentile Christianity.[198] If, namely, 21:23–22:14 and again 22:15–24:51 describe the "trial" of God against Israel with interrogation of the accused, pronouncement of guilt, and meting out and carrying out punishment (where in the first instance the sections are always linked together with repeated key words), then both strands close with the sharp warning to the church of Jesus that things will go exactly the same for it, if it does not keep the faith (22:11-14; 24:42-51). *To it* is given the final threat that they will "weep and gnash their teeth" (22:13; 24:51; also 13:42). It too can become a band of "hypocrites" (24:51). Conversely, the invitation to faith continues for the Jews even after Jesus' death (10:23; 17:27*a*). One could even ask whether 23:29, like Rom 11:25-26, does not expect that at least at the final coming of Jesus even Israel will acknowledge him. Yet the passage remains unclear.

26.7 Love as "Constitutional Law" Above the Jewish Laws. Thus Matthew consciously raises the question of the identity of the Jesus community. As already shown by the rhetorical forms ("this took place in order to fulfill what the prophet said"), no doubt adopted by Matthew from the tradition, this can only be considered by him in the category of fulfillment of the promises given to Israel. Thus community means the people of God gathered and re-created by Jesus and now extending worldwide (see 7.6 above), in whom evil and good live together until the last judgment (parables of the weeds and the fishing net, 13:24-30, 36-43, 47-50). Jesus is therefore first the one who does not abolish the law and prophets, but fulfills them (5:17). The law must be taught and kept (5:18-19). It is even presupposed in 24:20 that in order not to violate the sabbath (newly added vis-à-vis Mark 13:18), one may not use it for flight even when one's life is threatened. But where love is thereby put at risk, as in the food laws that are impossible for Gentiles (15:11), love is more important. The commandment to love one's neighbor is thus "constitutional law" that stands above all individual commandments, as the constitution of a country stands above the administrative laws. Therefore the Golden Rule, which is "the law and the prophets" (7:12), frames, together with 5:17, the heart of the Sermon on the Mount. Therefore the false teachers, against whom we are warned at the conclusion (7:22-23) are those who let love grow cold (24:11-12). Therefore it is said of the commandment to love one's neighbor in 22:40 that on it depends "all the law and the prophets," and it is expressly equated with the commandment to love God. It is also inserted in 19:19 in the material adopted from Mark, just as the Old Testament statement that God desires mercy, not sacrifice, was inserted into 9:13 and 12:7.

26.8 Jesus, the Wisdom of God. The antitheses are also to be understood from this standpoint: not just murder, but even hate, not just the consummated adultery, but even the desire offends God's good will, because it offends one's fellow human being (5:21-48). Jesus is thus primarily the teacher who gives the possibility of a new life and precisely in his good and helpful commandments will always be with his church (28:20). Yet the category of (wisdom) teacher (see 7.7 above) is not adequate. That is shown by a few observations worthy of consideration. Matt 11:19 explains that the wisdom of God is justified (vindicated before God and the whole world) by her deeds, and no longer, as originally and still in Luke 7:35, by her children; but 11:2 speaks of "the deeds of the Christ." Thus he is equated with the "Wisdom" that in the Jewish view was already at work with God at the creation (see 5.6 above). So also Wisdom's statement in Luke 11:49 is quoted in Matt 23:34 as statement of Jesus, and the assertions of Jesus in Matt 11:28-30 are handed down quite similarly in Sir 51:23-24 as assertions of Wisdom. Jesus is thus the Wisdom of God that has become human. Matthew could formulate it thus: "Wisdom" or "the Word (Greek *Logos,* often equated with Wisdom) became flesh," admittedly in a quite different sense from John 1:14, in the authoritative teaching of Jesus (see 7.8 above). Since Wisdom is already identified with God's law in Sir 24:23 (also in Bar 4:1), it is understandable how Jesus, as the law become human, can teach anew the commandments of the Old Testament in the sense willed by God. That the church can really fulfill the law in this way lies in the good gift of Jesus' teaching. It lives and will live until the end of the world because he came.[199]

26.9 Judgment and Forgiveness. Thus both are true: Jesus will also come again for his church as Son-of-man/judge (7:22-23; 13:30, 41; 16:27; 25:31), but judgment is decided by the application of love for the "least of these" (25:40, 45). And Jesus himself is above all the one who richly and unexpectedly rewards those who follow him (20:8-9), invites the people from the thoroughfares to the royal wedding feast (22:9), and is there precisely for those "who labor and are heavy-laden" (11:28-30). In him God's forgiveness of all guilt has come true in an unimaginable way (18:27; the sum owed amounts to 50 million denarii = days' wages!) and will come true again and again (6:12; 26:28; cf. 18:22). The title of honor of Jesus' disciples is "these little ones" (10:42; 18:6, 10, 14). The last will be first, even where they can scarcely display their own accomplishments (20:16).

While the messianic secret hangs over the Jesus of Mark's Gospel and comes to light only after Easter (Mark 9:9), in Matthew everything is concentrated on the earthly Jesus, who, as teacher and as the forerunner who makes the new life possible (28:20), is present in the decisions of the church (18:20). In him Wisdom that was always present with God and working with God became a human being. Guided by Wisdom, the church is on its way to a meeting with the "Son of man" in the last judgment. In this it remains the band of "little ones," who live from his forgiveness. What is new because of Easter—strictly speaking, because of Israel's decision against Jesus—is the explicit opening of the door to all nations through the missionary command.

27. THE GOSPEL ACCORDING TO LUKE

27.1 Author, Date, Place. Luke also knows Mark and Q, probably in a somewhat modified form and perhaps with his special material already attached (see 7.1, 4 above). In a change from the Markan text, Luke 21:20-24 clearly describes the fall of Jerusalem. One usually thinks of the eighties as the time of composition. A Luke is named in Philem 24; Col 4:14; and II Tim 4:11 as a companion of Paul. He cannot be the author, however, since some of the information in Acts does not agree with that in Paul's letters. According to Gal 1:17-18; 2:1 Paul was never in Jerusalem between his first visit and the apostolic council (vs. Acts 11:30; 12:25; yet see 9.1 above). Also, the emphasis on the absolute independence of Paul, who neither received the gospel from anyone nor was taught it (Gal 1:1, 12) is scarcely consistent with the role of Ananias in Acts 9:10-18. According to Acts 9:19-26 Paul remained in the city of Damascus "for several days" after his calling before he traveled to Jerusalem, where they still knew nothing of his conversion; according to Gal 1:17, before his first visit there he was in Arabia three years. In addition, in Jerusalem Paul did not see "the apostles" (Acts 9:27), but only Peter and the Lord's brother James (Gal 1:19). Beside Gal 2:6, the condition for the Gentile

Christians in Acts 15:20 cannot have been decided in the presence of Paul (see 9.1 above). The evident medical information does not go beyond what any educated person could have written. The author belongs to Gentile Christianity and writes somewhere in the Roman Empire. Perhaps his name was Luke, and he was not equated with Paul's companion until later, as it is first attested in Irenaeus around 180. Or the Gospel may have circulated without a name—which is hardly imaginable, since others already existed—or perhaps under another name, until on the basis of Acts with its "we" reports it was then ascribed to Paul's companion Luke.

27.2 Luke as Historian. In his preface Luke consciously reflects on what he is doing. He refers to "many" who have already written a gospel before him. He writes on the basis of tradition from "eyewitnesses" and explains that, "having followed all things closely for some time past," he wants "to write an orderly account." Thus he *wants* to be a historian. At this point he has already made a theological decision. In his opinion faith is fundamentally rooted in what happened historically "before us" and "beyond us," datable according to Roman emperors and Jewish authorities (1:5; 2:1-2; 3:1-2; cf. 3:23). What was implicitly achieved by Mark (see 25.8 above) is reflected and made conscious here. Faith is thus not just a philosophy that teaches the right knowledge and hence also the right attitude vis-à-vis the world and all that we encounter in it. One can adopt a philosophy without knowing where it comes from or who first taught it. Faith can obviously not be adopted without knowing what happened in the life, death, and resurrection of Jesus.

That, however, is only the one side. Secular historians also must investigate past events from the standpoint of their subsequent effects. They cannot possibly recount everything, of course; they must select the events that were really important, which can be known, however, only from the later course of history. Here one cannot set up laws so that one knows in advance what the effects of such events will be. Sometimes a victory unifies previously separated groups into one people; sometimes a defeat forces them to join together out of necessity in order to survive at all. Also, it is not simply human beings who make history. A hail storm can bring to naught a general's most beautiful plan, or a fog can spare a whole army from destruction. All of that must also be seen and considered by secular historians.[200] When Luke sees events as not simply coincidences but as the will of God, then that is naturally his decision of faith, just as it would also be a question of faith to trace the events back to pure coincidence (or to other causes). He knows, therefore, that being an eyewitness is not enough; one must also become a "minister of the word" (1:2) by inquiring into what God intended with the event. This is fundamentally true already in the selection of what one reports as history of Jesus. But it is also true for the consideration of why what is thus reported could be important for the readers of the Gospel. It is simply not the same for everyone and for every time, precisely because the gospel is not an eternally valid philosophy. That God is the living God also means that God's direction is involved in the historical effects of the life, death, and resurrection of Jesus. Therefore Luke writes the Acts of the Apostles, in which he makes clear that neither universally valid laws nor human power nor pure coincidence is responsible for how what is told in the Gospel has proved and continues to prove to be the salvation of the church and the world.

27.3 Structure and Special Material. In comparison with Mark we can see for the most part the same structure of Jesus' Galilean activity before the stay in Jerusalem, which Luke, however, no longer restricts to one week. To be sure, large sections are missing, above all Mark 6:46–8:27a (walking on the water, discussion of purity and food regulations, meeting with the Syrophoenician woman, healing of the deaf and dumb man, feeding the four thousand, demand for a sign, reproach of the disciples in the boat, healing of the blind man). In this way Peter's confession is moved to the vicinity of Bethsaida (9:10), where the disciples had gone, according to Mark 6:45. Thus it seems that this part was missing in the copy of Mark that Luke had before him, for he would scarcely have skipped over so much only in order to shorten or to omit what seemed inappropriate to him. Luke also places childhood stories at the beginning, but different ones from Matthew, and inserts Q material, probably in the order of the source he had before him (see 7.3 above), but in any case not concentrated in certain sections such as the Sermon on the Mount in Matt 5–7. This is related to the fact that Luke wants primarily to narrate and illuminate the history with Q sayings, while Matthew by contrast wants to instruct and thus sees the history more as a framework for the sayings of Jesus. Luke describes the second half of Jesus' activity emphatically as his way to Jerusalem and into suffering, so that the decision in this direction (9:51) more clearly marks a new section than Peter's confession does earlier.

What is important is that Luke's Gospel contains a large number of stories and parables that we find nowhere else, and which perhaps lay before him already gathered in a special source (connected with Q?): the Advent and Christmas stories (chaps. 1–2), the picture of the preacher in Nazareth (4:16-30), the story of the miraculous catch of fish and the calling of Peter (5:1-11), that of the widow in Nain (7:11-17), and of the prostitute in the house of the Pharisee (7:36-50), of the disciples who want to bid fire come down on the Samaritans (9:52-56), of the healing of the ten lepers of whom only one gives thanks (17:12-19), of the chief tax collector Zacchaeus (19:1-10), of Jesus' tears over Jerusalem (19:41-44) and his bloody sweat in Gethsemane (22:44), of his being brought before Herod (23:6-12) and his devotion to the thief (23:40-43), of his walking with the Emmaus disciples (24:13-35) and his appearance before the disciples in Jerusalem (24:36-53); then the parables of the good Samaritan (10:30-37), of the rich fool (12:16-21), of the lost coin and prodigal son (15:8-32), of the dishonest steward (16:1-8) and poor Lazarus (16:19-31), of the judge and the widow (18:1-8), and of the Pharisee and the tax collector (18:9-14). It is also striking how many female figures appear for the first time here or are more emphasized: beside Zechariah Mary receives her quite prominent position, and later also Elizabeth (1:5-56); beside the prophet Simon the prophetess Hanna (2:25-38); the mother of a dead child beside the father also named in Mark (7:11-17; 8:40-56); the sisters Mary and Martha beside the scribe (10:25-42); the women following Jesus beside the disciples (8:1-3); the pleading widow beside the pleading friend also known in Matthew (18:1-5; 11:5-8); the "daughter of Abraham" beside the "son of Abraham" (13:16; 19:9); and the woman with the lost coin beside the shepherd with the lost sheep also named in Matt 18 (15:4-10). Also the support for the poor and the warning against riches are clearly noticeable in Luke's special material. The disciples leave "everything" (5:11, 28; 14:33); blessed are the "poor" and those who "hunger" (without the additions of Matt 5:3, 6), and threatened are the "rich" and the "full" (6:20-21, 24-25; 16:14), also in the parables (12:15; 14:13-14; 16:19-31). Alms are recommended (11:41; 12:33; 19:8). Also prominent in the special stories cited is the love of Jesus for tax collectors, prostitutes, and the crucified criminal. In the passion story Luke tells many things differently, agreeing in part with John. On the night in which Peter denies Jesus, the latter is only arrested, and in the morning only *one* hearing takes place, but later on another one with Herod (23:6-12). It is not impossible that all of that, including the crucifixion of Jesus and his death, took place on the same day, but it is also not easy to imagine.

27.4 The Understanding of Christ. If one asks about the significance of Jesus, what is said appears at first to be curiously unclear. Of course, Luke not only, like Mark and Matthew, knows the polite conversational form of address for Jesus as "Lord," but also names him the "Lord" in his stories; but Acts 2:36 says that only the exaltation to God's right hand made him "Lord." Certainly Jesus is the "Son of God," although the Roman centurion under the cross avoids this title and only calls him "righteous" (Luke 23:47 vs. Mark 15:39), but in what way this is meant never becomes clear. According to Luke 1:35 it is in consequence of the virgin birth; according to 3:22—if the idea there is not just proclamation of Jesus' status—through the gift of God's Spirit; according to 3:23, 38, through his descent from Adam, the "son of God"; and according to Acts 13:33 through his resurrection, in which the word is fulfilled: "Thou art my Son, today I have begotten thee." Only Luke relates the title of God's "servant" to Jesus, but whether as a designation of the suffering one (Isa 53; thus Acts 3:13, 26) or of the royal Davidic ruler (Ezek 34:23-24 and elsewhere; thus Acts 4:25-30) is not specified. In central passages Jesus can simply be proclaimed as a ''man'' identified by miracles (Acts 2:22; cf. 10:38) or as the ''man'' whom God will one day have come as judge (Acts 17:31; 10:42). Therefore it is no wonder that when the high priest asks Jesus in the hearing whether he is the ''Christ,'' Jesus explains that they will see the ''Son of man'' at the right hand of God; then all declare that he is thus the ''Son of God,'' which Jesus accepts (Luke 22:67-70). Accordingly, it seems not to matter whether one calls him Christ, Son of man, or Son of God, because all these titles describe his unique relationship to God.

27.5 Significance of Jesus' Life and Death for Our Salvation. The manner in which Jesus conveys salvation is likewise unclear, though in Luke there are more references to his passion than in the other Gospels. He not only repeats the three announcements of suffering that Mark also knows—the second, incidentally, so that it speaks only of the handing over of the Son of man into the hands of men, without mentioning his resurrection. Even Moses and Elijah point to it at his transfiguration (9:11). Jesus himself speaks of the ''baptism'' waiting for him (12:50), the martyrdom of a prophet in Jerusalem of which he must also partake (13:33), and of the necessity of his suffering before the end times (17:25). Even more important is the whole shaping of his journey to Jerusalem as the way into suffering (from 9:51 on). Only Luke tells the parable of the tenants in the vineyard in such a way that only the son is killed, thus distinguishing his fate from that of the prophets (20:15). Only he quotes Isa 53 as a reference to the suffering righteous one: ''He was reckoned with transgressors'' (22:37). But again it remains unclear how this death is to be understood. The statement of Mark 10:45, that the Son of man has come to serve and to give his life as a ransom for many, is missing. In its place in Luke 19:10 is the saying, ''The Son of man came to seek and to save the lost,'' and a second in 22:27, in a kind of farewell address to the disciples: ''I am among you as one who serves.'' Inserted at this point also is the discussion of the disciples, which precedes Mark 10:45, concerning who is the greatest, and Jesus' assertion that the one who serves is the one who is truly great—though in a somewhat different form. Thus in both cases the whole work of Jesus is seen as this service, not only his death, which of course is certainly included, especially on the last evening before his crucifixion. In the word over the cup at the last supper the expression in Mark 14:24 of the blood ''poured out for you'' (Mark: ''for many'') is adopted, although it is not found in all manuscripts, but is curiously and mechanically appended without really being connected with the sentence. Literally it reads: ''in my blood [dative], that poured out [nominative] for you.'' Finally, we find in Acts 20:28 the reference to ''his own blood,'' with which God has redeemed the church; in the formula this refers to

God's blood, although naturally the blood of Jesus is intended. Again a common expression is more or less mechanically repeated.

This means that Luke is not especially interested in a correct title for Jesus or in precise formulations of his salvific action, but rather in the transmission in narrative fashion of the entire abundance of the special impact made by Jesus and his deeds.

27.6 Neither Ahistorical Proclamation nor Simple Acceptance as Truth. In Luke's time, even more than in Mark's (see 25.8 above), there was the danger of a development in the direction of Gnosticism, in which God's action in creation and history, as well as in the history of Jesus of Nazareth, became unimportant (see 20.2 above). By contrast, the (from a later standpoint, orthodox) church at large stressed the connection with the Old Testament and above all with Jesus. It formulated in its confession—though not expressly until later—what one must believe: incarnation, crucifixion, resurrection, second coming of Jesus Christ. With this the danger gradually arose that one would confuse faith with holding certain statements to be true. We do not know the extent to which this had already become visible in Luke's time and in the place where he lived, or whether he was aware of it. Neither Acts 8:9-11 nor 20:29-30 contain allusions to Gnostic heresies, and there is never any polemic against pure orthodoxy. But, to put it positively, his Gospel stands clearly against both extremes that would threaten his church in the future. Hence he narrates and stresses thereby the church's anchoring in history against any Gnostic detachment. God acted long before we perceived or believed anything. And he narrates in broad profusion without this being subject to summarization in a few central sentences, for example, on the significance of Jesus' death on the cross for salvation. He narrates against any mere holding of something to be true, without knowing already in advance which part of the narration will become God's living word that overwhelms the reader.

27.7 Jesus as *the* Parable of God. Thereby Luke incorporate anew what Jesus wants to express with his parables (see 2.3-4 above). For Jesus it is not a matter of conveying to his listeners instruction that they can take home as new information to supplement their previous knowledge or even to correct it, as pure "orthodoxy" easily misunderstands it. For him it is rather a question of awakening in them a chain of everyday experiences, so that experience with the kingdom of God that is coming upon them will come alive. Just as a parable can never be reduced to a statement interpreting it, so no statement, however correct, can take the place of the total, living abundance of Jesus' life, death, and resurrection. It is certainly true, for example, that Jesus is God's Son, but what "God's Son" means is perceived only by the one who submits to this abundance of Jesus' stories and sayings. Pure orthodoxy, the "kerygma," the

Christian doctrine without the narrative of the Gospels, is thus not enough. Conversely, however, it is clear that a parable in itself means nothing. All of Jesus' listeners know more or less how one bakes bread; he does not need to tell them that. Therefore everything depends on the fact that *Jesus* is recounting the parable and has the authority to introduce it with the formula, "The kingdom of God . . . is like leaven . . ." (13:20-21).

We must say it even more clearly: the story of Jesus becomes the "parable" of God because he, Jesus, *lives* it, and thus he himself is *the* parable of God.[201] Only Luke passes on the parable of the prodigal son, at the end of which the (almost) almighty father stands outside in the darkness with his older son, in the impotence of love that knows it can never compel love in return but can only wait for it, and which has nothing but a fervent heart and a few pitiful words of invitation. That is true because soon afterward the teller of this parable is hanging on a cross, all-powerful ("Do you think that I cannot appeal to my Father, and he will at once send me more than twelve legions of angels?"—Matt 26:53) and yet powerless, without being able to move hands or feet even an inch, waiting for people to open themselves to God's love. Therefore one can employ no other mythos—as Gnosticism did—that would illustrate the proclamation as well as the mythos of Jesus Christ. It is precisely not a question of a new self-understanding, an introspective movement of thought that one can express only through some kind of mythos instead of grasping it in precise sentences. The truth of the message of Christ depends on the fact that it happened in him, in his life, death, and resurrection. The narrated earthly Jesus, from his birth to his meeting with followers and disciples after Easter, is just as necessary a component of faith as the kerygma that proclaims the presence of God and his kingdom in Jesus of Nazareth.

27.8 Salvation History? Luke has been named the theologian of salvation history. This is correct if one wants thereby to designate his interest in the fulfillment of the Old Testament promise and in the providence of God, which carries and guides the apostle on his missionary journey and the church in its temptations. Both are already contained in I Cor 15:3-5: the crucifixion, burial, resurrection, and appearances of Jesus (which continue in meetings with over five hundred, with James, all the apostles, and finally Paul; 15:6-8) happen "in accordance with the scriptures." The Q sayings already explain the fate of Jesus as the end toward which all the destinies of the prophets move as their goal (Luke 11:50-51; 13:34; perhaps also 13:33). Preservation and divine guidance of the church until the Parousia is proclaimed by the eschatological talk in Q, as in Mark. If one thinks, however, of an overall plan according to which God's history of salvation unfolds, then it is to be found in Matt 1:2-16, where the history from Abraham to Jesus unfolds in three times fourteen generations; thus Jesus necessarily had to come at that particular place in history. The Lukan genealogical table (3:23-38) actually runs in a sequence of eleven times seven generations to Jesus as the beginner of the twelfth, messianic period, but we learn this only when we check the count. Luke did not do this and thus knows nothing about it or in any case does not want to tell his readers about it. Paul is familiar with a certain post-Easter course of history according to Rom 9–11: According to God's will Israel had to reject the gospel in order that it might come to the Gentiles and through their faith could then once again attract Israel to the faith, so that finally the multitude of the Gentiles and the whole of Israel will enter salvation. In contrast to this, with Luke all scriptural prophecies seem to have come to an end with the destruction of Jerusalem (Luke 21:22). Certainly God stands over the history of Israel. This is already seen in the fact that Paul turns to the Gentiles only after rejection by the Jews, and that it is also emphasized how three thousand, then five thousand, and finally "ten thousands" (no doubt a round number) of Jews faithful to the law in Jerusalem have accepted the gospel (Acts 2:41; 4:4; 21:20). The church is built on the foundation of Israel. But the salvation-historical summary of the time of the patriarchs and the Exodus from Egypt until David, the "man after God's heart, who did everything according to the will of God," which Paul offers in Acts 13:17-22, breaks off there in order to pass directly to the son of David, Jesus, the "Savior" who was proclaimed beforehand by John. The Old Testament prophets, who otherwise are important to Luke, are not mentioned at all in this historical sketch. Where the history of Israel to Jesus is really carried through, namely, in Stephen's speech (Acts 7), it is the history of Israel's disobedience and resistance. One might wonder whether in both cases the exemplary or the warning reaction of the people to God's offer is what is actually important, since in Acts 17:24-30 the creative acts of God are mentioned only to describe the reaction of humans, namely, their misunderstanding.

27.9 "Preexperiences." In any case, it is striking that the Gospel does not begin with "holy" history narrated in the scripture—as much as the Temple as showplace brings that to mind—but with experiences of a contemporary older couple in whom, of course, the experiences of Abraham and Sarah, Manoah and his wife, Elkanah and Hannah are repeated (1:5-25). Also the prophet and prophetess, who are in the Temple at the presentation of Jesus and proclaim his significance for salvation, are living people and not texts that have become scripture (2:25-38). Thus Luke connects with human experiences of God, and there is a certain historical coincidence in the fact that of the many childless couples precisely this one portrays the definitive, all-fulfilling experience of Mary. Thus the uniqueness of the Christ event consists not in something totally without analogy, not in Christ coming down like a meteor out of the blue. What is told in chapter 1 of the announcement to Mary (1:26-38) largely runs parallel to what also is reported of Zechariah and Elizabeth, who in turn experience what Old Testament couples have already experienced. The special nature of what happens to Mary is to be understood differently. Precisely because the two announcements are so parallel in structure and often even in wording, the differences are all the more important. The first story begins with the description of priestly background and calling, of the couple's great piety and righteousness under the law, and then mentions their plight: childlessness (1:5-7). It then tells how Zechariah goes into the Temple, does what a priest as a rule may do only once in his life, and while there encounters an angel (1:8-11). The second story begins with the angel, and Mary comes into the text only as the goal of his mission (1:26-27). She is a girl twelve to fourteen years old—the normal age for engagement and marriage—in an unknown small town which does not even appear among the many Galilean places named by Josephus. Nothing is said of piety or righteousness under the law, and she also becomes a descendant of David only through her future husband. In no way is she different from the thousands of other girls of her age. What happens to her is in unsurpassable radicality pure grace, unsubstantiated election traceable entirely to God alone: Mary is "filled with grace" (1:28). Even the virgin birth is certainly an enhancement compared to what happened to Elizabeth, but not without analogy at the time, since one assumed of many great figures in Greece and in the Hellenistic world, from Plato to Alexander the Great, that they were born without the action of a man, if also mostly not of a virgin.[202] Thus the uniqueness of Jesus lies in the idea that in him the grace of God has created the one in whom it will meet all people, surpassing and thus fulfilling everything that has gone before, without any sort of human achievement and greatness, indeed not even presupposing the activity of a procreating man. Here all the "preexperiences" of human suffering and divine help from Abraham and Sarah to Zechariah and Elizabeth receive their fulfillment and their meaning.

27.10 "Postexperiences." The time after Easter is, correspondingly, the time of "postexperiences." This is seen most clearly at the death of Stephen, who like Jesus prays for his enemies and commits his spirit into the hands of the Lord (Acts 7:59-60). But now the "Lord" is Jesus, who has appeared to him already as the Son of man so that he may die with a vision of the heavenly glory (7:55). Parallelism and fundamental difference are clear here. This is also true of Paul's journey to Jerusalem, which is similar to Jesus' journey there (19:21; 20:22; 21:4, 10-15). He too is "delivered" like Jesus (21:11; cf. Luke 18:32; 24:7), just as the blood of Stephen is "poured out" like that of Jesus (Acts 22:20; cf. Luke 22:20; 11:50). The disciples have already accompanied Jesus in all his trials (Luke 22:28) and have learned there that his church in general will "through many tribulations . . . enter the kingdom of God" (Acts 14:22). Therefore it is questionable whether one can regard Jesus' life as "the middle of time," framed by the Old Testament and church history, with creation at the beginning and the second coming of Jesus at the end.[203] It is probably better only to separate the time of fulfillment from that of promise, whereby Jesus' death, resurrection, and ascension naturally represent an important caesura within the time of fulfillment. But it is uncertain whether Luke at all expected a time of the church comparable to the Old Testment. In Luke 21:32 he repeats the statement, "This generation will not pass away till all has taken place," namely the coming again of Jesus with all its accompanying phenomena. In Luke 12:45 it is the *evil* servant who thinks, "My master is delayed in coming." In 19:12 Luke stresses redactionally that the Lord will "return," though without saying how quickly. In 21:25 he omits "in those days, after that tribulation" (Mark 13:24), so that the cosmic signs of the second coming follow directly the destruction of Jerusalem and "the times of the Gentiles." According to Acts 2:17-21 the "last days," added redactionally by Luke, have already begun, and the signs of the Spirit will change without interruption into the cosmic end times. The mission to Israel has ended (Acts 28:28) and perhaps also the mission to the Gentiles; in any case, in his "testament" Paul thinks only of the preservation of the church (Acts 20:28-32).

27.11 Continuity with Jewish Piety. We cannot say that in Luke Old Testament-Jewish piety changes without interruption into Christian piety, even if, for example, Paul's confession of his Pharisaism and the "God of our fathers" (Acts 23:6-8; 24:14-21) points in this direction (see 20.4 and n. 150 above). Certainly the Gospel begins and ends in the Temple, yet in the process this has become the place of Jesus' teaching (Luke 19:47; 21:37-38—Lukan additions) and will become the place from which the church begins its mission to the world (Acts 2:46; 5:42; 22:17). Its time has thus run out, as Stephen's speech critical of the Temple shows,[204] which leads to persecution and thus to missions among the Samaritans and Gentiles (Acts 7:47-50; 8:1-4; 11:19-21). More important still, Jewish piety already stands in the light of Advent only where people, like Zechariah and Elizabeth, Mary, Simeon and Anna, wait with empty hands and are totally oriented toward what new thing God will grant (Luke 1–2). Just like Paul, Luke knows that God has nothing to do with those who want to justify themselves, who trust in their own piety and righteousness under the law (Luke 10:29; 16:15; 18:9; 20:20). But he has extended that to everything in which humans put their trust and with which they believe they can survive, above all riches and possessions (16:14 beside 15; 12:16-21; 16:19-31).

28. THE ACTS OF THE APOSTLES

28.1 Author, Date, Sources. Certainly the Acts of the Apostles comes from the same author as Luke's Gospel. The style is the same. According to 1:2 the Gospel goes to the ascension (Luke 24:51; the omission in some manuscripts is later harmonization). But this is told again in Acts 1:9-11 and dated the fortieth day after Easter. Luke 3:20, however, also reports in advance the arrest of the Baptist; thus Luke 24:51 may anticipate the ascension, although it gives the impression that it happens on Easter Sunday evening. Or did Luke think that the resurrected one repeatedly came from heaven and on the fortieth day made his final departure? It is improbable that an originally unitary work was divided into two books and a new conclusion and foreword were written, because it is hardly imaginable that the contradiction was created by a redactor. Moreover, small but clear changes in style suggest that the author undertook the second part of his work only after the passage of some time.[205]

The problem of sources is difficult. Written in the *we* style are 16:10-17 (Troas to Philippi); 20:5-15 (Philippi to Miletus); 21:1-18 (Miletus to Jerusalem); 27:1–28:16 (Caesarea to Rome). That could derive from a terse travel report, scarcely more than a list of stops before Jerusalem, which may have come from a companion of Paul. We can already see in many manuscripts, however, that *we* was subsequently added in other places (11:28; 16:8, 13; 21:29; 27:19); therefore that could also have happened in the beginning.[206] Yet in the travel report in 27:9-11, 21-26, 31, 33-38 the sections in which Paul is the subject are clearly distinguished from those with *we* and *they;* the former also occasionally contradict the latter: in verse 11 only the captain and shipowner decide against Paul, in verse 12 the majority; in verse 20 a storm is described that leaves no more hope, in verse 21 Paul makes a speech standing up; according to verses 3*b* and 43 Paul is a prisoner, otherwise he appears free and even gives directions to the captain.[207] Many things also speak for an Antiochene source: the apostolic decree (15:20) is communicated to Paul according to 21:25 as if he had not been present (see 9.1 above); the number of apostles is slightly changed (1:13; cf. Luke 6:14-16); lists of names appear. Yet such a source cannot at present be more closely defined. The speeches of Peter and Paul, on the other hand, conform largely to a schema by which only the listeners (Jews, God-fearers, Gentiles) determine certain differences, but not the person speaking.[208] Finally, it is curious that in a number of manuscripts we have a quite different text, which is also longer by about one thirtieth, that is, by almost a chapter. Whether Luke[209] or someone else composed a kind of "second edition" can no longer be determined. Acts closes before the martyrdom of Paul (in the year 64?), to which *I Clem.* 5 (ca. A.D. 96) no doubt alludes along with that of Peter. This is hardly to be traced back to the fact that it was written before this date and thus before the Gospel, for 20:25 in fact presupposes the death of the apostle. Probably it closes thus because the relatively positive picture of the Roman authorities vis-à-vis the mission of Paul was not supposed to be disturbed. We begin to detect the exoneration of the Romans—who, naturally, do not permit themselves to be won for the faith, but with few exceptions (e.g., 24:26) treat Paul correctly—and, connected with this, the incrimination of the Jews. In this the Acts of the Apostles is an apology for Christianity that also colors historical fact.

28.2 The "Tactlessness" of the Acts of the Apostles? The title, the Acts of the Apostles, was not added until later. It is even more one-sided than the usual German translation, *Apostelgeschichte* ("apostle history"). If we understand the book in that way, we can also understand F. Overbeck's dictum that it is "a tactlessness of world-historical dimensions . . . to place an apostle history next to the gospel."[210] Actually, however, it is *God's* action in his post-Easter church that is described in historical perspective, and it is precisely this, theologically speaking, that is essential. The gospel is not only proclamation in the form of historical narrative; it also creates history on its own (see 27.2 above). This posthistory is also not to be comprehended in a particular system. In curious roundabout ways the gospel comes to Europe and finally to Rome. Piety that inquires after God's will (13:1-3) can have decisive consequences just as much as can human vices (24:24-27; cf. 26:32), pure misunderstandings (21:28-29), or the direct, unexpected intervention of God (16:6-10). God in his freedom may reveal from time to time something of his goals, and people may later understand the always surprising paths to those goals as God's guidance; but that is in any case not a schema that we could construct beforehand or afterward as having continuing validity. It is, of course, a question of experiences with God that are similar to what happened fundamentally in Jesus Christ (see 27.10 above); but such "postexperience" remains a testimony and sign of the absolute freedom of God, which is never at human disposal.

28.3 Jesus' Presence after Easter? Admittedly, one cannot simply expand the beginning of the book, "In the first book . . . I have dealt with all that Jesus began to do and teach . . ." (1:1) so that Acts describes what he continued to do and teach. The expression "began to" often occurs without any reflection about a continuation. Also Jesus scarcely appears in Acts as subject apart from the appearances to the eleven and Paul, in visions and dreams (7:56; 9:10; 18:9; 23:11), and in the one place, 16:14, according to which "the Lord [probably Jesus] opened her [Lydia's] heart." Otherwise it is the Holy Spirit, occasionally the "Spirit of Jesus" (16:7), the angel, the name, or the hand of the Lord that acts. The distinction from the earthly service of Jesus in the Gospel is thus preserved throughout, but what the disciples asked according to

146

Luke 17:5, "Lord, increase our faith," was fulfilled in Acts. This underlines that God's revelation in Jesus Christ is visible and is transformed into human faith only where God himself grants it.

28.4 The Conception of the Church. Luke also narratively proclaims how the various local churches, which are indebted to various messengers of Jesus, through God's action form a unity, which, however, is repeatedly in danger. The beginnings of the conception of a worldwide church of Jesus are already found in the letters to the Colossians and the Ephesians (see 17.7, 18.6 above), but no thought had been given to a thoroughly organized structure. Luke says nothing about the collection, which could best express and assure a unitary organization, although he knows about it (Acts 24:17). According to Gal 2:10, but not Acts 15, it is named as a condition for a worldwide mission. In its place comes a voluntary donation, recommended by charismatic prophets and understood purely as charity (11:27-30; 12:25). In this connection there appear for the first time Christian elders (11:30), such as are typical for the ordering of the Jewish congregation (Luke 7:3; Acts 4:5; etc.), without their function being named or their introduction even being mentioned. It is also mentioned in passing (14:23) that Paul and Barnabas, who according to Luke do not belong to the twelve apostles, also select elders in the newly founded churches (see 11.4 above). We learn from Paul's letters, not from Acts, that he sends various co-workers as his envoys into the churches, above all to Corinth. The apostolic letters of Paul, which represent a sign of a certain authority over the churches, are entirely missing; Luke does not know them or, in any case, does not use them. Paul himself, to be sure, receives a laying on of hands, but from an ordinary church member (9:17).[211] He is sent out together with Barnabas under the laying on of hands by the Antiochene "prophets and teachers" (13:1-3). Thus we find nothing about apostolic succession, the view that only the unbroken passing on of official authority through ordination by the first apostles until today authorizes an officeholder for his ministry. Rather, the emphasis is on the unique position of the apostle, who guarantees continuity to Jesus' earthly work, his crucifixion, and his resurrection, a function that is later assumed by the New Testament Scripture. Perhaps Luke consciously restricts the circle of apostles to eyewitnesses of the earthly Jesus (1:21-22) and has the period of God's revelation in Jesus Christ end with the ascension in order to forestall an overgrowth of erroneous prophetic revelations (cf. Eph 2:20). That could also be the reason that he reports nothing of the work of the prophets in the early church of Jerusalem (see 3.2 above). Also the founder of the mission to the Gentiles is one of the twelve, namely, Peter (11:18; 15:7), not Paul or the scattered Hellenists of 11:19-20. That is hardly historical, although Peter certainly did not block the mission to the Gentiles (Gal 2:6-9, 14-16), and there were also missionaries to the Gentiles before and in addition to Paul (e.g., in Rome).

Thus the special position of the twelve apostles (without Paul) is certainly emphasized as the foundation of the worldwide church of Jesus, but not the transmission of this authority in a particular office. In the unexpected freedom of God Paul is called, and he receives guiding visions or words of God, as once Peter did, but also as many more prophets do.

28.5 Baptism by Water and Spirit. A unified confession of faith in fixed form is also lacking. In 8:37 it was not inserted until later, and at Pentecost the requirement is repentance, not belief in a particular creed (see 27.4-5 above). Entry into the church, to be sure, always occurs through baptism. This presupposes, naturally, that the candidate for baptism learns beforehand who the "Lord" or "Christ" is under whose name he is placed (2:36; 8:5; etc.). Occasionally it may be declared of only one person that he (because of a special experience) has come to faith, and yet the baptism of his whole household is reported (16:31-33). Baptism is also not a rite that the church "administers" and which through its correct execution assures salvation. Luke knows no baptismal command. But in 1:5 and 11:16 he repeats the Baptist's saying of the baptism of the Spirit, which replaces the water baptism of John. Now, however, it is quoted as a saying of Jesus, and in 11:16 it defends precisely the baptism of the first Gentiles by water, which obviously in the Lukan understanding includes the baptism of the Spirit (2:38; 10:47). In this Luke seems not at all to be interested in whether the Spirit is given simultaneously with the water baptism (2:38 and throughout, where nothing is said of the gift of the Spirit) or exceptionally once beforehand (10:44-48) or afterward (8:15-16). In 1:5 and 11:16 he leaves out the word of baptism "with fire" (Luke 3:16). This shows that he no doubt sees in the Pentecost event the first fulfillment of this promise, but does not equate the "tongues as of fire" (2:3) with this baptism of fire. The fact that the already baptized disciples of John are again baptized with water in order immediately thereafter to receive the Spirit through the laying on of hands by Paul (19:5-6) shows how Luke closely connects water and Spirit baptism. The special position of the apostles is seen in the fact that they alone are not baptized with water, or at least that in any case it is nowhere reported (but different for Paul in 9:18!).

28.6 Scripture-Office-Dogma? Certainly Luke stresses the unalterable connection with the Jesus event reported in the Gospel; it is qualified as God's action by predictions in "the scriptures"; often only a general reference is given without indicating particular passages (Luke 18:31; 21:22; 24:25-27, 32, 44-46; Acts 3:18, 21, 24; 10:43; 13:27, 29; 17:2; 18:28; 24:14; 26:22, 27; 28:23); cf. I Cor 15:3-5. But the threefold authority of early Catholicism, scripture-office-confession of faith (dogma), has in any case not yet been achieved (see 20.3 and 24.5 above).

CHAPTER SIX

The Johannine Circle

29. THE GOSPEL ACCORDING TO JOHN

29.1 Sources? In this "child of sorrow of New Testament scholarship"[212] just about everything is disputed. The problem concerns what one regards as adopted tradition, what as work of the evangelist, what as still later redaction, and whether one must not at every stage deal with different hands or designs. Those who limit themselves to interpreting the Gospel in its present form must also ask whether its message lies above all in the great speeches, for which the stories serve as illustrations, or whether the miracle reports are crucial and the speeches only interpret them. It is also probable that a "sign source" was available.[213] The miracle in Cana is told as the first sign, the healing of the official's son as the second (2:11; 4:54), although according to 2:23; 3:2 Jesus did many signs in the meantime in Jerusalem. These sections are also stylistically different from the others. Probably also belonging to the same source are the feeding of the five thousand with Jesus' subsequent walking on water and the demand for a sign (6:1-31), which in their particulars are told differently from the other Gospels, but in the same order. Also the basic material of other miracle stories may go back to this source, so that 20:30-31 perhaps marks their end (see 7.2 above). Thus the statement that these signs are written down here so that the reader may come to faith could correspond more to the conviction of the author of this source than that of the evangelist. The fact that the latter adopted it, however, shows that he did not disagree with it. Whether there were other sources, for example, for the speeches, is very questionable.[214] For the passion story we may assume an independent tradition agreeing in some ways with Luke's (see 7.2 above), whether only oral or, more likely, already fixed in writing.

29.2 Differences from the Other Gospels. Presumably the author did not know the other Gospels, since compared to them he relates quite different stories or, at most, some of the special material that Luke also uses. Except for the passion story (cf. also 4.4 above) and the already mentioned feeding complex, only the purging of the Temple and the anointing appear to some degree similar, but in a different order than the first three Gospels. Moreover, we find Peter's confession in the middle of Jesus' activity in all the Gospels, but it reads differently in John 6:69 ("You are the Holy One of God"; cf. Mark 1:24). Only here, incidentally, is it said that Jesus had *twelve* disciples, apart from the traditional expression in 20:24. Quite different is the news of Jesus' more extensive activity in Jerusalem. Actually only the sections 2:1-12; 4:43-54; 6:1-7, 10, which probably belong to the sign source, clearly take place in Galilee. Three Passover feasts are also mentioned (2:13, 23; 6:4; 11:55; 12:1; 18:28), while in the other Gospels one gets the impression of only a one-year ministry of Jesus. No single healing corresponds to any mentioned in the other Gospels, and the driving out of demons is totally absent. Behind the healing of the official's son (4:46-54), to be sure, stands the same tradition as behind that of the servant in Capernaum (Luke 7:1-10 Q), but this shows precisely how differently it developed. Different also is the dating of Jesus' death. His passion is still on a Friday, but it is the day before, not on the Passover itself; historically, John is more probable at this point. Especially striking is the fact that except for the short comparison of the consequence of distress to the joy resulting from childbirth in 16:21, not a single parable is passed on, for the long "I am" speeches are something else (see 29.5 below). In general, in place of Jesus' short sayings, completely focused on the situation, we have long speeches and dialogues, even a three-chapter-long farewell speech to the disciples.

29.3 Author. There is no testimony that the author is the disciple John until the middle or end of the second century. In the Gospel the disciple "whom Jesus loved" (13:23) and who, according to 21:24, "has written these things" is never given a name. If "another disciple . . . known to the high priest" (18:15) is the same one, this points rather to someone from Jerusalem who did not belong to the twelve. Indeed, John never says that only the twelve sat at the last supper. This could also explain the concentration of this Gospel on Jerusalem, even if this disciple was only the beginning of an ongoing tradition. John came to mind because of the first four disciples called according to Mark 1:16-20, Andrew and Peter are named in 1:40-41, in 21:2 also the sons of Zebedee, one of whom, James, died early, however, according to Acts 12:2. Since, moreover, 1:41 states that Andrew "first" showed his brother to Jesus, it was assumed that the other (unnamed!) disciple (1:35, 37) was John (or perhaps James), so that John either came to Jesus as the first or was fetched by his brother. The author is familiar with the customs (2:6, 13; 6:4; 7:2-3, 8, 22, 37, 51; 10:22; 18:28; 19:31, 42) and the messianic expectations (1:25, 41, 49; 4:25; 6:14; 7:26-27, 40-42, 52) of Palestinian Judaism. Certainly 11:51 and 18:13 give the impression that the high priest is elected for only one year, but perhaps that is not the meaning. Nevertheless, the Gospel is not written by an eyewitness. How could one explain that the raising of Lazarus, the most miraculous of all Jesus' miracles, remained unknown to the other evangelists when it happened so publicly and with such impact (11:45-54; 12:9-11)? It is possible that the community from which the book came traced its tradition back to the disciple named in 13:23 etc. In 21:24 the *we* of those who end the Gospel with these verses is distinguished from the disciple "who is bearing witness to these things, and who has written these things" (referring to what?). Verse 23, incidentally, presupposes that he has already died.[215]

Chapter 21 is an epilogue after the closing in 20:30-31, presumably written by a different hand.[216] At the close of chapter 5 Jesus is in Jerusalem; 6:1 continues, "After this Jesus went to the other side of the Sea of Galilee, which is the Sea of Tiberias," as if Jesus were still, as in 4:46-54, somewhere on the west side in Galilee, from which in 7:10 he again goes up to Jerusalem. Also striking, if not inexplicable, is the reference in 7:23 to the sabbath healing of 5:1-11, as if it had just happened. If chapter 6 stood before chapter 5, everything would be much clearer. In 14:31 Jesus' talk to the disciples seems to be finished: "Rise, let us go hence"; but it still continues for two more chapters. If these were placed between 13:35 and 36, the continuity would be clearer here also. In any case, however one evaluates it, the Gospel was not finished in *one* draft, but expanded or assembled from individual pieces.[217]

29.4 Various Strata? Date. Did the "we" of 21:24 not only arrange but also expand? In 5:24-25 Jesus explains that whoever hears his word and believes has passed from death to life and will come no more to judgment, and therefore "the hour is coming, and is now," when the dead will hear Jesus' voice and live. Then verse 28 explains that the hour is coming (without "and now is") when all who are in the *tombs* will hear his voice (which in verse 24 is understood positively as "believe") and be raised to judgment. Similarly, in 6:39, 40, 44, 54 (cf. 12:48) the formula, "and I will raise him up at the last day," seems added on. Finally, in 6:51-58 the bread of life, about which Jesus says, "He who comes to me shall not hunger, and he who believes in me shall never thirst" (6:35), refers in a crass way to "eating" Jesus' body and "drinking" his blood in the Lord's Supper.[218] Is that a later elaboration more in agreement with church doctrine? Or can it be explained with the adoption of traditional statements, for example, from the liturgy of the church? In 3:3, 5 this is very likely, for John never otherwise speaks of the "kingdom of God" and thus adopted this from the tradition. Now verse 5 ("Unless one is born of water and the Spirit, he cannot enter the kingdom of God'') reminds us a lot of Matt 18:3 and thus could come from the baptismal liturgy. Verse 3 (''Unless one is born from above, he cannot see the kingdom of God'') would then be the more Johannized form, which mentions neither the water nor a (future) entrance into the kingdom of God, but a ''seeing'' already valid now. Thus the writer could also have adopted 6:51-58 from the Lord's Supper liturgy.[219]

We can only say with any certainty that the evangelist was an extraordinary theologian otherwise unknown to us, who had sources at his disposal and presumably had gathered around himself a circle of disciples or students, who edited or at least enlarged his work, and who also are possible authors of the three letters (see 30.1 below). He can hardly have written later than ca. A.D. 100, since a papyrus fragment found in Egypt proves that his Gospel was known there soon after that date.[220] Perhaps he is to be placed considerably earlier.

29.5 The ''I Am'' Speeches. It is clear that here we have a quite different kind of Gospel from the first three. Here the mystery of Jesus' identity is solved from the very beginning, and in his long ''I am'' speeches, furthermore, Jesus explains—always and only—who he is and what his coming means. Although in the other Gospels the activity of God's kingdom becomes visible in the words and deeds of Jesus, before Easter we do not see how that is connected with Jesus' relationship to God. On the one hand, to be sure, the Old Testament quotations in Mark 1:2-3 and the infancy narratives in Matt 1–2 and Luke 1–2 proclaim from the beginning that the topic here is the one in whom all of God's promises are fulfilled. On the other hand, the multiplicity of designations for Jesus in John (logos, Son of God, Son of man, Lamb of God, Messiah, the Holy One of God) point to the mystery of his person, for which none of these titles would be the single correct one. That is true even for the highest predicate that is attributed to Jesus here: *God*. It is not expressed in the sense of a formula of faith, but as a spontaneous cry of adoration (20:28), and probably also in the prologue, but there it is in mysterious connection with his character as Son (1:18).

Certainly Jesus' self-concept occurs in the ''I am'' speeches. Their nature is neither that of parable nor of allegory, but of direct identification. Strictly speaking, they do not say what Jesus is, but where community (''vine''—see 29.6 below), food (''bread'') and drink (''water''), knowledge (''light''), leadership (''shepherd''), and indeed the fullness of life (''the resurrection and the life'') are only to be found. *I* is not the subject, but the predicate that signifies the one who is everything that human beings are seeking and longing for. Therefore he is the ''true'' vine, the ''good'' shepherd, the bread ''of life.'' When we use these terms, it is always just in a faded, unreal sense. There is absolutely no earthly reality that can describe the Son of God, no earthly designations that can define him. At most they can, in a very preliminary way, point in the direction in which the encounter with him may be experienced.

With this we have again reached, in a curiously different form, what is crucial in Jesus' proclamation: There is no earthly reality that can define the reality of God. No earthly image can even come close to God. But God *becomes* reality, where Jesus encounters the world. Therefore Jesus spoke in parables, and their truth consisted in the fact that *he*, in his authority, told them (see 2.3 above). In the post-Easter church he was no longer the teller; therefore the church *had to* "christologize" them, that is, to make expressly clear that the parable that Jesus told becomes an event because in Jesus' actions and preaching the kingdom of God has really broken in (see 2.5 above). That is precisely what also happens in these Johannine speeches in which Jesus proclaims, "*I* am the true . . ."

29.6 The Conception of the Church. At the same time this says that Jesus, always is what he is in communion with his disciples, without abolishing the clear difference between him, who can say of himself, "*I* am the true vine" (15:1), and the disciples totally dependent on him, the individual "branches." In the Old Testament the vine is a regular image for Israel. A Jewish writing of the time says of Israel that its roots reached into the underworld and its branches into heaven.[221] In John 1:51 the "Son of man" is presented as the new Jacob (= Israel: Gen 28:12; 35:10). What the people of Israel represented in a very incomplete way, repeatedly pierced by contrary behavior, became reality in Jesus: the full response to God's grace in the trusting and obedient openness to God and hence oneness with the Father (10:30). As the true Jacob/Israel Jesus does not remain alone, but incorporates into himself all his disciples as his branches as long as they remain with him. At first this image corresponds fully to the Pauline image of the body and its members (see 11.4 above), but apart from the fact that it is related to Jacob/Israel, that is, to the people of God and not, as in Paul, to Adam (= "humanity" in Hebrew), it is important to John 15:1 to present Jesus as the only one in whom the "vine" signified by God is really to be found. Something similar is true of the shepherd and his sheep (10:11-18) or the grain of wheat and the fruit that it bears (12:24). In relation to this, Paul emphasizes the reciprocal ministries that the members afford each other; John, the immediacy of Christ to all "branches." No branch serves another, no sheep its fellow sheep, and no grain of wheat its neighbor. But they are one in that they all live from the true vine, are tended by the good shepherd, and are borne and nourished by the same wheat stem (see 30.4 below). Precisely in this oneness, then, they are also a testimony to the world (17:18, 21). Thus Jesus is the one in whom everything is to be found that humanity is seeking and striving for: in addition to fellowship, we have not only festivity and leadership and fruitfulness, but also food and drink, knowledge and abundant life. Only in Jesus can all this be found in a way that does not disappear again after a few hours or years. Therefore Jesus can bear witness to nothing else but his significance for the world. Thus exactly what became true in Jesus' whole activity, in word and deed and experience, is again expressed here in a very reflective way.

29.7 "Exaltation" to the Cross. Already in 3:14 the crucifixion of Jesus is foretold—albeit as a "lifting up" of the "Son of man." According to 6:62 "the Son of man ascending to where he was before" is even more scandalous and thus no doubt likewise indicates what is being played out in the crucifixion. In 12:32-34 Jesus says that the "Son of man" lifted up on the cross (also v. 23) will draw all people to himself, and that precisely this will be his "glorification," by which Jesus is troubled (vv. 27-28). Hence it is going to the cross itself that unites him with God, so that Father and Son become one (10:30). In a certain sense cross, resurrection, and ascension are thus seen as a single event (see 21.3 above),[222] just as also the last judgment, now already given over to the "Son of man" (5:27), will be executed according to 3:18 and 5:24 in the act of faith or unfaith vis-à-vis the one lifted up on the cross (3:14-15). Nevertheless, crucifixion and resurrection, from which according to 20:17 even the ascension (on Easter Sunday) seems to be distinguished, are *told,* that is, presented as a sequence. Historical thinking, which thinks in past-present-future, is thus not simply abandoned. Therefore the category of the future, even beyond death (if admittedly, apart from the epilogue in 21:22, also not expressly beyond the end of the world and second coming), is, even if one excludes passages like those named in 29.4 as later additions, also maintained:[223] 11:25-26; 12:25; 17:24; perhaps also 12:50; 14:23. Also according to 5:25, the "hour" is not just now; it is also "coming."

29.8 Present-day Interpretations. Must we see in John someone who stresses in Gnostic language, but in contradiction to Gnosticism (see 20.2 above), that salvation is paradoxically to be found in the one who "became flesh," goes through his life as a human being, and dies on the cross, yet who invites people not to understand themselves out of their own possibilities or to trust in them, but to open themselves entirely to God in a decision that is made ever anew?[224] But does John speak so nonvisually, so abstractly of the faith as if it were a human decision anchored only in paradox? Does he not adopt crass miracle reports? Even with the statement, "Blessed are those who have not seen and yet believe" (20:29), he may only mean his readers, who according to verses 30-31 are supposed to be won over precisely through the reports of Jesus' signs, which they have not seen themselves. Should one, conversely, see in him the naive Gnostic who describes a God walking on earth, who remains untroubled even in his passion, untouched by suffering? For the cry of 12:27, "Now my soul is troubled," is immediately corrected: "What shall I say,

'Father, save me from this hour'? No, for this purpose I have come to this hour. Father, glorify thy name.''[225] Yet 9:22 and especially 16:1-4 show that the church is being persecuted—and only by the Jews, contrary to the synoptic writers—and has experienced exclusion from the synagogue (which robs it of any protection through the Jewish community) and even executions. Such a readership has no illusions about what the crucifixion of Jesus meant, even if nothing of Jesus' suffering is indicated. If one can locate this situation historically only in the east Jordan territory (say, on the present Golan Heights), because only there did Jews have such power, then maybe, because of this proximity to Galilee, the humanity of Jesus' life was known and was an obvious presupposition for both parties. That could explain why the Christian community stressed only the divinity of Jesus that was doubted by the Jews.[226] Even if in the meantime the Johannine community may have emigrated into other areas (Asia Minor?), the persecution situation still shaped the addition to the healing story in 9:13-29 and the farewell speech in chapters 15–16. Or should one perceive in Jesus above all the prophetic messenger sent by God?[227] Yet the central ''I am'' statements cannot be explained merely by the self-concept of a messenger who points to his employer. Perhaps the Johannine view is well described by the recommendation of a ''residence Christology,'' in which Jesus to some extent takes the place of the Temple.[228] Against the background of the seemingly all-destroying fate of the temple destruction, we must ask, where then can God now take up residence in Israel? That could explain why John has pushed to the beginning of the Gospel the cleansing of the Temple and Jesus' saying of the destruction of the old Temple and the raising up of the new in Jesus' resurrected body (2:13-22). That alone, to be sure, is not enough; we must at least add the Johannine radicalization, which regards everything earthly as darkness and only the higher world of God as light.

29.9 The Paraclete. However one interprets it, the Gospel of John is in any case the one that most consistently sees the life of the earthly Jesus from the standpoint of the post-Easter period of the church. It is no longer the earthly Jesus who calls his disciples to himself, but rather the witness who already knows the significance of Jesus as the bringer of salvation and proclaims him as the ''lamb of God, who takes away the sins of the world'' (1:29), that is, first the Baptist, then each disciple won for Jesus (1:35-51). As the earthly one, Jesus has taken his leave from the disciples, and that is good and necessary (16:7), for much of what Jesus said to them will not be understood until afterward (2:23; 12:16). He explains to them the way in which he will be with them from now on: in the ''Paraclete'' (''Counselor''),[229] the ''Spirit of truth'' (14:16-17), who will ''bring to your remembrance all that I have said to you'' (14:26) and together with the disciples ''will bear witness to me'' (15:26-27). This is precisely what happens in the Fourth Gospel, which bears such witness.

In it Jesus himself speaks (16:13-14), and in this proclamation the worldwide judgment is actually accomplished. Now we see what sin is. Only since Jesus, and in him God himself, came into the world has there been sin in the real sense (15:22). It consists in the fact that the world still thinks it "sees" and does not notice how much it needs the shepherd who brings life also for it (9:40–10:21). Thus not to believe in Jesus, as 16:9 defines sin in the deepest sense, means not simply the rejection of a confession of faith, but the belief that one can survive through one's own wisdom. God's "righteousness," on the other hand, shows itself in that he stands with Jesus and gives him his due in his return to God's world (16:10). As in I Tim 3:16 (see 5.12 above), this is designated as Jesus' "vindication."

29.10 "It Is Finished": Dualism and World Mission. Finally, in the preaching of the gospel the ultimate defeat of the "ruler of this world" is proclaimed, that is, of all the powers who seem to rule the world and in whom it believes (16:11). With this the abyss that divides everything between light and darkness, truth and falsehood, world above and world below, God and devil (3:11; 8:23, 42-44; etc.), and thus separates the people who come either from this side or that, is seemingly forever closed. Yet this is, in the experience of the believer, an expression of the character of everything given to us as a pure gift of grace. That not only challenges us to "remain" in Jesus and hence in love (15:5-17 etc.), but also to witness in the world and for the world (17:18, 21). Only thus can the tone of this Gospel be properly understood. In Mark and Matthew the only word of the crucified one expresses the distress endured here: "My God, my God, why hast thou forsaken me?" (Mark 15:34). In Luke we see the devotion of Jesus to his persecutors, to the criminal crucified with him, and to his Father in heaven (23:34, 43, 46). The Johannine Jesus (19:26, 28, 30) still makes arrangements from the cross for his mother and his disciple, speaks of his "thirst" only to fulfill the scripture, and his last word is the victory cry, "It is finished" "accomplished," "fulfilled," which precisely through this Gospel echoes throughout a persecuted and anxious church (16:1-3, 33).

30. THE JOHANNINE LETTERS

30.1 Author. Like the letters of Peter, James, and Jude, these are named after their author, because the first letter does not have the character of a letter, but is directed at a larger circle of readers who are in no way more closely designated, the second is addressed to "the elect lady," which is a symbol for a (not named) church,[230] and the third to a Gaius unknown to us. In terms of content and style they are closely related to what is proclaimed in the Fourth

Gospel. In the second and third letter the author calls himself "the elder." As in Papias (ca. A.D. 130-40), that probably designates a man from the first generation of the church, because there is no reference to an office of elder (see 29.3 and n. 215 above and 30.4 below). Besides the Zebedee John, Papias also knows an elder John.[231] The three letters are close and could come from the same author, but one might also think of two different members of a Johannine "school."[232] It is unlikely that the evangelist wrote all or even one of them. Since they were presumably written after the Gospel and were familiar with it,[233] one can only ask whether a redactor, who added chapter 21 and perhaps other supplements to the Gospel, is not also a candidate for author of the Johannine letters. In any case, vis-à-vis the Gospel as a whole, the language is more monotonous, without Semitic overtones, and even different sometimes in the selection of words, as much as it remains related to the Gospel. Decisive, however, are the differences in content, which can hardly be explained only through the different situation of struggling against a heresy.

30.2 Peculiarity in the Rejection of False Teachers. The three letters can be characterized as "Johannine pastoral letters."[234] This means that the first letter is more "ecclesiastical" vis-à-vis the Gospel. That is seen already in the understanding of time. While the Gospel stresses almost entirely the already experienced fulfillment of salvation in Christ (see 29.4 above), in I John 2:28; 3:2 the still delayed final "appearance" of Jesus is expressly called the "Parousia." Different from the present, we will then "see him as he is." Even the emergence of the false teachers ("antichrists") is a sign of the "last hour" (2:18). Contrary to all "progressive" activity, "abiding in the doctrine" must be inculcated (II John 9). One must hold fast to the confession of Jesus as the Christ (5:1) and thus the Son of God (1:3; 4:15; 5:5), indeed the "true God" (this is probably what 5:20 means). It is not enough to repeat it, however; it must also be interpreted. There is some question, namely, as to whether Christ really "has come in the flesh" (4:2; II John 7). What fundamentally led to the composition of Gospels at all (see 25.8 above) appears again as a problem in a new form in view of the special character of the Gospel of John. Is the statement of the Word becoming flesh (John 1:14) not to be understood only in the sense that God's wisdom took shape in the teachings of Jesus, which live on in the church's proclamation (see 26.8 above)? That is, could not the teachings of the revealer, which are present through the Paraclete, be sufficient? This even seems to have already taken shape with the heretics in the concept attested in a later Gnostic, Cerinth,[235] namely, that the heavenly Christ (that is, the divine authority) bound himself to the man Jesus at the baptism in the Jordan, but left him again before the crucifixion. Apparently defending against this is the assertion that Jesus came "not with water only but with the water and the blood" and that "the Spirit is the witness" to this (in the sacrament?—5:6-8;

cf. also John 19:34).[236] Since Gnosticism (see 20.2 above) is not uniform, but took shape gradually from various sources, it is entirely possible that a theology that was interested only in the "wisdom" taught by Jesus and portrayed in his life, was expressed, as by Cerinth, even if perhaps in fewer mythical images. The danger here is also the depreciation of the historical Jesus of Nazareth, not of course in such a way that everything is concentrated in the "kerygma," the message of cross and resurrection, but that only the "glory" appearing in the wisdom teacher Jesus and his proclamation remains important as the presence of the "wisdom of God" (see 7.7 above). In any case, the letter sees in this the teaching of the "antichrist" (see 19.1 above), who is supposed to come in the "last hour," whereby this mythical figure presents itself as more than one false teacher ("antichrists"—2:18, 22; 4:3; II John 7). They have gone out from the community (2:19), and thus it is still a question of an intrachurch conflict, in which the Johannine letters emphasize the anchoring of faith in the history of the one who "became flesh" and really died. It is his "blood" that cleanses from all sins and represents the expiation for them (1:7; 2:2, 12).

30.3 Dualism: Church and World. The Johannine view, in which Jesus Christ is everything and in which light and darkness, the world above and below are sharply separated (see 29.10 above), is also maintained here. Therefore one must clearly separate oneself from the false teachers (II John 10-11), and the believer must not love the world that is passing away (I John 2:15-17), even though Jesus is the expiation for the whole world (2:2). God and the world, children of God and children of the devil are clearly separated (3:10; 4:4-6; 5:4, 19). Totally different from Paul, who wants to become all things to all people in order to win them for Christ (I Cor 9:19-22), and who thus moves consciously into the world with his message in order to proclaim it in the language of this world, the Johannine community works more or less in isolation as a model of a new life (see 29.6 above). That is why Jesus' exhortation to brotherly love (John 15:12-17) is so emphatically embraced: keeping God's commandments means loving one another: I John 2:3; 3:11-18, 22-23; 4:7-8, 20-21; II John 5–6. Such love remains unmistakably the gift of God and is never simply human achievement. Because God is love (I John 4:8, 16), *love* means fundamentally *his* openness to humanity (4:10), which among us becomes and must become love for one another (4:11). The "birth from above," as John 3:3 formulates it, or "regeneration," as it is in Titus 3:5, is according to I John 4:7-10 this very experience of God's love that becomes brotherly love: "He who loves is born of God." Still more soberly 2:29 speaks of "every one who does right," and 3:10 links the two; 3:9 and 5:18 even explain that one born of God no longer commits sin. That is fundamentally true (cf. end of 16.5 above), although in 1:8–2:2 the author knows very soberly that sin occurs anyway, indeed that anyone who asserts that he or she has no sin is lying. Therefore now the "Comforter" is no longer the Holy Spirit, as in the Gospel, but Jesus, who as the "expiation for sin" works with the Father on our behalf. Whenever our hearts condemn us, God is greater and gives us confidence on the day of judgment (3:20; 4:17-18). Thus this defends against the danger of a self-satisfied security that relies on election valid once and for all and is no longer moved by the love of God still maintained in the confession—as well as against a doubt-filled anxiety that lives in constant uncertainty.

30.4 The Conception of the Church. In the Johannine letters we also have an unusual view of the church. At about the same time as the pastoral letters (see 20.3 above), or in any case not very much earlier, the conception of the church, as we find it in Jerusalem and in Paul, developed in precisely the opposite direction from the description in the pastoral letters. The writer of the Gospel of John (see 29.6 above) knows no office besides those of Judas (13:29), the high priest, whose official authority is strongly emphasized (11:51), and Pilate, of whom the same is true (19:10-11). Only in the supplementary chapter is Peter, as the one who denied Jesus three times and who explained three times that he loved him, given the task of tending Jesus' sheep (21:15-17), but this is immediately balanced by the position of the other disciple, whom Jesus loved (21:20-23). Fundamentally I John 2:20, 27 stresses: "You all know [or: know everything] . . . and you have no need that any one should teach you; as his [i.e., the Lord's through the Holy Spirit] anointing teaches you about everything, and is true, and is no lie." This almost unbelievable confidence in the leading of the Spirit is, to be sure, linked with the confidence that the Spirit will proclaim nothing other than what has been taught "from the beginning," that is, in the apostolic tradition (2:24; 1:1-3).

Unfortunately, the situation of the Third Letter of John remains unclear. Many things indicate that the author represents a strongly charismatic group, perhaps a band of itinerant preachers (see 3.1, 9 above) and defends himself against Diotrephes, the officeholder of a church becoming more and more institutionalized, who rejects his envoy.[237] Yet other solutions are also possible. Nonetheless, whatever the concrete situation here may have been, in the Johannine writings we certainly see an understanding of the church that represents the immediacy of Christ to each individual church member and full confidence in the teaching and acting of the Spirit.

30.5 Alternatives in the Conception of the Church. Thus at the end of the New Testament both initiatives toward the development of the coming church (and a few middle positions) are present: (1) the emphasis on correct tradition, doctrine, and institution, though secured by the presupposition that the prophetic Spirit designates before ordination the officeholder to be installed, and (2) the emphasis on the free access of every individual to the exalted Christ and the absolute freedom of the Spirit, though secured by the presupposition that the Spirit teaches nothing other than what was true "from the beginning."

CHAPTER SEVEN

The Prophetic Book

31. THE REVELATION TO JOHN

31.1 Author, Date, Place. The author calls himself "John" in 1:1, 4, 9; 22:8 and designates himself a "servant of God" and "your brother" who shares "with you"; his words are "prophecy" and his brothers "the prophets" (1:3; 22:7, 9, 18). The names of the twelve apostles are engraved on the foundation stones of the heavenly Jerusalem (21:14), without the author ever indicating that he himself is one of them. He is certainly not the person who wrote the Fourth Gospel. The style is different down to the smallest, insignificant details, even if we wanted to explain the strong echo of Semitic forms as consciously archaic-holy language. The most important Johannine ideas and concepts are missing, for instance, the opposition of light and darkness, love and hate, God and world, and "being from God" and "remaining in God/Christ." While the Gospel of John almost exclusively speaks of present salvation and hardly ever of its future, or at most says that what is already present "remains" or is perfected, it is precisely the still delayed future of God that is the theme of Revelation.[238] If the incarnation of God's Logos is the heart of the Gospel, that place in Revelation is filled by his present and above all future position as the exalted ruler who will come again. Both speak of Christ as the "Lamb," as do also Isa 53:7 (= Acts 8:32) and I Pet 1:19 (cf. I Cor 5:7); but Revelation uses another word,[239] which can also designate the ram. There are certainly similarities with John's Gospel, for example, the designation of Christ as the Logos (John 1:1-14, yet only in the prologue [see 5.13 above]; Rev 19:13), the view of faith as a "preserving" (of Jesus' sayings), and the importance of "bearing witness." Yet such similarities are also found in Paul and especially in the Letter to the Hebrews. At the beginning of the fourth century Eusebius suggested the elder John (see 30.1 above) as the author.[240] That is possible, although the title of elder in Revelation is given only to the twenty-four heavenly elders (4:4, 10).

The time must be that of the first great persecution, in which being a Christian as such was punishable even in Greece and Asia Minor, thus perhaps the time of Domitian in the nineties. The number 666 (13:18) goes back to number games. Since Greek letters (like Hebrew) are also number symbols, one can, for instance, put them together and use them as the key to a name: "I love the one whose number is 545."[241] Christian Gnostics have also claimed to prove with this that Christ and the Holy Spirit are one, because alpha and omega (Rev 1:8) yield 801, the same number as the sum of the letters of *peristera* ("dove"—Luke 3:22 etc.).[242] Written with Hebrew letters, "Caesar Nero" yields 666;[243] with Greek letters the same result comes from "M. Nerva," the successor of Domitian, who ruled only from summer 97 until spring 98 (Rev 17:10?).[244] Yet there are so many other possibilities that it behooves us to follow the warning of Berengaudus and abandon the calculations, because otherwise the result could be one's own name.[245] Total martyrdom is, to be sure, the exception (2:13); nevertheless, "Nero," about whom the story was told that he would come again as an even more terrible tyrant, and "Nerva" at the end of the great persecution are logical possibilities.

The addressees are located in Asia Minor (chaps. 2–3), and the seven churches, of course, symbolically represent the worldwide church, whose fate is described in what follows. The author is on the island of Patmos off the coast of Asia Minor (1:9). In contrast to I Peter, the pastoral letters, and Ignatius somewhat later, there is curiously hardly any feeling of Pauline influence. The question of the law, for example, plays absolutely no role anymore. Thus in the churches of Asia Minor very different influences seem to have been at work, especially if we were also to locate the Johannine Gospel and letters here. Perhaps that can be explained in part by the fact that itinerant prophets (see 31.2 below) and settled churches developed in different ways.

31.2 Prophetic Character. Within the New Testament canon the book is important because it is the writing of a prophet. Prophets played an important role in the early church:[246] Matt 5:11-12; 7:22; 23:34; 24:11-12 (see 26.5 above); Acts 2:17-18; 11:27-28; 13:1; 15:32; 19:6; 21:9-10 (see 3.2 and 8 above); Rom 12:6; I Cor 12:28; 14:1; I Thess 5:20 (see 10.4 above); Eph 2:20; 4:11 (see 18.3 above); I Tim 1:18 (see 20.3 above); III John (see 30.4 above). Naturally there is hardly any written tradition from them. The prophet speaks God's message ever anew in concrete situations, so that decisions are made (I Cor 14:24-25). That is more essential than the foretelling of the future (which is also true of Revelation!), although in the process of speaking to a concrete situation, a certain judgment of the one coming to the church is involved and actual predictions also occur (Acts 11:28; 20:23; 21:11). Distinct from these prophets resident in the churches are the actual itinerant prophets, who take Jesus' call to discipleship literally even after Easter, leave home and family, and without possessions move from church to church with their message (Matt 10:41; see 3.1 above). Above all the *Didache* (a Syrian church discipline of the nineties?) describes how these prophets let themselves be cared for by the churches, but sometimes also settled down in them (10:7; 11:4-12).[247] Such wandering prophets presumably even took Paul to task (I Cor 9:3-18) for having taken (self-earned!) money along on his missionary journeys (into not yet Christian areas—Rom 15:20!). They are attested well into the third century and compose one of the roots of the emerging monastic movement in the fourth century.[248]

31.3 The Meaning of the World of Images. The strange, but also theologically important thing is the overflowing abundance of the most curious images. In a strange way the book takes up something that is already visible behind the parable talk of Jesus (see 2.3 above), the Johannine "I am" speeches (see 29.5 above), the Lukan concentration on narrative (see 27.7 above), but also in the Pauline assertions that we can only know God by *being known by* God (I Cor 8:2; 13:12). God cannot be described and thus, in the strict sense, cannot be taught, but can no doubt be perceived in his encounter with humanity. This is totally different from the Greek conception of the logos, in which the macrocosmos, the universe, is structured analogously to the microcosmos, the human being, and is ruled by the same spirit, the logos. God could then be discovered in the regularity of the laws of the universe, which can be examined, and thus could be comprehended by reason. The Greeks praise God when they discover in the most curious animal forms the same constant and immutable laws of blood circulation that also are valid for themselves. The author of Job 38–41, on the other hand, is struck by the abundance and movement of life and is astonished precisely by the unexpected and incomprehensible, by the hippopotamus that "eats grass like an ox," whose "bones are tubes of bronze," and whose tail rises up "stiff like a cedar" (40:15-18). In this he perceives the incomprehensible creative power of God, his Lord. Something of this is seen in the world of images of Revelation. When before God's throne there are four creatures who are "full of eyes all round and within" (4:8), one cannot draw it, for it is unimaginable; but it means that whoever approaches God's throne, from front or back, from left or right, is watched by countless eyes. That is much more impressive and true, because more appropriate to the reality of God, than when we explain abstractly, "God is omniscient." Such images express the truth that we can never get the better of God, not even mentally, and thus can never be "finished" with him, and that we can only meet him by being seen and known by him. Knowledge of God

163

happens only when he touches and moves us in the totality of our lives—however we then react to it. Therefore the Old Testament, even into the later apocalyptic, starting with chapters like Isa 24–27 written after the exile and above all Daniel, is interested in history, not in constant laws of nature.

31.4 Description of a Historical Development? In contrast to the Old Testament prophets, in whom the word of God is occasionally accentuated through images, in the Jewish apocalyptists images move into the foreground and are interpreted by God's word. Dreams and visions become more and more important. That is also true of the Revelation to John. He too wants to describe something like the history of God's action until the consummation. The visions of seven seals (6:1), seven trumpets (8:2, 6), and seven bowls (15:7) do not repeat the same period three times, but are rather to be understood as unfolding a new series out of every seventh plague. Now in terms of history, church, or eschatology one can hardly construct a development in which the images of Revelation could be directly identified with coming (or already past) events within our world history or in the thousand-year kingdom beginning shortly before the last day, as is appropriate, for example, for Dan 11. One even wonders how far the seer in general is thinking of a still comprehensible temporal sequence and is not, rather, overpowered by an abundance of images that describe the nature of the coming of God and the resistance of the powers and the people who have fallen under their influence.[249]

31.5 The Relationship to Jewish Apocalyptic. Agreement with and difference from the apocalyptists of Judaism are equally important. In agreement is knowledge of the God who is not at our disposal, whose decisive action lies still in the future, though in such a way that it is approaching the reader, because it is the unfolding and fulfillment of already experienced action that can also be experienced in the present. It must be transcribed into images, which only become false when, disconnected from the linguistic event in which speaker and hearer are involved, they become objective descriptions of a predictable and hence controllable future history. Also in agreement is the dimension in which thought and language take place: the world, which reaches far beyond the salvation of the individual soul; further, the knowledge of the otherness of God, whose action does not let itself be dissolved into the voice of one's own inner being and one's reaction to it; and finally the perception that God manifests himself in his action: God is and remains the living God.

Differences, however, are also visible. While for the Jewish apocalyptists all salvation lies in the future and the present is felt to be largely abandoned by God and his spirit, John begins with the already accomplished fulfillment of salvation in Jesus Christ. The Lamb, still bearing the wound of the sacrificial knife, has already assumed the throne (5:6). Therefore, Jewish apocalyptists all

164

write in the name of a figure in God's past salvation history (Adam, Enoch, Daniel, et al.), but John signs with his own name and describes even the story of his calling (1:9-20). He knows that the present is already the time of God, even if not of the perfected world. It is not skipped over in one's enthusiasm. Its sufferings are taken seriously. In chapter 13, however one interprets in detail, visible behind the two beasts is the power of the state, which is severely persecuting the church. The situation has now become so different from Rom. 13 (see 16.1 above), the pastoral letters (see 20.4 above), and I Peter (see 23:6 above) that resistance against it is also possible and necessary, no matter how much the suffering of the church still forms its true answer in the hope of God's future. An enthusiasm that believes it already has everything in faith, so that the distress of the church and the world no longer must be acknowledged, is impossible. Nor can the church, however, escape into dreams of the glorious future. That becomes very clear in the proposed missionary writings that are emphatically promise and admonition for the present (chaps. 2–3) and hold the present-day "work" of the reader to be absolutely important.

CHAPTER EIGHT

Afterword

32. THE FORMATION OF THE NEW TESTAMENT

32.1 Neither Canon nor Oldest Tradition as Guarantee of Truth. In a rather long process the writings contained today in the New Testament were declared canonical, and some of them (Heb, Jude, II Peter, II and III John) continued to be disputed into the fifth century, Revelation into the tenth. Occasionally, on the other hand, the *Letter of Barnabas* or the *Shepherd of Hermas* appeared in the canon.[250] Thus the boundary of the canon long remained fuzzy, and one could ask whether the *Gospel of Thomas* or the *First Letter of Clement* belongs there rather than the Letter of Jude. That does not, however, change the fact that by and large it contains the writings that have persevered, that is, those in which the church has repeatedly heard the word of its God, the message by which it lives.

Theologically this must be delineated vis-à-vis two extreme standpoints. (1) This does not mean that the end product, the canon as such, represents a guarantee that is at the church's disposal. It must decide again and again whether, for example, it will read the pastoral letters critically from Paul's viewpoint and John's Gospel from the standpoint of the first three—or vice versa. It must judge where in its particular situation it has to place the emphasis. It will have to ask itself repeatedly to what extent the later writings are an enlightening and continuing development, to what extent they no longer contain essential assertions of earlier writings but perhaps consciously presuppose them and thus can only be read together with them. (2) That does not mean, on the other hand, that the oldest witness still available is decisive. Certainly one can and should inquire back from the present Gospels into earlier tradition, for example, into Q, or from the letters of Paul into the confessional formulas and hymns they contain. But this in no way means that the developed message of Mark or of the Letter to the Romans has not understood what happened in Jesus Christ more clearly and distinctly than the underlying tradition.

32.2 The Canon Oriented Toward Past, Present, and Future. The church in which the New Testament canon arose and was recognized knew that the message from which it lives is clearly anchored in the history of Jesus of Nazareth. Already at the oral stage the first confessional formulas and hymns distinguished the incarnation or birth, crucifixion, and resurrection with appearances to the disciples as essential events. The first collections placed Jesus' words and deeds into his life. So the church adopted the *Gospels* into the canon as witnesses that pointed back to that time, to the *past,* which, however, still lives. At the same time it knew that God is a living God, a God who takes seriously human beings, their needs, questions, dangers, and their possibilities, gifts, and ministries. Therefore the gospel cannot be reduced to definitive information about historical facts, even if one explains that these, naturally, continue to have influence, as do all relevant historical events. Nor can it be reduced to teachings of Jesus fixed once and for all, even if one explains that these must be repeatedly applied to new problems. Jesus lived a life that with its totally unexpected and unpredictable outcome defies any final mastery, and he spoke in parables that do not permit resolution into summarizing statements that definitively fix their meaning. Therefore the church adopted into the canon the *letters* of the apostle and the apostle's disciples, which repeatedly spoke anew to the particular situation as witness to the *present* significance of the gospel in the canon. In all of this it did not forget that the gospel also cannot be resolved into a successful hearing and being moved, which, under the impact of Jesus' word and activity and destiny, re-create people in their times and situations. God does not work only in individual souls and only indirectly through them. Jesus' sayings and parables of God's dominion and the Son of man also speak of the God who is building his kingdom and of the coming consummation. Apocalypses such as Mark 13, the maranatha cry of the earliest worship services, and parts of letters such as I Cor 15 bear witness to this often glowing expectation of the final intervention of God. Therefore the church also adopted into the canon the *Revelation of John* as the witness to God's consummate action pointing into the *future,* because God's action creates history: it does not just meet and move individual people in their present situations. It goes without saying that this division of the canon is correct only in regard to a certain accentuation. In the Gospels, as in the letters, as in Revelation, the topic is repeatedly the living Jesus Christ who always spans past, present, and future, and as "the Alpha and Omega" is "the first and the last, the beginning and the end" (Rev 22:13).

32.3 The Relative Authority of the Canon. This involves two things. (1) From its beginning on, the church continued to develop. In the process all the testimonies of the New Testament were composed at a particular stage, against particular dangers, and with particular memories and hopes. The social situation of the writer and the addressed readership was always involved. Therefore the message also had to develop. Here one can distinguish between documents that are very strongly shaped by their situation and the front on which they are fighting, such as, in my opinion, the Letter of James, and others that in a more central way try to formulate a message that is valid in any place and at any time, such as, in my opinion, the Letter to the Romans. This, however, does not change the basic point that again and again the Christ who lives today and speaks to today's church must be heard. (2) Nevertheless, the church has not simply heard him in recurrent prophetic sayings, but has subjected its whole proclamation to the standard of the New Testament writings. As much as the message must always be formulated anew, so must this new formulation always be measured against the church's basic experiences of Jesus as they are gathered in pre- and post-Easter testimonies in the New Testament. Today, new formulations may express the message more clearly, at least for a particular time and situation, than the first assertions of the New Testament period, even than the words of Jesus himself, but one must always ask critically whether they remain fundamentally consonant with what was attested then. As much as God remains a living God who always meets us anew, so also he remains true to himself and neither today nor tomorrow will be the opposite of what he was yesterday. Hence, being anchored in the life, death, and resurrection of Jesus—as this is also witnessed in the first formulations of the post-Easter proclamation and will be completed in God's final creative act, the new earth under a new heaven—preserves the New Testament from losing its historical contours and being reduced to an intrapersonal psychic event.

32.4 Demarcation from "Early Catholicism." The first of these two points designates a boundary against an "early Catholic" understanding according to which the church at any time can officially determine what the canon, understood only as foundation, now means. But the argument that the acceptance of the New Testament canon then also requires that of a more or less simultaneously determined official church structure of bishop-elder-deacon and thus guarantees this forever valid order[251] cannot be maintained in this way. For the canon is first of all not simply sacrosanct but a living voice to be heard critically again and again, and within its variety emphases must be placed. Then, however, the church at the end of the second century did not simply declare the literature of the time to be canonical, but only testimonies of the first century, of which only a few may have extended into the second century. Thus over against contemporary writings it relied in a thoroughly critical fashion on testimonies which were already over a century old, with the intention of letting itself be questioned and reshaped by them. It declared canonical neither the *First Letter of Clement* nor the letters of Ignatius, in which its order was extensively described and declared exemplary. It adopted instead, for example, even the Johannine letters and the Gospels, which scarcely know anything of such an order, and the reports of the activity of early Christian prophets. This is all the more remarkable since in the time shortly before and after 200 a wave of charismatic and prophetic religiosity with corresponding preaching and healing activity spread widely through the Montanists and became dangerous for the church at large. In spite of this the church had experienced the salvation-creating power of God only in the entire fullness of the New Testament writings and had also let itself be critically defined by them. Therefore it emphatically strove for no collection of maximally uniform assertions, but regarded the whole variety of the message as essential for its future. Thus it made allowance for the ever possible blossoming of alternatives (see 30.5 above), even though it had seen precisely in regard to the Montanists that the church cannot survive in the long run without a certain amount of order.

32.5 Demarcation from Gnosticism. The second point, however, also designates the boundary against a "Gnostic" understanding, for which only the words of the still living Christ (Spirit) and the still occurring miraculous deeds[252] represent an authority, and no longer the Jesus Christ embedded in history—expressed in modern terms: only the doctrine of salvation proclaimed today in the Spirit of Jesus and a modern lifestyle that needs to be connected only loosely with the Jesus of Nazareth attested in the New Testament and the resurrected one who appeared to the disciples. Thus openness and limitation belong together in the New Testament as in the life of the church. Only where the word really speaks to the current situation in all openness to new questions and answers and to new dangers of prejudgment is it the living word of God. But it is also this only where, in clear distinction to what happened in Jesus Christ, it rejects wrong questions and answers and prejudgments.

32.6 Canon (and Dogma) as "Guardrails." Perhaps we can picture it this way: Along a divided highway there are guardrails and white lines at the edge of the roadway. They continue mile after mile and are thus not simply the same ones encountered at the beginning, but in spite of all the curves they form continuous lines. Their function is that of keeping the driver from a dangerous crossover into the opposing lanes of traffic or from a plunge down into the abyss. Naturally, anyone who stops in the first ten feet in order to be quite safe and not cross the guardrails or guidelines will go absolutely nowhere, and anyone who confuses the white lines or even the guardrails with the roadway itself and tries to drive on them will probably meet with quick disaster. In freedom drivers must decide how they want to drive in the open space on the road between these guidelines and guardrails, whether they follow someone and brake or want to turn left, accelerate and overtake, and so forth. In similar fashion, certain New Testament assertions, even in continuous but still changing form, must always mark the boundaries that may not be overstepped. What faith is, however, is not to be confused with the boundaries themselves. Neither holding fast to them nor driving on them is possible or wholesome; faith must seek its own way in the open space between them (which is much larger than a four-lane highway). Thus the New Testament, with its unconditional connection with Jesus of Nazareth and his resurrection, with its taking seriously of the post-Easter message, and with clear orientation toward God's final creative deed, limits the roadway and precisely in this way grants the church of every age and land the freedom of its own journey.

ABBREVIATIONS

AB—Anchor Bible

ANRW—Aufstieg und Neidergang der römischen Welt

ATANT—Abhandlungen zur Theologie des Alten und Neuen Testaments

BEvT—Beiträge zur evangelischen Theologie

BHT—Beiträge zur historischen Theologie

BJRL—Bulletin of the John Rylands University Library of Manchester

BZ—Biblische Zeitschrift

BZNW—Beihefte zur *ZNW*

CBQ—Catholic Biblical Quarterly

CNT—Commentaire du Nouveau Testament

EKKNT—Evangelisch-katholischer Kommentar zum Neuen Testament

EvT—Evangelische Theologie

FRLANT—Forschungen zur Religion und Literature Des Alten und Neuen
    Testaments

FS—Festschrift

GTA—Göttinger theologische Arbeiten

GNT—Grundrisse zum Neuen Testament

HBT—Horizons in Biblical Theology

Hist. Eccl.—Historia Ecclesiastica

HKAW—Handbuch der klassischen Altertumswissenschaft

HNT—Handbuch zum Neuen Testament

HTKNT—Herders theologischer Kommentar zum Neuen Testament

HTR—Harvard Theological Review

HUT—Hermeneutische Untersuchungen zur Theologie

JBL—Journal of Biblical Literature

KD—Kerygma und Dogma

MeyerK—H. A. W. Meyer, Kritisch-exegetischer Kommentar über das Neue Testament

NIGTC—The New International Greek Testament Commentary

NovT—Novum Testamentum

NTD—Das Neue Testament Deutsch

NTS—New Testament Studies

PRSt—Perspectives in Religious Studies

SANT—Studien zum Alten und Neuen Testament

SBLDS—SBL Dissertation Series

SBS—Stuttgarter Bibelstudien

SQS—Sammlung Ausgewählter kirchen und dogmengeschichtlicher Quellenschriften

ST—Studia theologica

SUNT—Studien zur Umwelt des neuen Testament

TBl—Theologische Blätter

TDNT—G. Kittel and G. Friedrich (eds.), Theological Dictionary of the New Testament

THKNT—Theologischer Handkommentar zum Neuen Testament

TLZ—Theologische Literaturzeitung

TRE—Theologishe Realenzyklopädie

TU—Text und Untersuchungen

TZ—Theologische Zeitschrift

UB—Die Urchristliche Botschaft

UTB—Uni-Taschenbücher

WA—M. Luther, Kritische Gesamtausgabe (= ''Weimar'' edition)

WMANT—Wissenschaftliche Monographien zum Alten und Neuen Testament

WUNT—Wissenschaftliche Untersuchungen zum Neuen Testament

ZNW—Zeitshrift für die neutestamentliche Wissenschaft

ZRGG—Zeitshrift für Religions und Geistesgeschichte

ZTK—Zeitshrift für Theologie und Kirche

NOTES

The book can also be read without the notes, which are here only to facilitate further scholarly work.

1. Cf. P. Stuhlmacher, *Vom Verstehen des Neuen Testaments*, GNT 6 (1979), 206.
2. E.g., W. G. Kümmel, *Introduction to the New Testament*, (Nashville: Abingdon, 1986); H. M. Schenke and K. M. Fischer, *Einleitung in die Schriften des Neuen Testaments*, vols. 1 & 2 (Berlin, 1978/1979); E. Lohse, *Die Entstehung des Neuen Testaments*, 4th ed. (1983).
3. *Ann.* 15.44.
4. *Claud.* 25.4.
5. *Ant.* 18.63-64; 20.200.
6. Str-B 1:1023 (5b).
7. For more detail see H. Conzelmann, *History of Primitive Christianity*, (Nashville: Abingdon, 1973), 29-31.
8. F. Herrenbrück, "Wer waren die Zöllner?" *ZNW* 72 (1981): 178-94. Further: Conzelmann (n. 7), 148-57; on the social position of the craftsman: H. G. Kippenberger and G. A. Weevers, *Textbuch zur neutestamentlichen Zeitgeschichte*, GNT 8 (1979), 84-85; E. Lohse, *Umwelt des Neuen Testaments*, GNT 1 (1971), 106-9.
9. G. Theissen, "Gewaltverzicht und Feindesliebe," in *Studien zur Soziologie des Urchristentums*, WUNT 19 (1983), 160-97, esp. 183-88; "Wanderradikalismus," ibid., 79-105 (= *ZTK* 70 [1973]: 245-71); and *The Miracle Stories of the Early Christian Tradition*, (Philadelphia: Fortress, 1983), 277-80.
10. This is a somewhat modified and expanded version of "The Testimony to Jesus in the Early Christian Community," 1. Roots of the Tradition, in *HBT* 7/1 (1985): 77-85.
11. H. Gese, "Psalm 22 und das Neue Testament," *ZTK* 65 (1968): 1-22, esp. 11-12, 17-18.
12. Theissen, *Wundergeschichten* (n. 9), 57-83.
13. Ibid., 84, 133-43, 279. In the Hellenistic realm in that period there seem to have been individual reports of miracles (especially from holy places), but no collections: P. J. Achtemeier, "The Origin and Function of the Pre-Markan Miracle Catena," *JBL* 91 (1972): 200-202.
14. C. Dietzfelbinger, "Vom Sinn der Sabbatheilungen Jesu," *EvT* 38 (1978): 281-98, esp. 294-98.
15. J. D. Crossan, *In Parables* (1973), 13. For bibliography on the parables, see E. Schweizer, s.v. "Jesus Christus," *TRE* 16:715-17.
16. H. Weder, *Die Gleichnisse Jesu als Metaphern*, FRLANT 120 (1978), 95-98.
17. U. Luz, in *Sie aber hielten fest an der Gemeinschaft*, ed. by C. Link, U. Luz, and L. Vischer (Zurich-Basel, 1988), 49-59.
18. Schweizer (n. 15), 720-21. In passages like Ps 89:26 *Father* is clearly symbolic (like *Rock*).

19. W. Stenger, "Sozialgeschichtliche Wende und historischer Jesus," *Kairos* 28 (1986): 11-22, esp. 14-15; W. H. Kelber, *The Oral and the Written Gospel* (Philadelphia, 1983), 29. Cf. Theissen, "Wanderradikalismus" (n. 9), 79-105.

20. W. Stenger, "Die Seligpreisung der Geschmähten," *Kairos* 28 (1986): 56-57; Theissen, "Gewaltverzicht" (n. 9), 183-95.

21. G. Klein, s.v. "Eschatologie," *TRE* 10:274-75; J.D.G. Dunn, *Unity and Diversity in the New Testament* (London, 1977), 176-78.

22. *Did.* 10:6; presumably also I Cor 16:22, if the letter was read in worship before the celebration of the Lord's Supper (G. Bornkamm, *Das Ende des Gesetzes* [Munich, 1952], 123-32; versus Dunn [n. 21], 55; G. Delling, *KD* 10 [1964]: 76). In view of the frequency of the assertions about the coming of God and the rarity of petition for it in the Old Testament and Judaism (D. E. Aune, "The Apocalypse of John and Graeco-Roman Revelatory Magic," *NTS* 33 [1987]: 492; but different in Hellenism!), one must—in spite of Rev 22:20—also take seriously "The Lord comes" (or even: "has come"?) as possibly the original meaning.

23. E. Käsemann, "Sentences of Holy Law in the New Testament," in *New Testament Questions of Today,* (London: SCM, 1969, 66-81.

24. Kelber (n. 19), 30.

25. R. H. Gundry, "Hellenization of Dominical Tradition and Christianization of Jewish Tradition in the Eschatology of 1–2 Thessalonians," *NTS* 33 (1987): 170.

26. Ibid. and R. Bauckham, "Synoptic Parousia Parables and the Apocalypse," *NTS* 23 (1976/77): 165-69; "Synoptic Parousia Parables Again," *NTS* 29 (1983): 129-30.

27. Josephus *Ant.* 17.299-303, 339: Archelaus competes in Rome for royal status and afterward kills his opponents.

28. G. Kretschmar, "Ein Beitrag zur Frage nach dem Ursprung frühchristlicher Askese," *ZTK* 61 (1964): 27-41.

29. Kelber (n. 19), 193.

30. Stenger (n. 19), 17.

31. Kelber (n. 19), 195.

32. E. Schweizer, on Acts 1:16-22, *Neotestamentica* (Zurich, 1963), 416-17.

33. Kelber (n. 19), 187-99.

34. Cf. E. Schweizer, s.v. "Jesus Christus," *TRE* 16:677-85.

35. Or "Christ Jesus" or "the/our Lord Jesus," always with the relative pronoun or participle expressed.

36. R. A. Horsley, "The Background of the Confessional Formula in I Cor 8:6," *ZNW* 69 (1978): 130-35; R. Kerst, "1 Kor 8:6—ein vorpaulinisches Taufbekenntnis?" *ZNW* 66 (1975): 130-39.

37. Philo *Cher.* 125; *Leg. Gai.* 115; *Decal.* 64; cf. *Hermas* 26:1 (= *Herm. Man.* 1:1).

38. Only in the Stoic expectation of a renewal of the cosmos after the conflagration do we occasionally find a purposive "to" (E. Schweizer, *Der Brief an die Kolosser,* 2d ed., EKKNT 12 [1980], nn. 144-45).

39. H. W. Bartsch, "Zur vorpaulinischen Bekenntnisformel im Eingang des Römerbriefs," *TZ* 23 (1967): 329-39; cf. E. Käsemann, *Commentary on Romans,* (Grand Rapids: Eerdmans, 1980), 11-13.

40. E. Schweizer, "Zum religionsgeschichtlichen Hintergrund der 'Sendungsformel' Gal 4,4f.; Röm 8,3f.; Joh 3,16f.; 1 Joh 4,9," in idem, *Beiträge zur Theologie des Neuen Testaments* (Zurich, 1970), 83-95; idem, "What Do We Really Mean When We Say, 'God Sent His Son . . .'?" in *Faith and History: Essays in Honor of Paul W. Meyer* (Atlanta: Scholars Press, 1991), 298-312.

41. N. A. Dahl, "Formgeschichtliche Beobachtungen zur Christusverkündigung in der Gemeindepredigt," in *Neutestamentliche Studien für R. Bultmann,* BZNW 21 (1954), 4-5. M. Wolter ("Verborgene Weisheit und Heil für die Heiden," *ZTK* 84 [1987]: 297-319) shows the roots in the understanding of divine revelation to be in the Jewish wisdom and apocalyptic literature. From this standpoint Paul describes in I Cor 2:6-10 the knowledge of salvation in the cross of Jesus as God's gift, in contrast to the wisdom of the world. Such passages as II Tim 1:9-10; I Pet 1:20; Ign. *Magn.* 6:1; *Herm.* 89:2-3 (= *Herm. Sim.* 9:12:2-3) draw from the same source in order to say that God has already established his plan of salvation with Jesus from eternity. In the Revelation schema, however, the interest lies elsewhere. Here the crucial

assertion is the turning point between the pre-Christian blindness of all nations to God's love and their present participation in salvation on the basis of Paul's preaching to them.

42. On the distinction from *homologies:* W. H. Gloer, "Homologies and Hymns," *PRSt* 11 (1984): 115-32.

43. G. Delling, "Zum gottesdienstlichen Stil der Johannes-Apokalypse," *NovT* 3 (1959): 107-37; F. Hahn, "Liturgische Elemente in den Rahmenstücken der Johannesoffenbarung," in *Kirchengemeinschaft—Anspruch und Wirklichkeit,* FS G. Kretschmar (Stuttgart, 1986), 43-57.

44. J. Heriban (*Retto PHRONEIN e KENŌSIS* [Rome, 1983]) understands, according to *TLZ* 111 (1986): 748-50, verse 6 in reference to the incarnate one, which cannot be supported.

45. Contrast O. Hofius, *Der Christushymnus Phil 2:6-11,* WUNT 17 (1976), 33-34, 41-55, 67-74. The limitation to angels and living and dead people is, in any case, not acceptable in Paul's understanding; cf. "all things" in 3:21, victory over all enemies, even death itself, and dominion over "all things" I Cor 15:25-28.

46. On the religious-historical background see 17.3-5 and on John 1:1-18 see 5.13.

47. This distinction is found in N. Walter, "Geschichte und Mythos in der urchristliche Pärexistenzchristologie," in *Mythos und Rationalität* ed. by H. H. Schmid (Gütersloh, 1988), 224-34. The parallels to John's prologue in the wisdom literature and in Philo have already been collected in C. H. Dodd, *The Interpretation of the Fourth Gospel* (Cambridge, 1953), 274-77. Cf. G. Schimanowski, *Weisheit und Messias,* WUNT 2/17 (1985), esp. 153-94 and the survey, 204-5. Against this Walter (n. 9) correctly registers his concern that even before the Christian concept of preexistence, wisdom attributes were transferred to the Messiah. *I Enoch* 48:6 would be the only Jewish passage that speaks of a hidden existence, even before creation, of the son of man, who is no doubt to be equated with the Messiah. But apart from the question, to what extent the Ethiopian translation agrees with the original (see 9.4 and n. 78 below), the age of *I Enoch* 37–71, which is missing in the fragments found at Qumran, is quite uncertain. Statements competitive to Jewish-Christian assertions would thus be conceivable, even where there is no direct influence.

48. Koch, *Was ist Formgeschichte?* 3rd ed. (1974), 111: changes in the oral tradition are primarily unintentional and smooth, and an addition to a text is a conscious act; E. Güttgemanns, *Offene Fragen zur Formgeschichte des Evangeliums,* BEvT 54 (1970), 86-91: "fragmentation" (87), "form-historical change," "reshaping in regard to structure and function" (88); Kelber (n. 19); L. H. Silbermann, ed., "Orality, Aurality and Biblical Narrative," *Semeia* 39 (1987): esp. 27-45, 107-33; F. Hahn, "Zur Verschriftlichung mündlicher Tradition in der Bibel," *ZRGW* 39 (1987): 307-18; G. Sellin, "'Gattung' und 'Sitz im Leben' auf dem Hintergrund der Problematik von Mündlichkeit und Schriftlichkeit synoptischer Erzählungen," *EvT* 50 (1990): 311-31.

49. WA 10:1.1: 17:7-12 in G. Ebeling, *Dogmatik des christlichen Glaubens* (Tübingen, 1979), 3:260-61.

50. Kelber (n. 19), 33.

51. T. J. Weeden, *Traditions in Conflict* (1971); cf. "The Heresy That Necessitated Mark's Gospel," *ZNW* 59 (1968): 145-58; Kelber (n. 19), 210, yet already in "Mark 14:32-42: Gethsemane," *ZNW* 63 (1972): 166-87.

52. H. von Campenhausen, *Die Begründung kirchlicher Entscheidungen beim Apostel Paulus,* Studienhefte zur Altertumswissenschaft 2 (1957), 32-34. Paul adopts quite different confessions of faith, and never the same one twice (Luz [n. 17], 98).

53. As early as E. Lohmeyer, *Das Evangelium des Markus,* MeyerK 1/2 (1937), 10; also H. Weder, "'Evangelium Jesu Christi' (Mk 1,1) und 'Evangelium Gottes' (Mark 1,14)," in *Die Mitte des Neuen Testamentes,* FS E. Schweizer, ed. by U. Luz and H. Weder (Göttingen, 1983), 400-401.

54. Circa A.D. 130-40, handed down in Euseb. *Hist. Eccl.* 3:39:16 (ca. A.D. 313); here Matthew is mentioned *after* Mark! If the reference here is not to the words *of* Jesus but those *about* Jesus (thus U. H. Körtner, *Papias von Hierapolis,* FRLANT 133 [1983], 159-63), then we would have to consider an actual gospel that, of course, would have been of a different genre from those we have and not the Hebrew original of Matthew (see 26.1 below). Could we, however, relate the quotation to our Greek Gospel and translate it: "Now, Matthew put the words of the Lord into literary form in Hebrew style; each one presented them as he was able" (J. Gnilka, *Das Matthäusevangelium,* HTKNT [1988], 2:517-18)?

55. Sellin, "Das Leben des Gottessohnes," *Kairos* 25 (1983): 237-53.
56. J. Gnilka, *Das Evangelium nach Markus*, EKKNT 2/1 (1978), 20.
57. R. Pesch, *Das Markusevangelium*, HTKNT 2/2 (1977), 1-27: already written in Aramaic by A.D. 37 (p. 21) and then translated into Greek for the Hellenists (21-26). He also posits a pre-Markan collection of miracle stories (HTKNT 2/1 [1974], 277-81).
58. The proclamation of Jesus as Son of God is presupposed in Luke 4:3/Matt 4:3 (Q). Thus Q must also have told of the voice of God at Jesus' baptism, although in the baptism pericope itself only the word for heaven being "opened" and the formulation "upon him" (instead of literally "into him" in Mark 1:10) are in agreement vis-à-vis Mark, which, naturally, is not enough for reconstruction of a Q version.
59. J. M. Robinson, "LOGOI SOPHON: on the Gattung of Q," in *Trajectories through Early Christianity*, H. Koester and J. M. Robinson (Philadelphia: Fortress, 1971), 72-113. W. Schmithals (*Einleitung in die drei ersten Evangelien* [Berlin, 1985]) is skeptical: Jesus' own proclamation can at most still be detected in an early draft of Q (Q¹), which was still quite unchristological (pp. 399-402), but it led a very limited life of its own and is hardly to be reconstructed (404); Mark already presupposes Q, and the evangelist is perhaps the final redactor of Q (403).
60. Luke 10:1 is redactional according to S. Schulz, *Q* (Zurich, 1972), 404.
61. Originally belonging to Q: ibid., 332, and the works named there, cf. 335.
62. Cf. works named in I. H. Marshall, *The Gospel of Luke*, NIGTC (Grand Rapids: Eerdmans, 1978), 410.
63. Cf. ibid., 434.
64. I have briefly indicated this in "Die Christologie von Phil 2:6-11 und Q," *TZ* 41 (1985): 258-63.
65. Previous publication in English (n. 10) in *HBT* 7/1 (1985): 86-98.
66. H. E. Tödt, *Der Menschensohn in der synoptischen Überlieferung*, 2d ed. (1963), 244; cf. H. Koester, "One Jesus and Four Primitive Gospels," and J. M. Robinson "Kerygma and History in the New Testament" in Koester and Robinson (n. 59) 158-204, and 20-70; Schulz (n. 59), 28-32; E. Schillebeeckx, *Jesus* (Freiburg, 1975), 355-88; K. M. Fischer, *Das Urchristentum* (Berlin, 1985), 55-56.
67. G. Theissen, "Legitimation und Lebensunterhalt," *Studien* (n. 9), 201-30, esp. 214-26 (= *NTS* 21 [1975], 205-14); also R. Scroggs, "The Sociological Interpretation of the New Testament," *NTS* 26 (1980): 174-75.
68. Cf. also Papias (Euseb. *Hist. Eccl.* 3:39:15), the Apocryphon of John, and, in reference to the word of the apostle, Jude 17.
69. Euseb. *Hist. Eccl.* 3:39:4.
70. Documentation in C. K. Barrett, *The New Testament Background: Selected Documents*, (New York: Harper & Row, 1987), citation 9, (pp. 13-14).
71. Orosius *Historiae adv. paganos* 6.6.15-16; cf. Schenke and Fischer (n. 2), 1:134-35; Kümmel (n. 2), section 13.
72. Thus Schenke and Fischer (n. 2), 1:55-56, cf. 60.
73. G. Lüdemann, *Paul, Apostle to the Gentiles*, (Philadelphia: Fortress, 1984), 237-44; the apostolic council could then be equated even with Acts 18:22 (ca. A.D. 51): p. 165; similarly J. M. Suggs, "Paul's Macedonian Ministry," *NovT* 4 (1960): 60-68, and R. Jewitt, *Pauluschronologie* (Munich, 1982), 141; cf. also U. Schnelle, "Der erste Thessalonicherbrief und die Entstehung der paulinischen Anthropologie," *NTS* 32 (1986): 208-9. Then the calling would be placed in the fall of 37 (Jewitt, 58-63, 156-57). Critical of this view is T. Holtz, *Der erste Brief an die Thessalonicher*, EKKNT 13 (1986), 20-23. A detailed presentation of the various views and critiques is in G. Sellin, "Hauptprobleme des 1. Korintherbriefes," *ANRW* 25.4 (1987), 2986-90. He assumes that the visit in Jerusalem and Antioch (Acts 18:22) is only a Lukan addition, so that in the strict sense one cannot speak of three journeys, but only of initial activity in southern Asia Minor and subsequent extended activity in Asia Minor and Europe.
74. Since leather tents hardly existed, the conception of Paul as a "leather worker" is probably false. Tentmakers were middle-class craftsmen (P. Lampe, "Paulus-Zeltmacher," *BZ* 31 [1987]: 256-61).
75. The ancient letter writer always thinks from the standpoint of the recipient: "I have written" does not need to refer to what has preceded, but is equivalent to "I am writing" in our language.

76. W. Speyer, *Die literarische Fälschung im Altertum*, HKAW 1/2 (1971), 137-38, 140, 143, 145, 237, cf. index; for Judaism: M. Hengel, "Anonymität, Pseudepigraphie und 'literarische Fälschung' in der jüdisch-hellenistischen Literatur," in *Pseudepigrapha* (Geneva, 1972), 1:231-329; also N. Brox, ed., *Pseudepigraphie in der heidnischen und jüdischen Antike*, Wege der Forschung 484 (1977).
77. N. Walter, *Der Thoraausleger Aristobulos*, TU 86 (1964), 150-66.
78. E. Schweizer, "Menschensohn und eschatologischer Mensch im Judentum," in idem, *Neues Testament und Christologie im Werden* (Göttingen, 1982), 113.
79. W. O. Walker, "The Burden of Proof in Identifying Interpolations in the Pauline Letters," *NTS* 33 (1987): 610-18. W. Schmithals (*Die Briefe des Paulus in ihrer ursprünglichen Form* [Zurich, 1984]) assumes thirteen letters to Corinth (pp. 19-20), five to Thessalonica (111, with additions by the redactor), three to Philippi (99), two to Rome (125), and one (Rom 16) to Ephesus (158).
80. N. Brox, *Falsche Verfasserangaben*, SBS 79 (1975), esp. 45-48, 57-67. For all letters and newer literature cf. *ANRW* 25.4 (1987). Cf. also D. L. Mealand, "Positional Stylometry Reassessed: Testing a Seven Epistle Theory of Pauline Authorship," *NTS* 35 (1989): 266-86; D. Trobisch, *Die Entstehung der Paulusbriefsammlung*, NTOA 10 (1989).
81. Survey: O. Merk, "Paulusforschung 1936-1985," *TRu* 53 (1988): 1-81.
82. G. Bornkamm, *Paul*, (New York: Harper & Row, 1971) 105-6, 230-1, 232-33 (= E. Bloch).
83. Aggressively formulated in 1966 in K. Stendahl, *Paul among Jews and Gentiles* (Philadelphia, 1976), esp. 12-17, 78-96; then E. P. Sanders, *Paul, the Law and the Jewish People* (Philadelphia, 1983), summary on 207-10; also M. D. Hooker, in *Paul and Paulinism*, FS C. K. Barrett (London, 1982), 47-56; J. D. G. Dunn, "The New Perspective on Paul," *BJRL* 65 (1983): 95-122; E. Schweizer, *TLZ* 109 (1984): 666-68; balanced: P. Stuhlmacher, "Paulus und Luther," in *Glaube und Eschatologie*, FS W. G. Kümmel (Tübingen, 1985), 285-302.
84. L. E. Keck, *Paul and His Letters* (Philadelphia, 1979), 46.
85. W. G. Kümmel, "Jesus und Paulus," *TBl* 19 (1940): 209-31, esp. 221-22; E. Jüngel, *Paulus und Jesus* (1962); J. Blank, *Paulus und Jesus*, SANT 18 (1968); H. Weder, *Das Kreuz Jesu bei Paulus*, FRLANT 125 (1981), 34-44, esp. 38-40; H. Braun, *Jesus* (Stuttgart, 1984), 259-70; and in general: *From Jesus to Paul*, FS F. W. Beare (Waterloo, Ont., 1985).
86. Thus, for example, Schenke and Fischer (n. 2), 65-71, which, however, assumes a totally different order of the individual sections.
87. Verse 1:6 speaks of "imitators . . . of the Lord" and thus presupposes at least the knowledge of Jesus' joyful confidence in God even in suffering.
88. Lüdemann (n. 73), 238, also calls attention to this.
89. For discussion see Holtz (n. 73), 97, esp. n. 431; W. Trilling, "Die Briefe des Paulus an die Thessalonicher," *ANRW* 25.4 (1987): 3391.
90. For an survey of all previous attempts and his own recommendation, see G. Sellin (n. 73), 2964-82. Chapter 13 should not be removed from the context of chapters 12–14, since also in Rom 12:9a the summons to "love" closes the section on the gifts of grace (3-8) and provides transition to behavior in the church (and in the world—9b-21); cf. E. Schweizer, in *Charisma und Agape (1 Kor 12-14)*, Ben., monogr. Reihe 7 (1983), 43. The unity is established by A. Strobel, *Der erste Brief an die Korinther*, Zürcher Bibelkommentare (1989), 12 (except for the gloss 14:33b-35 [ibid., 223-24]).
91. G. Theissen, "Social Integration and Sacramental Activity: An Analysis of 1 Cor. 11:17-34" in *The Social Setting of Pauline Christianity*, (Philadelphia: Fortress, 1982), 145-174; cf. idem, "Christologie und Sozialerfahrung" (on I Cor 12) = *Studien* (n. 9), 326-30. G. Schöllgen ("Was wissen wir über die Sozialstruktur der paulinischen Gemeinden?" *NTS* 34 [1988]: 73) stresses that things looked different in small towns, e.g., in Galatia. It seems, however, to be a misunderstanding that a temple to the goddess of love existed there with a thousand prostitutes; even in Corinth prostitution was apparently a purely secular matter (Sellin [n. 73], 2995).
92. R. E. Oster ("When Men Wore Veils to Worship," *NTS* 34 [1988]: 481-505) considers whether a Roman custom lies behind the instruction to cover one's head. That men and women were admonished in the same way is advocated by J. Murphy-O'Connor, "I Cor 11:2-16 Once Again" (*CBQ* 50 [1988], 265-74). On 14:33b-35 see n. 90.
93. Camphausen (n. 52).

94. G. Sellin, "Das 'Geheimnis' der Weisheit und das Rätsel der 'Christuspartei'" (on I Cor 1-4), ZNW 73 (1982): 80-81; idem (n. 73), 3026; see 5.7 and n. 41 above. Different is F. Bovon, "Connaissance et expérience de Dieu selon le N.T.," in La Mystique, ed. by J. M. van Congh (Paris, 1988), 69.

95. Sellin (n. 73), 3015.

96. Because "body of Christ" for Paul always describes the church, he is not speaking of this when he talks about the uniting of the individual with Christ, but of the "one spirit" with the Lord (v. 17).

97. Cf. n. 92 and S. C. Barton, "Paul's Sense of Place: An Anthropological Approach to Community Formation in Corinth," NTS 32 (1986): 234-43 and n. 3. Also 12:12-13 makes it clear that it is a question of the universal body of Christ, the church at large which is lived, however, in the local church; cf. also 1:13; Gal 3:28.

98. Philo Leg. All. 3.246-47.

99. Sellin (n. 73), 3025 with bibliography; also see 5.2 above.

100. This is referred to by 12:18 ("Did Titus take advantage of you?"); if the letter is unified, 7:14 likewise designates the recommendation on the occasion of the first visit, but with a division that places chapters 10–13 before 1–9, it refers to the visit of 12:18.

101. Thus G. Dautzenberg, "Der zweite Korintherbrief als Briefsammlung," ANRW 25.4 (1987), 3050, n. 21.

102. On 6:14–7:1 cf. J. Murphy-O'Connor, "Philo and 2 Cor 6:14-7:1," RB 95 (1988): 55-69. Purely coincidental juxtaposition such as the senseless connecting of Barn. 5:7ff. and Pol. Phil. 9:2 in some Greek mss. (Die apostolischen Väter, SQS II 1/1, 1924, XL) is of no concern here.

103. Sellin (n. 73), 2981, and W. Schenk, "Der Philipperbrief in der neueren Forschung (1945-1985)," ANRW 25.4 (1987): 3284-85.

104. Dautzenberg ([n. 101], 3051-52) points to the warning against false teachers (Acts 20:29-30; I Tim 4:1-3; II Tim 4:6-9), the necessity of powerful leadership (Acts 28:28, 31), and hard admonitions (Heb 12:21; Rev 2–3), which repeatedly make the intervention of the apostle necessary (I Tim 3:14-15; 4:13).

105. Often 2:14–6:13 is allotted to a special "intermediate letter" (Zwischenbrief), but 7:5 repeats 2:13 and cannot be directly attached to it; also the change from "my mind could not rest" (2:13) to "our bodies had no rest" (7:5) is hardly comprehensible if they originally stood immediately beside each other. Thus, at the very least, one would have to assume that the redactor reshaped 7:5 on his own.

106. E.g., C. J. Hemer, "Observations on Pauline Christology," in Pauline Studies, FS F. F. Bruce (1980), 12-13, 15-16.

107. J. L. Martyn, "Apocalyptic Antinomies in Paul's Letters to the Galatians," NTS 31 (1985): 410-24; "Paul and His Jewish-Christian Interpreters," USQR 42 (1988): 1-15. He is also preparing the commentary on Galatians in the Anchor Bible.

108. Thus H. D. Betz, Galatians (Philadelphia, 1979); also R. G. Hall, "The Rhetorical Outline for Galatians—A Reconsideration," JBL 106 (1987): 277-87: exordium, 1:1-5; proposition, 1:6-9; proof: a. narration, 1:10–2:21, b. further headings, 3:1–6:10; epilogue, 6:11-18, whereby Hall assumes the outline of a deliberative talk, not that of a court speech as Betz does.

109. W. Harnisch, "Einübung des neuen Seins," ZTK 84 (1987): 286-87. Cf. J. G. Barclay, Obeying the Truth (Edinburgh, 1988).

110. This is the only passage in Paul that gives such a name to the church of Jesus composed of Jews and Gentiles—unless a special Jewish-Christian church (house church) is intended (G. Schrenk, "Was bedeutet 'Israel Gottes'?" Judaica 5 [1949]: 81-94). Cf., however, I Cor 10:18.

111. Cf., e.g., B. W. Schenk, Die Philipperbriefe des Paulus (Stuttgart, 1984), esp. 334-38; research report: idem (n. 103), 3280-84, and B. Mengel, Studien zum Philipperbrief, WUNT 2/8 (1982), 297-316 (with survey of the research).

112. Perhaps even before Paul's arrest (despite the mention of his "trouble" in 4:14). 4:21-23 is occasionally drawn to the second letter.

113. Thus, e.g., Schenk (n. 111), 291-98; idem (n. 103), 3296-98.

114. Mengel (n. 111), 293-94, 314-16, who assumes a longer interruption before 2:25 and again

before 3:2. The fact that 3:2 mentions no new information is, to be sure, a problem for this solution.

115. D. F. Watson, "A Rhetorical Analysis of Philippians and Its Implication for the Unity Question," *NovT* 30 (1988), 57-88.

116. W. Schenk, "Der Brief des Paulus an Philemon in der neueren Forschung (1949-1987)," *ANRW* 25.4 (1987): 3483; for Ephesus: P. Stuhlmacher, *Der Brief an Philemon*, 2d ed., EKKNT 18 (1981), 21.

117. Perhaps in Rome there were only house churches flourishing beside each other, see 16.2 below (W. Schmithals, *Der Römerbrief als historisches Problem*, SNT 9 [1975], 69, taken up in Wilckens [n. 70], 43, n. 111). On the house churches in general cf. Stuhlmacher (n. 116), 70-75 (there all the evidence); cf. also Theissen (n. 91), esp. *Studien* (n. 9), 302-9, and "Social Stratification of the Corinthian Community," in *The Social Setting of Pauline Christianity*, (n. 9), 69-120; also Scroggs (n. 67), esp. 170.

118. On the whole letter cf. also D. M. Derrett, "The Functions of the Epistle to Philemon," *ZNW* 79 (1988): 63-91.

119. Wilckens (n. 70), 35-39.

120. Schenke and Fischer (n. 2), 1:135-36.

121. Wilckens (n. 95), 39-41:

122. M. Hengel, "Jakobus der Herrenbruder—der erste 'Papst'?" in *Glaube und Eschatologie*, FS W. G. Kümmel (Tübingen, 1985), 71-104; W. Pratscher, *Der Herrenbruder Jakobus und die Jakobustradition*, FRLANT 139 (1987), 93-100.

123. H. Hübner, s.v. "Galaterbrief," *TRE* 12:9-11.

124. Wilckens (n. 70), 30-33.

125. Sanders (n. 83), 65-91, esp. 75.

126. Ibid., 93-122; cf. also Wilckens (n. 70), passim, in concentrated form already in EKKNT 5/1 (1969), 72-77. On the question of the righteousness of God and the meaning of the law cf. also I. Baldermann, *Einführung in die Bibel*, UTB 1486 (1988), 60-73, 212-15, which summarizes the most important matters very elegantly in a generally understandable form.

127. Cf. J. Jervell, "Der Brief nach Jerusalem," *ST* 25 (1971): 61-73.

128. One thinks of the role that the Letter to the Romans has played in Augustine, then in Luther's lectures on it, and again after the First World War in Karl Barth's interpretation. J. Blank has also called my attention to some lines from *The Fall* by Albert Camus (New York: Knopf, 1956): "I am inclined to see religion rather as a huge laundering venture—as it was once but briefly, for exactly three years, and it wasn't called religion" (p. 111). "They have hoisted him onto a judge's bench, in the secret of their hearts, and they smite, they judge above all, they judge in his name. He spoke softly to the adulteress: 'Neither do I condemn thee!' but that doesn't matter; they condemn without absolving anyone. In the name of the Lord, here is what you deserve. Lord? He, my friend, didn't expect so much. He simply wanted to be loved, nothing more. Of course, there are those who love him, even among Christians. But they are not numerous" (p. 115). "He who clings to a law does not fear the judgment that reinstates him in an order he believes in" (p. 117). "But they believe solely in sin, never in grace" (p. 135). Here too the Letter to the Romans is revived in completely new form.

129. W. Bujard, *Stilanalytische Untersuchungen zum Kolosserbrief als Beitrag zur Methodik von Sprachvergleichen*, SUNT 11 (1973).

130. E. Schweizer, "Christus und Geist im Kolosserbrief," in *Christ and Spirit in the New Testament*, FS C. F. D. Moule (Cambridge, 1973), 297-313 = Schweizer (n. 78), 179-93.

131. Thus the majority, e.g., P. Pokorny, *Der Brief des Paulus an die Kolosser*, THKNT 10/1 (1987), 9-15.

132. Evidence for both: Schweizer (n. 38), 19, nn. 1 and 2.

133. E.g., P. Benoit, "L'hymne christologique de Col 1:15-20," in *Christianity, Judaism and Other Greco-Roman Cults*, FS M. Smith (Leiden, 1975), 254; E. P. Sanders, "Literary Dependence in Colossians," *JBL* 85 (1966): 45.

134. Thus offered for discussion: E. Schweizer (n. 38), 26-27; in more detail: "Der Kolosserbrief—weder paulinisch noch nachpaulinisch?" in idem (n. 78), 150-63.

135. E. Schweizer, "Slaves of the Elements and Worshipers of Angels: Gal 4:3, 9; Col 2:8, 18, 20," *JBL* 107 (1988): 455-68 (correct *prosperity* to *posterity* in 8.3 and on p. 465, middle).

136. Aristobulos: Euseb. *Praep. Ev.* 13:12:9-16; M. Hengel, *Judaism and Hellenism,* (Philadelphia: Fortress, 1974), I 243ff. (with n. 877); Walter (n. 77), 66, n. 2, and 158-71.
137. Schweizer (n. 135), 3.5 and n. 46.
138. Basically correct in his critique, even if occasionally a little too critical, is A. Vögtle, *Das Neue Testament und die Zukunft des Kosmos* (Düsseldorf, 1970), 183-208 (on Rom 8) and 208-33 (on Col 1).
139. On this problem: H. J. Gabathuler, *Jesus Christus, Haupt der Kirche—Haupt der Welt,* ATANT 45 (1965), 150-67; Schweizer (n. 38), 202-5.
140. E. Schweizer, s.v. *"soma," TDNT* 7: 1037, 1043-1044, even Sir. 43:27!
141. Ibid., 1037; 1054. The fact that Col 1:18; 2:19 talks about "the body" (not, as in Paul, his or Christ's body) corresponds to this Hellenistic use of language. While Paul, moreover, sees the local church as "body of Christ," though in such a way that the church as a whole lives in it (see 11.4 and n. 97 above), Colossians speaks of the universal church in analogy to the Hellenistic understanding of the cosmos. There is disagreement over whether the cosmic-god concept of Hellenism is the origin of the body-of-Christ concept, so that Paul consciously reshaped it, while the author of Colossians went back to the history-of-religion model (thus K. M. Fischer, *Tendenz und Absicht des Epheserbriefs* [Berlin, 1973], 54-78), or whether it was the writer of Colossians who on the basis of this model reshaped the differently formulated Pauline view (thus Schweizer, 1072-79). As Fischer himself has shown (taken up in Schweizer, 1090-92), it is certain that Gnosticism could not have been the origin.
142. Cf. R. Schnackenburg, *Der Brief an die Epheser,* EKKNT 10 (1982), 193-96 (with the position of E. Schweizer). Like Schweizer, now also U. Luz, "Ueberlegungen zum Epheserbrief und seiner Paränese," *Neues Testament und Ethik,* FS R. Schnackenburg (Freiburg, 1989), 392, n. 62.
143. H. Merkel, "Der Epheserbrief in der neueren exegetischen Diskussion," *ANRW* 25.4 (1987): 3220.
144. Cf. U. Luz, "Erwägungen zur Entstehung des 'Frühkatholizismus,'" *ZNW* 65 (1974): esp. 94-101; "Charisma und Institution in neutestamentlicher Sicht," *EvT* 49 (1989): esp. 90-94.
145. W. Trilling, *Untersuchungen zum 2. Thessalonicherbrief,* ETS 27 (1972), summary on 157-58; "Die beiden Briefe an die Thessalonicher: Eine Forschungsübersicht," *ANRW* 25.4 (1987): 3365-403; G. S. Holland, *The Tradition That You Received from Us,* HUT 24 (1988), 130: end of the first century.
146. W. Schenk, "Die Briefe an Timotheus I und II und an Titus (Pastoralbriefe) in der neueren Forschung (1945-1985)," *ANRW* 25.4 (1987), 3404-7: the trito-Paulines.
147. Nag Hammadi Codices 1:3, pp. 45-46 (J. Leipoldt and W. Grundmann, ed., *Umwelt des Urchristentums* [Berlin, 1967], 2:370). On the Jewish and Hellenistic background of Gnosticism cf. E. Grässer, "Das wandernde Gottesvolk," *ZNW* 77 (1986): 162-67.
148. The Gnostics were, of course, reproached by their ecclesiastical opponents for such libertinism, but it does not seem to be typical of Gnosticism. It is important to note that there is no "normative" Gnosticism, but only principal ideas that appear in very different forms and, above all, only develop over a long period of time (J. Blank, "Die Irrlehrer des ersten Johannesbriefes," *Kairos* 26 [1984]: 167).
149. E. Schweizer, *Gemeinde und Gemeindeordnung im Neuen Testament,* 2d ed., ATANT 35 (1959), 154-56 (= *Church Order,* 3d ed. [London, 1979]). That is true for *office* in the sense of leadership, honor, and voluntary service (*archè, timè, leiturgia*), also for the word stem *hier-,* which denotes priestly service (at most Rom 15:16 for the apostle). Concrete, ordered ministries are naturally named, in I Tim 3:1 also the *episcopè,* the "supervision" (of the "bishop").
150. On the basis of such similarities A. Strobel ("Schreiben des Lukas?" *NTS* 15 [1968/9]: 191-210) thought of Luke as the author of the pastoral letters; cf. N. Brox, "Lukas als Verfasser der Pastoralbriefe," *JAC* 13 (1970): 62-77, with critical inquiries.
151. Thus F. Overbeck, *Zur Geschichte des Kanons* (1880), 1: "like a Melchizedekian being without genealogy."
152. M. Rissi, *Die Theologie des Hebräerbriefes,* WUNT 41 (1987), 13. Voting for a genuine letter is H. Feld, *Der Hebräerbrief,* EdF 228 (1985), 20-33.
153. The frequent designation of the addressees as "saints" does not need to point to the Jerusalem church; cf. Rom 1:7: "called to be saints."

154. R. E. Brown, in idem and J. P. Meier, *Antioch and Rome* (New York, 1983), 2-8. Perhaps, however, Acts 7:47-51 only means that God is greater than the Temple and that the sin consists in interpreting the statements of Stephen as rejection of the Temple (D. D. Sylva, "The Meaning and Function of Acts 7:46-50," *JBL* 106 [1987]: 261-75). Nevertheless, that remains questionable.
155. F. F. Bruce, "'To the Hebrews': A Document of Roman Christianity?" *ANRW* 25.4 (1987): 3513-19; H. Feld, "Der Hebräerbrief," ibid., 3588-93.
156. Heb 9:1-10. Also according to the Old Testament the latter did not stand in the holy of holies, yet on the basis of its function one could draw that conclusion from certain passages (A. Strobel, *Der Brief an die Hebräer*, NTD 9 [1975], 169-70).
157. Brown (n. 154), 149-51; Rissi (n. 152), 12-13.
158. E.g., Josephus *Ant.* 3.123, 180-83, cf. 8.107-8; *Bell.* 5.212-17; and Philo *Vita Mos.* 2, esp. 98, 101, 117, 133-34, where the robe of the high priest symbolizes the universe that he brings before God.
159. Rissi (n. 152), 41, 89-90. Schenke and Fischer differ (n. 2), 2:250-51; G. W. Buchanan, *To the Hebrews,* AB 36 (1972), 96, with reference to I Macc 14:41; Josephus *Ant.* 16.163.
160. Schenke and Fischer (n. 2), 2:252.
161. E. Grässer, *Heb 1:1-14,* EKKNT 5/3 (1971), 76-77.
162. Idem (n. 147), 165-67, 179, in disagreement with O. Hofius. Cf. Fischer and Schenke (n. 2), 2:263-69.
163. Cf. here Rissi (n. 152), 114-15; Feld (n. 155), 3584-85: Is only the church at large intended?
164. Also Rissi (n. 152), 119, who refers to O. Cullmann.
165. Josephus *Ant.* 20.200; Hegesipp in Euseb. *Hist. Eccl.* 2:23.
166. B. R. Halson, "The Epistle of James: 'Christian Wisdom'?" in *Studia Evangelica,* ed. R. L. Cross, TU 102 (1968), 4:312-14 (a catechist "school"). H. Paulsen (s.v. "Jakobusbrief," *TRE* 16:492) dates it A.D. 70-100. J. A. T. Robinson (*Redating the New Testament* [London, 1976], 139) sees it as the oldest New Testament writing. W. Popkes (*Adressaten, Situation und Form des Jakobusbriefs,* SBS 139 [1986], 184-88) assumes a basic model of an "instructional talk," which could go back to James, but was modified and enriched with additional material (e.g., the Sermon on the Mount!).
167. Pratscher (n. 122), 209-13, 218-21.
168. *Herm.* 59:3 (= *Herm. Sim.* 5:6:3); 69:5 (= *Herm. Sim.* 8:3:5); Justin *Dial.* 14:3; 11:2. On the law of liberty cf. R. Schnackenburg, *Die sittliche Botschaft des Neuen Testaments,* HTKNT Sup 2/2 (1988), 206-10.
169. Pratscher (n. 122), 214-16.
170. Chr. Knoch in Link et al. (n. 17), 81.
171. Schenke and Fischer (n. 2), 1:203.
172. H. Preisker, *Der erste Petrusbrief,* 3rd ed., HNT 15 (1951), 156-62. Summary and critique of efforts to date in N. Brox, *Der erste Petrusbrief,* 2nd ed., EKKNT 21 (1986), 19-24, which correctly posits a unified "circular letter."
173. Philo restricts this general priesthood to the day of Passover, on which any Israelite can slaughter the lamb (*Spec. Leg.* 2.145; *Vita Mos.* 2.224; *Decal.* 159 [as exception]). On I Peter cf. E. Schweizer, "Zur Christologie des 1. Petrusbriefes," in *Anfänge der Christologie,* FS F. Hahn (Göttingen, 1991), esp. 374-77.
174. In 5:5 the "elders," in contrast to the "younger," are probably the older generation. In more detail: E. Schweizer, "Das Priestertum aller Glaubenden," *Im Gespräch mit der Bibel* (for P. Frehner), ed. by V. Weymann (Zurich, 1987), 11-20.
175. F. Hahn, "Randbemerkungen zum Judasbrief," *TZ* 37 (1981): 212. An original image of "impurities in your agates" that was incorrectly read (W. Whallon, "Should We Keep, Omit, or Alter the *hoi* in Jude 12?" *NTS* 34 [1988], 156-59) is improbable.
176. Only in verse 4 is it *krima* as in Rom 3:8, but in verses 6, 15 *krisis:* G. Sellin, "Die Haeretiker des Judasbriefes," *ZNW* 77 (1986): 209-12. He is thinking not of Gnostics in the true sense, but rather of itinerant teachers who experience pneumatically effected ectasies (p. 224).
177. Hahn (n. 175), 209-10, 213-15.
178. Ibid., 215-18.

179. M. Rese, "Besprechung von E. Fuchs/P. Reymond, La deuxiéme épître de Saint Pierre. L'épître de Saint Jude," *TLZ* 109 (1984): 266.
180. Ibid.
181. E.g., also Philo *Spec. Leg.* 2.146.
182. Käsemann, "An Apologia for Primitive Christian Eschatology," *Essays on New Testament Themes* (Philadelphia: Fortress, 1982), p. 169: "perhaps the most dubious writing in the canon."
183. A.D. 130-40, passed down in Euseb. *Hist. Eccl.* 3:39:15 (ca. A.D. 313); see also A. Delclaux, "Deux témoignages de Papias sur la composition de Marc?" *NTS* 27 (1980/81): 401-11, who believes Papias attests composition still during Peter's lifetime.
184. Thus, e.g., E. Brandenburger, *Markus 13 und die Apokalyptik,* FRLANT 134 (1984), 74-83.
185. In chapter 13 Mark follows an apocalyptic model; according to 14:17 Jesus comes "with the twelve," of whom two had already been sent ahead according to verses 12-16, presumably because it was that way in a traditional section on the last supper.
186. Cf. E. Schweizer, *The Good News According to Mark,* (Richmond: John Knox, 1970), 384-386; for others who see it similarly, cf. idem, *Matthäus und seine Gemeinde,* SBS 71 (1974), 13-14, n. 22; now also M. de Tillesse, "Evangelho secundo Marcos," *Revista Biblica Brasileira* (1988): 89-117, 137-56. Pesch (n. 57, 2/1:32-40) sees the structure similarly but separates the second from the third main part at 6:29/30.
187. Ibid., 2/1:277-81. Cf. E. Schweizer, "Zur Christologie des Markus," in idem (n. 78), 86-90 (in English in *God's Christ and His People,* FS N. A. Dahl [Oslo, 1977], 29-31).
188. R. Pesch, "Der Schluss der vormarkinischen Passionsgeschichte und des Markusevangeliums: Mark 15:42–16:8," in *L'évangile de Marc,* ed. M. Sabbe (Gembloux, 1974), 402-3.
189. P. Pokorný, *Die Entstehung der Christologie* (Stuttgart, 1985), 157-58.
190. For more detail on the following paragraph: E. Schweizer (n. 187), 90-100 (32-37).
191. Chapter 13 is presumably an apocalyptic vision of the future, perhaps from the time of A.D. 44, possibly a catechetical collection of various and variously aged traditions, as G. Beasley-Murray (*Jesus and the Kingdom of God* [Exeter, 1985], 323) now also recognizes. I will gladly concede to C. Breytenbach (*Nachfolge und Zukunftserwartung nach Markus,* ATANT 71 [1984], 331-37) that the orientation toward the future is perhaps even more important to Mark than I see it.
192. Cf. U. Luz, "Das Geheimnismotiv und die markinische Christologie," *ZNW* 56 (1965): 9-30; rpt. in *Das Markus-Evangelium,* ed. R. Pesch, Wege der Forschung 411 (1979), 211-37; E. Schweizer, "Zur Frage des Messiasgeheimnisses bei Markus," ibid., 1-8; rpt. in idem, *Beiträge* (n. 40), 11-20.
193. E. Schweizer, "Die theologische Leistung des Markus," *EvT* 24 (1964): 337-55; rpt. in idem, *Beiträge* (n. 40), 21-42, and in *Das Markus-Evangelium* (n. 192), 163-89.
194. U. Luz, *Das Evangelium nach Matthäus,* EKKNT 1/1 (1985), 62-64, 70-71; R. Hummel, *Die Auseinandersetzung zwischen Kirche und Judentum,* BEvT 33 (1963), 28-33 (no complete detachment from the synagogue).
195. On the following see Schweizer, *Matthäus* (n. 186), 20-22.
196. G. Bornkamm in idem, G. Barth, and H. J. Held, *Überlieferung und Auslegung im Matthäusevangelium,* WMANT 1 (1961), 48-53. On the transparency of the historical for the time of the church cf. the distinctions in W. Schenk, *Die Sprache des Matthäus* (Göttingen, 1987), 343-44. Cf. Luz (n. 194), ½ (1990), 20-30.
197. M. J. Suggs, *Wisdom, Christology and Law in Matthew's Gospel* (Cambridge, Mass., 1970), 120-27. J. Dupont (*Les béatitudes,* Ebib [1973], 3:327-29) has already shown that 5:13-16 belongs to 5:11-12.
198. Schweizer, *Matthäus* (n. 186), 116-25. Yet it remains doubtful that according to 27:52 "the murder victims" (23:31-32) appear as witnesses against Israel (P. Hoffmann, "Das Zeichen für Israel," in *Zur neutestamentlichen Überlieferung von der Auferstehung Jesu* [Darmstadt, 1988], 449-50).
199. Cf. Suggs (n. 197), 30-61, 98-127.
200. Cf. Weder (n. 85), 49-119.
201. E. Schweizer, *Jesus Christ: The Man from Nazareth and the Exalted Lord* (Macon, Ga., 1987), 88-90, and the works named there; also idem (n. 15), 724-25.
202. Documentation: G. Delling, "parthenos," *TDNT* 5:829-30. Soon after Luke, Plutarch

(Numa 4.6) explained that the Egyptians held it possible that the spirit of God could produce certain beginnings of life in a woman.

203. Thus H. Conzelmann, *The Theology of St. Luke,* (New York: Harper and Brothers, 1961).
204. Cf., however, n. 154.
205. G. Schneider, *Die Apostelgeschichte,* HTKNT 5/1 (1980), 1:76-79.
206. J. Wehnert *(Die Wir-Passagen der Apostelgeschichte,* GTA 40 [1989]) sees in this a means of rhetorical style.
207. R. Pesch, *Die Apostelgeschichte,* EKKNT 5/2 (1986), 284-88. On sources in general: Schenke and Fischer (n. 2), 142-45.
208. Schenke and Fischer (n. 2), 145-49; also E. Schweizer, "Zu den Reden der Apostelgeschichte," *TZ* 13 (1957): 1-11 = Schweizer (n. 32), 418-28.
209. Thus M. E. Boismard, *Texte occidentale: reconstruction et réhabilitation* (Paris, 1984), 8-9.
210. *Christentum und Kultur* (1919), rpt. (Darmstadt, 1976), 78.
211. It no doubt conveyed, according to tradition, the receiving of the Spirit (cf. the same formulation in 2:4), while Luke himself stresses the recovery of sight.
212. J. Becker, *Das Evangelium nach Johannes,* Ökumenischer Taschenbuch-Kommentar 4/1 (1979 = GTB 505), 27.
213. J. Blank (n. 148), 168-69; cf. now R. T. Fortna, *The Fourth Gospel and Its Predecessor* (Edinburgh, 1989). Different is M. Hengel, *The Johannine Question* (London: SCM, 1989), 90-92 and nn. 72, 81.
214. L. Schenke ("Der 'Dialog Jesu mit den Juden' im Johannesevangelium," *NTS* 34 [1988]: 573-603), to be sure, posits a source for the talks in chapters 3–10 and end of 12.
215. B. Bonsack ("Der Presbyteros des 3. Johannesbriefes und der geliebte Jünger des Evangeliums nach Johannes," *ZNW* 79 [1988]) sees in him the current bearer of the office of witness among the teachers of the community: he "remains," that is, "the gospel" remains (60-62). R. A. Culpepper *(Anatomy of the Fourth Gospel* [Philadelphia, 1983], 215) distinguishes the disciple named in 13:23 at the last supper from the one mentioned later in 19:26; 20:2; 21:7, 20.
216. Different is P. Minear, "The Original Functions of John 21," *JBL* 102 (1983): 85-98.
217. J. Becker, "Aus der Literatur zum Johannesevangelium," *TRu* 47 (1982): 279-301, 305-47; "Das Johannesevangelium im Streit der Methoden," *TRu* 51 (1986): 1-78; H. Thyen, s.v. "Johannesevangelium," *TRE* 17, esp. 200-218. Cf. now Hengel (n. 123), 102-8.
218. M. Barth *(Das Mahl des Herrn* [Neukirchen, 1987], 203-59) claims to see here only symbolic talk for the act of faith. This lecture is available in English in an abridged version: *Rediscovering The Lord's Supper,* (Atlanta: John Knox, 1988), 77-102.
219. Survey in e.g., R. Schnackenburg, *The Gospel According to John* (London: Burns and Oats, 1980) vol. 2, 56-59; cf. also E. Schweizer, "sarx" *TDNT* 7:139-140.
220. The dating is, of course, not entirely certain: G. Strecker, "Die Anfänge der johanneischen Schule," *NTS* 32 (1986): 47, n. 50 (up to A.D. 100 is possible).
221. Ps 80:8-16; Hos 10:1; Joel 1:7; Isa 5:2 (LXX); Jer 2:21; 6:9; Ezek 15:6; 19:10; IV Ezra 5:23; *Bib. Ant.* 12:8 Cf. R. E. Brown, The Gospel According to John XIII-XXI, AB 29A (1970), 669-72.
222. This could also have been related to the fact that the Johannine church orginally observed Easter on the Jewish Passover and thus celebrated Jesus' death and resurrection in worship on the same night (J. Blank, "Die Johannespassion," in idem, *Der Prozess gegen Jesus* [Freiburg, 1988], 179).
223. The return at the last day may be intended in 14:3, but that remains uncertain since the farewell speeches do not mention it, but rather only the coming of the Spirit, in which Jesus actually comes again to his disciples (see 29.9 below).
224. Thus R. Bultmann—all evidence, also for the following, in Schweizer (n. 15), 705-7.
225. Thus L. Schottroff under the influence of E. Käsemann.
226. Thus K. Wengst.
227. Thus J. A. Bühner.
228. Thus J. Blank (n. 148), 175.
229. The Greek word from which *Paraclete* is derived means "summon, exhort, comfort." It is, however, a passive form, so that one can only think of the one "summoned" (Latin *advocatus*), and thus of a "supporter, intercessor, advocate." On his role cf., e.g., E. Franck, *Revelation Taught—the Paraclete in the Gospel of John,* CB.NT 14 (1985).

230. Documentation of the Hellenistic churches (ekklesiai): W. Bauer, W. F. Ardnt, et al., *A Greek-English Lexicon of the New Testament* (Chicago: 1958), s.v. *"kyria"* 2.

231. Euseb. *Hist. Eccl.* 3:39:4.

232. See R. A. Culpepper, *The Johannine School,* SBLDS 26 (1975), esp. 259. Critique: E. Schüssler-Fiorenza, "The Quest for the Johannine School: The Fourth Gospel and the Apocalypse," *NTS* 23 (1977): 406-10.

233. For the opposite view: Strecker (n. 220), 31-47. It may be granted to Hengel (n. 213, p. 105) that "a towering creative teacher" (104), in the span of a long life, may show very different reactions to very different problems. Thus it is not impossible—though improbable—that the same author wrote and finished the Gospel and is responsible for, or at least encouraged, the writing of the letters.

234. Of I John: E. Lohse, *Grundriss der neutestamentlichen Theologie,* 2nd ed., ThW 5 (1974), 144, which adopts H. Conzelmann's formulation ("Was von Anfang war," in *Neutestamentliche Studien* [n. 41], 201).

235. Irenaeus *Haer.* 1:26:1 (Harvey 21:1).

236. To me it seems grammatically impossible that only the blood of Jesus was designated as the all-purifying water (*gen. epexeget.,* M. C. de Boer, "Jesus the Baptizer: I John 5:5-8 and the Gospel of John," *JBL* 107 [1988]: 87-106). Cf. a similar, but more carefully formulated idea in Barth (n. 218), 238-41 (and 245-47) (German edition).

237. Thus A. von Harnack, *Über den dritten Johannesbrief,* TU 15/3 (1897); for other solutions: H. Conzelmann and A. Lindemann, *Arbeitsbuch zum Neuen Testament,* UT 52 (1975), 297-98; J. W. Taeger, "Der konservative Rebell," *ZNW* 78 (1987): 267-87, which, conversely, sees in the elder someone who strives for a monarchical position, while Diotrephes is conservative.

238. A timeless solution (Lohmeyer) is just as much to be excluded as a clear temporal order (Rissi): T. Holtz, *Die Christologie der Apokalypse des Johannes,* TU 85 (1971), 216-18. Cf. O. Böcher, "Die Johannes-Apokalypse in der neueren Forschung," *ANRW* 25.5 (1988): 3850-93.

239. It is also found in the epilogue in John 21:15, but for church members (cf. P. Whale, "The Lamb of John," *JBL* 106 [1987]: 289-95).

240. *Hist. Eccl.* 3:39:6. J. Roloff (*Die Offenbarung des Johannes,* Zürcher Bibelkommentare [1984], 15-16) shows the relationship between the beginning of Revelation and the beginnings of Pauline and post-Pauline letters.

241. R. Schütz, *Die Offenbarung des Johannes und Kaiser Domitian,* FRLANT 50 (1933), 63.

242. Irenaeus *Haer.* 1:14:6 (Harvey 8:7); Hippolytus *El.* 6:49:5.

243. L. Brun, "Die römischen Kaiser in der Apokalypse," *ZNW* 26 (1927): 148, n. 1 (as questionable possibility). More in L. Kreitzer, "John and the Nero *Redivivus* Myth," *ZNW* 79 (1988): 92-115, esp. 92, n. 2: possible in Greek would be *Nerōn Kaisar ōn.*

244. Thus H. Kraft, *Die Offenbarung des Johannes,* HNT 16a (1974), 222.

245. In E. Stauffer, *666,* CNT 11 (1947), 237.

246. See esp. U. B. Müller, *Prophetie und Predigt im Neuen Testament,* SNT 10 (1975).

247. Körtner (n. 54, 129-32) is thinking of itinerant prophets also being the authorities to which Papias refers.

248. Schweizer, *Matthäus* (n. 186), 163-70; now also Theissen, "Wanderradikalismus" (n. 9), 83-101 and nn. 20, 64; on I Cor 9: Theissen (n. 67).

249. For an survey of the various interpretations, see G. Maier, *Die Johannesoffenbarung und die Kirche,* WUNT 25 (1981), summary on 619-24. E. Lohse ("Wie christlich ist die Offenbarung des Johannes?" *NTS* 34 (1988): 323-24) shows that adopted images and creative rewriting are connected.

250. H. Conzelmann (n. 7), 139-147.

251. Carefully designated as analogy in H. Schürmann, "Auf der Suche nach dem 'Evangelisch-Katholischen,'" *Kontinuität und Einheit,* FS F. Mussner (Freiburg, 1981), 354. See also E. Schweizer in *Charisma und Institution,* ed. T. Rendtorff [Gütersloh, 1985], 332-33, n. 77).

252. In Gnostic-Christian writings as a rule one finds only revelation speeches of the resurrected one (the extent to which the *Gospel of Thomas* is Gnostic is questionable) and miracles of *apostles* (see 2.1 above and Achtemeier [n. 13], 199, n. 3: even in the apostolic fathers).

(Listed passages are in addition to any section given in parentheses. Q is quoted mostly according to Luke.)

187

SUBJECT INDEX

(References are to section and subsection. Especially important passages are in italics.)

Abba, 2.9
"*Amen*, I tell you," 7.5
Anthropology, 10.3; 11.4-5. *See also* Soul
Apocalyptic, 31.5
Apothegmatization, 3.1; 6.3
Apostolic council, 9.1. *See also* Acts 15; Gal 2:1-10
Apostolic succession, 28.4
Aquila and Priscilla, 9.1; 11.1; 15.3; 16.1; 21.1

Baptism, 29.4
  of Jesus, 2.6
  water/Spirit, *28.5*
Body of Christ, 11.4; 17.7; 18.3. *See also* Church

Canon, 32.1-3, 6. *See also* Scripture
Christ
  as title, 2.7; 7.8
  descent into hell, 23.4
  "in/with Christ," 14.7
Christology
  Absence of Jesus after Easter, 6.1; 25.4
  in Acts, 5.5
  Christ = God, 19.1; 29.5; 30.2
  cosmic, 17.5
  habitation of God, 29.8
  high priest, 21.2-6
  Lamb, 5.4; 31.1
  Lord (*kyrios*), 5.1; 7.8
  in Luke, 27.4
  in parables, 2.5; 27.7; 29.2, 5; 31.3
  preexistence, 5.6; 7.10; 21.2
  in Q, 7.5, 8

Son (of God), 2.9; 5.3, 6; 7.4, 7; 8.6; 25.6
  wisdom, 26.8. *See also* Wisdom Christology
Church, 2.8 (founded by Christ?); 3.2 (foundation?); 18.4-5 (bride of Christ); 23.5-6 (general priesthood); 26.4 (group of disciples); 28.4 (Acts); 29.6; 30.4-5 (John). *See also* Office, House churches, Jewish Christians, Body of Christ
Collection, 12.2, 6; 13.1; 28.4
Cosmos, 5.11; 7.8; 17.5, 7; 31.3
Creation, 5.11; 17.5; 24.4

David's son, 5.3; 26.6
Delivering of Jesus, 5.4
Dialogue character of the message, 9.5; 11.2; 20.4. *See also* Scripture
Discipleship, 3.1, 9-10; 6.2; 7.7; 21.5; 26.4

Early Catholicism, 24.5; 28.6; 32.4
Easter
  as caesura, 3.10; 8.6; 9.6; 25.3-4; 28.3
  Good Friday/ascension, 21.3; 29.7
Elemental spirits, elements, 17.3-4
Eschatology, 2.2; 3.3, 5-7; 7.6; 14.4; 18.6; 19.1-2; 24.4
Exaltation (of Jesus), 5.10, 12-13; 7.7-9; 8.8; 29.7
Experiences, 2.3; 27.7, 9-10; 28.2

Faith, 2.1; 5.1-6 (confessional formulas); 9.6; 13.5; 20.1; 22.3-4; 23.3; 27.2, 6; 28.2; 29.5